the
American
Dimension

CULTURAL MYTHS
and SOCIAL REALITIES

the American Dimension

CULTURAL MYTHS and SOCIAL REALITIES

W. ARENS, *SUNY, Stonybrook*
SUSAN P. MONTAGUE, *Northern Illinois University*

Alfred
PUBLISHERS

ALFRED PUBLISHING CO., INC.

Library of Congress Cataloging in Publication Data
Main entry under title:

The American dimension.

Bibliography: p.
1. United States—Social life and customs—1971-
—Addresses, essays, lectures. 2. Ethnology—United
States—Addresses, essays, lectures. I. Arens, W.,
1940-   II. Montague, Susan P., 1942-
E169.02.A6483   301.29′73   76-2411
ISBN 0-88284-030-4 pbk.

CONTENTS

CONTENTS

PREFACE

The student of anthropology rightly expects that his course of study will introduce him to the variety of human experiences. Yet, rarely, if ever, does this include the study of American culture. This is an unfortunate oversight, because American culture is as rich and as deep as any other, and, if looked at objectively, can often appear as bizarre and irrational. Consequently, we feel that this collection of essays, with Americans as the natives, fills a gap in a discipline that purports to examine the cultural universe. The analyses offered will not only tell us something about our hidden selves, but will help us to understand others in a more meaningful way.

The following essays fall into two distinct categories: American culture, and social strategies. Those selections that analyze cultural phenomena are concerned primarily with the message content of mass media. Many of the contributors have chosen this area because the media present a body of highly standardized information aimed at a large, voluntarily participating audience (i.e., television and film viewers). Thus it can be assumed that what is presented reflects the ideas and interests of a large segment of the American populace. Further, the information is readily accessible and thus is far easier to obtain than data collected by interviewing many individuals.

These essays treat one particular body of mass media data, the information transmitted through entertainment channels, which include television programs; motion pictures; magazines; and staged performances such as concerts, plays, and sports events. It is readily noticeable that the information content of such entertainment stresses certain topics, while others are given rather short shrift. Entertainment productions deal with the content of interpersonal relationships, that is, how individual actors act vis a vis other actors in various situations. Even impersonal topics such as politics and economics are treated in terms of the actions of specific individuals, and how their decisions affect their lives as well as those in their immediate social circle. The entertainment media are frequently accused of being shallow and void of meaningful content, but this is pseudointellectual pretension. In fact, entertainment deals with the most important issues Americans face: how to best live their daily lives; what it means to be an American and to live in American society. These issues underlie more commonly recognized social issues such as what type of political or economic system is most appropriate for our society. It is not too surprising that although we disapprove of political censorship in societies that directly equate morality with the existing political order, we at the same time heavily censor our own entertainment media. Television is the most obvious case, with pretaping and bleeps to avoid inadvertent intrusions of objectionable material. Movies are also censored and coded for various audiences. Magazine publishers face at least threats of prosecution when their subject matter, usually sex, is perceived as a threat to social mores. Rock stars are arrested with considerable frequency, and concert goers may be hassled by the police. Even sports figures are vulnerable and subject to expulsion from athletic competition when their personal behavior violates the expected, overly idealistic moral code. Questions of major changes in sports, such as the advisability of allowing women and men to compete with each other, or the use of drugs to enhance performance, are treated in terms of their implications for the morality of the entire society. In short, the mass media constitute a forum for depicting and, to a certain extent, debating current morality. They offer the viewer situational models that can be adapted and used in the individual's own life. Far from being shallow or meaningless, popular entertainment painstakingly examines what it is to be human in our society, dissecting and reconstructing the most basic social situations and providing an ongoing discussion of our very essence. In short, the media provide a gold mine of useful information for the analysis of American culture.

The second section deals with social strategies, or with how people adapt and use information to formulate real behavior in various social contexts. These selections are concerned with the construction of social action in a host of situations, and treat such diverse topics as volunteer fire departments, moonshining, and poker playing. As such, they are concerned with how people actually act, rather than with ideology. Instead of obtaining data from ideological channels, information is derived from observing people interacting with one another in common real-life situations. The regional scope of these essays is indicative of cultural variation in the United States, and thus we learn something about the differences between East and West or rural and urban America.

We hope that the essays will be insightful and will raise significant questions for further analysis. Because the essays deal with our own culture, the reader is also the native, and therefore has the opportunity to consider and debate the analysis and conclusions arrived at. We offer the book as a beginning effort in what we think will be a fruitful exploration into the topic that has always interested us the most: ourselves.

We would be remiss in our responsibilities as editors if we did not conclude this preface by acknowledging our debt to the many individuals who have been of great assistance in seeing this volume through its metamorphosis. The majority of the essays were originally presented at the 1974 meetings of the American Anthropological Association at the symposium, "North of the Border." At that time, we were privileged to have with us as discussants Professor Robert Manners of Brandeis University and Professor Harold W. Scheffler of Yale University. Their comments and reflections on the papers were appreciated by all concerned and in a variety of ways have been incorporated into this final presentation. They deserve our collective thanks and appreciation for sharing their thoughts with us. We hope that we have succeeded in putting their advice into practice by examining the seemingly trivial side of American social life without being trivial ourselves.

At a later stage, we were fortunate in being able to call on the expert assistance of Jeffrey Steinberg and the services of Mrs. Mari Walker for an unending supply of bad puns and good typing, both of which were essential to the task. Finally, we would like to dedicate this book to our respective mentors. Although they may not have participated in this project directly, they provided us with the intellectual perspective that resulted in the study of American culture.

the American Dimension

CULTURAL MYTHS
and SOCIAL REALITIES

INTRODUCTION

A quipster once defined anthropology as "the study of the exotic by the eccentric." As inexact and uncomplimentary as it may be, there is an important element of truth in this definition. After all, who but an eccentric would spend years observing and then a lifetime writing about the exchange of shells by a few hundred natives on a remote Pacific island? Yet, this type of behavior is exactly what is expected of the aspiring anthropologist in order to gain admission into the ranks.

However, these expectations are changing to some extent, and this book reflects the trend. Although all of the contributors have carried out traditional fieldwork in another part of the world, these essays focus on American culture from the anthropological perspective. This is not to imply that this has never been done before, but in the past, such studies have tended to focus on the relatively exotic nooks and crannies of our own society that are as foreign to many of us as an African kinship system. This emphasis on the little-known aspects of American society by anthropologists is in direct contrast to the normal procedure in the study of another culture, where the aberrations and peculiarities are ignored in favor of understanding regularities and dominant themes. In this collection, the major interest is on the analysis of the American mainstream, or what has lately come to be known as "Middle America." It is our contention that the sports, films, television shows, hobbies, and general life style of the ordinary American are also suitable grist for the anthropological mill. In retrospect, what is odd is that this area of inquiry has been ignored for so long, because when pressed to rationalize its own worthiness, anthropology has always claimed that in studying other cultures we would then be in a better position to understand our own. Although this may not have been put into practice, the argument remains valid and the topic eminently worthy.

A first step in this process requires an understanding of what is meant by the concept of "culture." It has been difficult to arrive at an exact and acceptable definition of the term. Most anthropologists would now agree with Clifford Geertz that culture is a system of meanings embodied in symbols. This implies that most human behavior is not innate or instinctive, but rather is learned and based on our linguistic ability to manipulate symbols to construct a universe of meaning. The goal of the anthropologist, then, is to examine and analyze the phenomenon of culture in order to better understand how we as human beings construct and conduct our uniquely human existence.

Thus the utility of anthropological investigations is measured not by what we gain in knowledge about others, but what we learn about being human in the process of looking at others. The ultimate goal is to know oneself. In this respect anthropology does not differ from the other social sciences; but it does differ in the previously stated assumption that it is by looking at others that we can best learn about ourselves. This is based largely on the idea that in order to see any phenomenon clearly it is necessary to first stand at a distance from it. A problem, therefore, in viewing American culture is that as native participants we are not always detached observers. Prior fieldwork in another society helps in providing the necessary objective framework.

Another difficulty is the factor of magnitude. The more people in the society, the greater the potential for cultural variation. Anthropologists, in their initial efforts to define the basic principles around which cultural systems operate, prefer to look at small-scale societies. Consequently, we have been reluctant to focus attention on our own society. Only recently have anthropologists in sizeable numbers been turning to writing directly about "us" rather than about "them." Why this fairly sudden turnabout? To answer this question, it is necessary to look briefly at the history of the discipline.

Modern anthropology evolved simultaneously in two separate, though interrelated lines, the British and the American. The first direct fieldwork which involved something more than a brief visit, was conducted more or less simultaneously by both the British and Americans in the early years of this century. Bronislaw Malinowski and A. R. Radcliffe-Brown led the way in England with their work in the Trobriand and Andaman Islands. At the same time, Franz Boas' American students at Columbia University also carried out their pioneering studies, notably among them Margaret Mead in Samoa. Although understanding another culture was the common aim, the theoretical interests of the two groups differed radically. The British focused on social structure, that is, the institutionalized patterns of interpersonal behavior between members of a group. This involved the examination of kinship, political, and economic systems and the relationships among them in a single society. To these social anthropologists, culture was somehow unreal and thought of as merely an ideological support for social organization. Their American counterparts, on the other hand, were interested in culture per se, but often approached it from a psychological point of view and attempted to account for cultural differences through the application of Freudian psychoanalytic theory.

Neither of these methodologies proved particularly useful for the analysis of Western society and culture. It is difficult enough to conceptualize the social network of a small village with two hundred people, and virtually impossible to do the same for a society of two hundred million. Freudian psychology also turned out to be of minimal explanatory value, because although it is carried by individuals, culture is a group phenomenon, and therefore must be approached from a different perspective.

In the 1960s French structuralism gained prominence, primarily through the works of Claude Lévi-Strauss. In addition to having a general impact on anthropology, structuralism, with its concern for the universal properties of the human mind, stimulated a renewed interest in cultural analysis. At this point, Geertz's definition of culture as a system of meaning embodied in symbols was adopted. Since it is employed in many of the essays, a number of implications of this definition should be made explicit.

First, as defined, culture can be viewed as a communication system. This means that all the people using the culture must share a body of basic standardized definitions and ideas, or else they could not interact in a meaningful way. Second, these broad, shared definitions and ideas are generative—they may be combined and recombined to create a multitude of messages. In this sense, the basic units of culture are like the words in a language, which are combined and recombined to make sentences whose meaning is different from each of the words utilized in the construction. There are also rules governing these combinations, determining which possess meaning and which do not. In language, this is known as grammar, and these rules are unconscious in the sense that speakers are not always aware of them even as they use them. We are not yet sure how unconscious these rules are for culture. Certainly, the actors are not completely aware of them, but we do not know whether they are as irretrievable as language grammar. What we are learning about is the basic "words" that are used to construct cultural systems, and again, informants learn these intuitively and are not conscious of them. Fortunately, though, they can recognize them once they are pointed out. Thus, it becomes possible to directly ascertain the content of basic cultural symbols and to map how they are combined to create ideological systems. From this standpoint, there is no reason why anthropologists cannot directly confront the symbolic underpinnings of their own culture just as easily as they confront those of foreigners. Further, since all members of the culture must share these meanings, their number becomes irrelevant for analysis.

Anthropology today not only possesses a body of theory that promises to offer significant insight into American culture, but also occupies an advantageous position because it has analyzed so many other cultures. Looking at others increases our own self-consciousness because it makes us realize that ideas we may take for granted as intrinsic to human reality are in fact not inherently real or necessary, but rather only our way of seeing things. For example, when the Trobrianders were asked for their opinions as to what should be included in a report of their culture, they indicated that the anthropologist should collect yam recipes and write a cookbook. The fact that a cookbook would be an unusual anthropological monograph, to say the least, raises questions about how cooking is classified in American culture. Clearly, it occupies a very different position in Trobriand culture than in ours, if they feel that by understanding their cooking one can understand them. But the matter of looking at others to see ourselves is really a bit more complex, for it actually involves a feedback process. Every time we see ourselves differently we also see them differently, and this in turn leads us to see ourselves differently anew. This is another reason for the significance of anthropologists devoting at least part of their energies to the formal analysis of their own culture. We can be aware that we differ from others, but unless we consciously look at our own system, it is all too easy to continue our peculiar assumptions about human reality.

Part I

SYMBOLIC ANALYSIS
OF
CULTURAL
PHENOMENA

PROFESSIONAL FOOTBALL

An American Symbol and Ritual

W. ARENS

O, you sir, you! Come you hither, sir. Who am I, sir?
OSWALD. My lady's father.
LEAR. 'My lady's father'! my lord's knave! you whoreson dog! you slave! you cur!
OSWALD. I am none of these, my lord; I beseech your pardon.
LEAR. Do you bandy looks with me, you rascal? *[striking him.]*
OSWALD. I'll not be strucken, my lord.
KENT. Nor trip'd neither, you base football player.

King Lear. Act I, Scene 4.

A school without football is in danger of deteriorating into a medieval study hall.

—Vince Lombardi.

Attitudes toward football players have obviously changed since Shakespeare's time. Today the once "base football player" occupies the throne and rules the land. In fact, to have played too many games without a helmet seems to be a prerequisite for high office in our country. The prominent role football assumes in our society deserves comment . I would contend that although only a game, it has much to say about who and what we are as a people.

3

Although I am a professional anthropologist by training and have carried out fieldwork in another culture, this essay owes its impetus to the years I have sat in front of a television watching hundreds of football contests. Out of a feeling of guilt, I began to muse in a more academic fashion about this game and turned to the numerous books written by players and also to the rare anthropological accounts of sport in other societies. This has led me to believe that if an anthropologist from another planet visited here he would be struck by the American fixation on this game and would report on it with the glee and romantic intoxication anthropologists normally reserve for the exotic rituals of a newly discovered tribe. This assertion is based on the theory that certain significant symbols are the key to understanding a culture. It might be a dreadful thought, but nonetheless true, that if we understood the meaning of football we might better understand ourselves.

I emphasize a symbolic analysis because this game that intrigues us so much is engaged in by relatively few, but highly skilled individuals. Most of us at one time or another have played golf, tennis, basketball, softball, or even baseball, but only the "pros" play football. Touch football must be discounted because it lacks the essential ingredients of violent physical contact and complexity of game plan. The pleasure derived from football therefore is almost totally vicarious. This sport's images and messages satisfy our collective mind, not our individual bodies.

An appreciation of this argument requires an initial short detour in time to examine the evolution of this American sport from its European origins. The enshrined mythology states that the game was first played by a group of English soldiers who celebrated their victory over a Viking settlement by entering the losers' burial ground and using the skulls of the enemies' dead in a kicking match. Sometime later, an animal's inflated bladder was substituted for the skull, and the sport of "Dane's Head" became known as football. During the early Middle Ages, the game was a disorganized all-day competition between neighboring towns. The ball was placed midway between two villages and the object was to kick it along the countryside into the village and finally onto the green of the opposing community for a score. The game became so popular with the English peasantry that Henry II banned the pastime in the twelfth century because it interfered with the practice of archery. The sport was not reinstated until the seventeenth century, by which time the longbow had become an obsolete weapon.

According to Reisman and Denny (1969), who have charted the game's evolution, the kicking aspect remained dominant until 1823 when, as popular legend has it, a scoundrel named William Ellis, of Rugby School, "with a fine disregard for the rules of football, as played in his time, first took the ball in his arms and ran with it." This innovation on soccer was institutionalized at the school, and shortly thereafter was adopted by others; hence the name "rugby"—and the association of this sport in England with the educated elite.

Although both games were exported to America, only rugby was modified in the new setting. The claim has been made by the participants, and officially adopted by the National College Athletic Association that the first intercollegiate game took place between Rutgers and Princeton in 1869. However, since that contest followed soccer rules, the honor of having played the first game of what was to emerge as American football rightly should go to Harvard and McGill in 1874, when rugby regulations were the order of the day. In the remaining decades of the nineteenth century, the sport began to take on a more American form as a definite line of scrimmage and the center snap replaced the swaying "scrum" and "heal out" of English rugby. This meant that possession of the ball was now given to one team at a time. However, the introduction of the forward pass in the early years of this century signaled the most radical break with the past. These revisions on rugby resulted in greater structure and order, but at the same time more variety and flexibility, because running, kicking, and forward passing were incorporated as offensive maneuvers. Football had become an American game.

As a result of this process, football has emerged as an item of our cultural inventory that we share with no other country but Canada, where it is not nearly so popular. Does football's

5

uniqueness and popularity say something essential about our culture? Rather than dismiss this question as trivial, we should be aware that we share our language, kinship system, religions, political and economic institutions, and a variety of other traits with many nations, but not our premier spectator sport. This is important when we consider that other societies have taken up baseball, a variation of cricket, and basketball, a homegrown product. Like English beer, the American brand of football is unexportable, even to the colonies. No one else can imagine what the natives see in it. On the other hand, soccer, the world's number one sport, has not been a popular success in America. In a peculiar social inversion, though, the educated and well-traveled American middle class has taken some interest in this sport of the European working classes. Nonetheless, football is uniquely American and little else can be included in this category.

Also, football, as compared to our language and many values, is not forced upon us. It is an optional aspect of our culture's inventions, which individuals choose to accept. Our society, like any other complex one, is divided by race, ethnicity, income, political affiliation, and regionalism. However, 79 percent of all the households in the country tuned in the first Super Bowl on TV, implying that the event cut through many of the divisive factors just mentioned. Personally, I can think of precious little else that I have in common with our former or current president, with a rural Texan, or an urban black other than a mutual passion for this game. Football represents not only "Middle America," as is so often claimed, but the whole of America. When we consider football, we are focusing on one of the few things we share with no one outside our borders, but do share with almost everyone within it.

The salient features of the game and of the society that created and nourishes it reflect some striking similarities. The sport combines the qualities of group coordination through a complex division of labor and minute specialization more than any other that comes to mind. Every sport exhibits these characteristics to an extent, but in football the process has surely reached the zenith. Every professional and major college team finds it necessary today to include a player whose only function is place kicking, and another for punting. Some have individuals whose sole responsibility is to center or hold the ball for the point after a touchdown. Football is also a game in which success now demands an extensive reliance on sophisticated electronic technology from telephones to computers while the match is in progress. In short, football, as opposed to its ancestor, rugby, epitomizes the spirit and form of contemporary American society.

Violence is another of our society's most apparent features. This quality of American life and its expression in football clearly accounts for some of the game's appeal. That football involves legitimate bodily contact and territorial incursion defines it as an aggressive sport par excellence. It is hardly surprising therefore that books by participants are replete with symbolic references to war. For example, Jerry Kramer, a Green Bay Packer during their glory years of the 1960s, divides his book, *Instant Replay,* into the following sections: Preliminary Skirmishes; Basic Training; Mock Warfare; Armed Combat; War's End. Frank Leahy, a former coach of Notre Dame and in his time a living symbol of America, wrote in his memoirs:

> . . . the Stars and Stripes have never taken second place on any battlefield. With this in mind, we ask you to think back and ask yourself where our young men developed the qualities that go to make up a good fighting man. . . . These traits are something that cannot be found in textbooks nor can they be learned in the lecture room. It is on the athletic fields that our boys acquire these winning ways that are as much a part of the American life as are freedom of speech and of the press (1949: 230).

Mike Holovak (1967), a former coach of the New England Patriots, waxed even more lyrical in reminiscing about his World War II military service. He refers to those years as the time he was on "the first team" in the "South Pacific playground" where the tracers arched out "like a long touchdown pass" and the artillery fired "orange blobs—just like a football."

To single out violence as the sole or even primary reason for the game's popularity is a tempting oversimplification. There are more violent sports available to us, such as boxing, which allows for an even greater display of legitimate blood spilling. Yet, boxing's popularity has waned over the last few decades. Its decline corresponds with the increased interest in professional football, in which aggression is acted out in a more tactical and sophisticated context. Football's violence is expressed within the framework of teamwork, specialization, mechanization, and variation, and this combination accounts for its appeal. A football contest more adequately symbolizes the way in which our society carries out violence than does a sport that relies on naked individual force. An explanation of football's popularity on the basis of violence alone also overlooks the fact that we are not unique in this respect. There have been many other violent nations, but they did not enshrine football as a national symbol.

Although the "national pastime" may not have suffered the same fate as boxing, interest in baseball has also ebbed. If my analysis of football is correct, then baseball is not in step with the times either. The action in baseball does not entail the degree of complexity, coordination, and specialization that now captures our fancy. I think this is what people mean when they say that baseball is boring. The recent introduction of the designated hitter and the occasional base-running specialist who never bats or fields are moves to inject specialization and heighten the game's appeal to modern America. In essence, baseball belongs to another era, when life was a bit less complicated.

To return to our original interest, one final point must be made on the symbolism of football. Earlier I wrote that football represented the whole of America and overcame traditional differences in our society. However, the importance of the division between the sexes, which has more recently become part of our consciousness, was not mentioned. Football plays a part in representing this dichotomy in our society because it is a male preserve that manifests and symbolizes both the physical and cultural values of masculinity. Entrance into the arena of football competition depends on muscle power and speed possessed by very few males and beyond that of most females. Women can and have excelled in a variety of other sports, but football generally excludes them from participation. It was reported in a local newspaper that during a game between female teams the players' husbands appeared on the sidelines in women's clothes and wigs. The message was clear: if the women were going to act as men, then the men were going to transform themselves into women. These "rituals of rebellion" involving an inversion of sex roles have often been recorded by anthropologists. It is not surprising that this symbolic rebellion in our culture was aimed at a bastion of male supremacy.

If this argument seems farfetched, consider the extent to which the equipment accents the male physique. The donning of the required items results in an enlarged head and shoulders and a narrowed waist, with the lower torso poured into skin-tight trousers accented only by a metal cod-piece. The result is not an expression, but an exaggeration of maleness. Dressed in this manner, the players engage in handholding, hugging, and bottom patting, which would be ludicrous and disapproved in any other context. Yet, this is accepted on the gridiron without a second thought. Admittedly, there are good reasons for wearing the gear, but does that mean we must dismiss the symbolic significance of the visual impression? The game could just as easily be played without the major items, such as the helmet, shoulder pads, and cleats. They are as much offensive as defensive in function. Indeed, in comparison rugby players seem to manage quite well in the flimsiest of uniforms.

The preceding discussion puts us in a better position to ask the question hinted at earlier—are we in effect dealing with an American ritual of some meaning? The answer depends upon how ritual is defined. A broad anthropological view suggests that it is a standardized, repetitive activity carried out for the purpose of expressing and communicating basic cultural ideals and symbols. A ritual therefore does not necessarily imply communication with the supernatural. The inauguration of a president or the playing of the national anthem are common examples of nonreligious rituals in America. An objective evaluation of the problem also demands recognizing that an act can have a sacred and a secular character at the same time. Consequently, at one level, football can be viewed simply as a sport and at another level as a public ritual. Considering some of the players' activities from this perspective furnishes some interesting and supportive observations.

If we view the game as a ritual and therefore in some respects as a sacred activity, we would expect the participants to disengage themselves from the profane world of everyday affairs. This is a common aspect of ritual behavior in any part of the world. Especially relevant for the participants is the avoidance of what anthropologists refer to as "pollution"—an impure ritual state—as the result of contact with contaminating acts or situations. Association with this profane realm renders a participant symbolically unfit to engage in a sacred performance.

In many rituals performed entirely for and by males, sexual contact with females must be avoided. Abstinence under these conditions is almost a cultural universal because the sexual act is an expression of man's animal or profane nature. In many a rite of passage for boys about to enter adulthood, the participants are taken out of the community, isolated from the opposite sex, and may not be seen by them. In other societies, prior to a significant activity such as the hunt or warfare, the community members are admonished to refrain from sexual behavior for fear of disastrous consequences. Is it really surprising then that in the world of sport, and with football in particular, sex before the event is viewed with suspicion? In this context I am reminded of Hoebel's (1960) statement that: "The Cheyenne feeling about male sexuality is that it is something to be husbanded and kept in reserve as a source of strength for the great crises of war." This compares well with the attitude at the virtually monastic world of football training camps. At these facilities all of the players, including those married, are sequestered together during practice days. They are allowed to visit their wives, who must be living off the grounds, on Saturday night only, since there is no practice on Sunday. As is to be expected they must return to the all-male atmosphere on Sunday evening in consideration of Monday's activities. The result is that sex and football, the profane and the sacred, are segragated in time and space. During the season a variation of the procedure prevails. The players and staff spend Saturday night together since the contest takes place on Sunday. In each instance there is a clear-cut attempt to avoid the symbolic danger of contact with females prior to the event.

This was impressed on me when I traveled with my university's team by chartered bus to a game to be played at the opponent's field. Since there were a few unoccupied seats, two of the players asked the coach if their girlfriends could ride along. He said in all seriousness that they could not ride to the game with us, but that they could join us on the bus on the way home. A writer who spent the season with the Rice University football squad mentioned a similar instance (Tippette, 1973). When the team bus pulled up in front of the dormitory where they would spend the night on the opponent's campus, a number of the girls from the college entered the vehicle and began to flirt with the players. The Rice coach, who was in an accompanying car, stormed onto the bus and ordered the girls off immediately. He then told the players that they should have known better, since the incident was a dirty trick instigated by their foe. Dirty trick or not, somebody planned the exercise, well aware of the unsettling effect that it would have on the team.

One further example is from the professional arena. Describing the night before the first Super Bowl, when the Green Bay Packers were allowed to bring along their wives as a reward for championship play, Jerry Kramer wrote: "My wife's been here for the past few days, and so has Chandler's. Tonight we're putting the girls in one room, and Danny and I are sharing one. It's better for the girls to be away from us tonight. We're always grumpy and grouchy before a game" (1968).

There are, of course, some perfectly reasonable arguments for segregating the players prior to a game. For one, the coaches argue that they are assured that the team members get an undistracted night's sleep. Thus it is assumed that the players will be better able to concentrate on the upcoming event. At the same time, when these vignettes are considered, the theme of possible pollution through contact with females is not altogether absent. In any event, the inhibition of sexual activity prior to an athletic event has no apparent scientific rationale. The latest position based on research argues that sex is actually beneficial, since it induces a more restful night's sleep.

The New York Times recently reported that a British physician who has advised and interviewed his country's Olympic

11

competitors mentioned that one informant admitted setting the world record in a middle distance track event an hour after sexual intercourse. Another confessed that he ran the mile in less than four minutes an hour and a half after the same activity. One must look beyond rationality for an explanation of the negative attitude toward sex on the part of the elders who control professional football. However, if we grant that the sport involves a significant ritual element, then the idea does make some sense. From this standpoint scientific reasoning is not relevant.

Accounts of rituals in other cultures also indicate the prevalent belief in symbolic contamination through contact with illness or physical imperfection. Examples of this sort of avoidance also crop up in football. Players report that those who become sick to their stomachs in the summer heat of training camp are avoided and become the objects of ridicule. In a similar vein, participants are rightfully admonished to stay away from an injured player so that the trainer can attend to him. However, they do not appear to need the advice since after a momentary glance they studiously avoid a downed colleague. Injured, inactive players on the team I was associated with as faculty sponsor were not allowed to mingle with the active participants during the game. The loquacious professional Jerry Kramer also writes that when he was hurt and disabled, he felt like an "outsider," "isolated" and "separated" from the rest of the group. Others have written that they were ignored during these times by their teammates and coaches. I do not want to push this argument too far because there are many sound reasons to explain this patterned reaction. At the same time, I can think of similar arguments for the behavior of people in other cultures after having come into contact with illness or death.

Eating is another profane act, since it is a further indication of our animal nature. As in every society, contact with certain foods renders an individual unfit to participate in rituals. However, in contrast to sexuality and physical imperfection, nourishment cannot be avoided for any length of time. Instead, under controlled conditions, the act of eating is incorporated into the ritual, and the food becomes charged with a sacred character. Consequently, not just any type of food is acceptable, but only specified types with symbolic significance may be ingested by ritual participants. What would be more appropriate in our society than males eating beef prior to the great event? Imagine the scorn that would be heaped on a team if it were known that they prepared themselves for the competition by eating chicken.

The problem with a purely functional interpretation is that this meat, which, it is believed, must be eaten on the day of the competition, is not converted into potential energy until hours after the game has ended. Although the players must appear for this meal because it is part of the ritual, actually very few eat what is presented to them. Instead, in contradiction to the ritual experts, the participants prefer a high-energy snack, such as a pill, which they realize has more immediate value. Nevertheless, those who control the players' behavior, as in the other instances, adhere to a less functional course by forcing their charges to confront a meaningful symbolic substance. If this situation were presented to an anthropologist in the heart of the Amazon, I wonder how long it would take to suggest ritual cannibalism on the part of the natives.

I have tried to make it clear that I am well aware that there are a number of secular, functional explanations for the behavior that has been described. However, it bears repeating that a ritual has a variety of levels, components and consequences. The slaughter of a white bull during a rite of passage for males among cattle-keeping people in Africa has an obvious nutritional benefit for those who consume it. At the same time, though, this does not obviate the ritual significance of the act. If I am making too much of the symbolic element of American football, then perhaps we ought to reconsider the ease with which we accept this type of analysis for other supposedly simpler cultures. Accounts of team log racing among the Shavante Indians of Brazil as an attempt to restore harmony to a social order beset by political divisions (Maybury-Lewis, 1967) and the analysis of cock fighting in Bali (Geertz, 1972) as an expression of national character, have caused little stir. Unless we consider ourselves something special, our own society is equally suited to such anthropological studies. It is reasonable that if other people express their basic cultural themes in symbolic rituals, then we are likely to do the same.

13

REFERENCES

Geertz, Clifford, 1972, "Deep Play: Notes on a Balinese Cockfight." *Daedalus.* Winter.

Hoebel, E. Adamson, 1960, *The Cheyenne.* New York: Holt, Rinehart and Winston

Holovak, Mike, 1967, *Violence Every Sunday.* New York: Coward-McCann.

Kramer, Jerry, 1968, *Instant Replay.* New York and Cleveland: World Publishing Company.

Leahy, Frank, 1949, *Notre Dame Football.* New York: Prentice-Hall.

Maybury-Lewis, David, 1967, *Akwe-shavante Society.* Oxford: Clarendon Press.

Reisman, David and Denny, Reuel, 1969, "Football in America: A Study in Cultural Diffusion." In J. W. Lory, Jr. and G. S. Kenyon. eds. *Sport, Culture and Society.* New York: Macmillan.

Tippette, Giles, 1973, *Saturday's Children.* New York: Macmillan.

A STRUCTURALIST APPRECIATION OF "STAR TREK"

PETER J. CLAUS

I . . . want to emphasize the fact that anthropology should be not only the study of savage custom in the light of our mentality and our culture, but also the study of our own mentality in the distant perspective borrowed from Stone Age man.

—Bronislaw Malinowski, "Myth in Primitive Psychology"

The "distant perspective" I bring to bear on television as our symbol of technological and cultural sophistication is that of the savage intellect revealed in myth by the theories and methods of Claude Lévi-Strauss. When Lévi-Strauss first used structural analysis in his study of the Oedipal myth (1955), his findings bewildered the academic world. He was variously accused of crediting myths with more and less than the savage mind was capable; by and large, though, his work was mistakenly considered to be a mere aberrancy. Not until Edmund Leach added a more pragmatic flavor to the theories and applied the methods to several classical Biblical and Hindu myths (Leach, 1961, 1962a, 1962b, 1966) did the English-speaking world become familiar with the technique.

Lévi-Strauss, meanwhile, was already conducting advanced exploration into the vast dimensions of the human mind as revealed by his methods (1963a). His work on myth—*mythologiques,* as he calls it—has culminated in a tedious four volumes (1964, 1967, 1968, 1971). Tedious—his techniques reveal such

15

complexity in even a simple story that the resultant labyrinth is again met with bewilderment and skepticism by even his close followers. However, his advocates are now legion and under his influence a variety of scholars have once more returned to seek the universal truths of human nature in myths of the ancient and the innocent.

Lévi-Strauss's structural analysis has been applied imaginatively and rewardingly to a wide variety of oral traditions over the last decade.[1] In this paper I illustrate how a new medium, television, can be approached in a similar manner. My reasons for suggesting the application of structural analysis to this realm are not simply to add another study to the numerous ones already existing, nor to suggest that different methods are needed and different structures forthcoming, but rather to apply structural analysis to a tradition that we can all judge critically. A most surprising result of this approach is that it demonstrates that despite the enormous complexity afforded by an electronically transmitted visual dimension, the basic structural features of most television programs are virtually identical to the nonindustrial traditions analyzed by Lévi-Strauss and other structuralists. As a result, I shall be particularly concerned with demonstrating the similarities between television serials (using "Star Trek" as an example) and myth when compared in terms of Lévi-Strauss's formula $(f_x A : f_y B :: f_x B : f_{a-1} Y)$; and discussing the nature of mediation and mediators in modern myth.

We need not concern ourselves with an elaboration of this cryptic formula or the use of the word "mediator" at the present time since these are discussed at length later. However, for those readers who hate to be left in the dark about the conclusion of a paper, the formula, briefly, states that the principal characters or imagery of a myth always stand in an initial relationship of opposition to one another; hence, the left-hand side of the formula. This opposition is resolved through the narrative of the myth by a series of mediating characters and processes in such a way that the characters partake in one another's character and function ("f"). This mediation is what the right-hand side "explains." This, Lévi-Strauss claims, is a structure (i.e., the formula or rule) common to all myth, which he views as many mental attempts at reconciling and transforming the basic contradictions between nature and culture, the real and the ideal.

MYTH AND TELEVISION SERIALS

Most structuralists would probably agree that it is not wise to define myth too rigorously. Although Levi-Strauss places it at one extreme of verbal expression in opposition to poetry (1955), others have found it necessary to distinguish mythic structure from that of other oral traditions (Köngäs-Maranda and Maranda, 1971). In this study I have taken inspiration from Lévi-Strauss's advice to "broaden one's perspective, seeking a more general point of view which will permit the integration of forms whose regularity has already been established . . . but [are] incompletely analyzed or viewed in too narrow a fashion" (1963a: 46). Certainly television, like myth, is at the opposite end of the expressive spectrum from poetry.

From this perspective it could be argued that much of a weekly television schedule potentially qualifies as myth. Clearly, westerns, gangster shows, espionage thrillers, and others have a social function for our society similar to that of myths among many nonindustrial peoples. I shall choose "Star Trek," strictly speaking a "prophecy tale," for my analysis and try to reveal the common internal, logical grounds it shares with myth. Each of the characteristics linking "Star Trek" to myth are internal ones. There is also an external correspondence, for as with myth in relation to religion, "Star Trek" has a cultlike following of believers whose association is perpetuated by some truths and values they distill from the program.

The features commented on are time, the logic of fantasy, narrative structure, and levels of reality represented and linked by myth.

Time

Though myth is placed in period long ago, in another sense it is also timeless. Lévi-Strauss has written: "[myth] explains the present and the past as well as the future" (1963c: 209).

17

"Star Trek," despite its futuristic time setting, is clearly meant to carry a message for the present. Given the fantastic machines and exotic forces of the universe that make up the scenarios, many of the episodes actually leap back into our own American past for their plots and settings. The promiscuous use of temporal settings achieves the same end as that achieved by using a temporal setting long ago in the past: ability to create an ideal model of existence bearing a "genetic" similarity to the present, but lacking all the annoying facts of the real world.

The Logic of Fantasy

The essence of myth is that it contradicts the elements and the logic of ordinary existence. Upon closer inspection, however, it is clear that myth is restrained by both physical and human nature. For those who adhere to its peculiar tradition, myth is enhanced by an extraordinary (though not exactly irrational) truth-value. "Star Trek," while frankly acknowledged as fantasy, expresses fundamental values of American society precisely because they are seen to persist "victoriously" (to use Maranda's term) in what could have been an utterly imaginary future situation. From the perspective of a projected future, it is apparently reassuring to see that our present values have withstood time to confront the as yet unknown world of the future. The fantasy of television has a particularly powerful link to reality since there always persists the feeling that "seeing is believing."

Narrative Structure

Myth, as Lévi-Strauss has demonstrated, consists of meaningful units, mythemes, or gross constituent units that exist "at the sentence level" (1963c: 210-212). While myth is presented diachronically in narrative strings of such related units, the repetition of mythemes throughout the narrative creates bundles of related unit-relationships through which the meaning of the myth is expressed. Analysis consists of abstracting these sets of relationships and expressing them in a model that can be used for the purpose of comparing different versions of the same myth and for comparing different myths.

Since it is this aspect of Lévi-Strauss's technique that aroused so much skepticism when it was first presented, it is perhaps advisable to present a brief example of this style of analysis.

Hammel (1972) provides us with an excellent example of a structural analysis of the familiar tale of "The Three Bears." I abstract aspects of a synchronic analysis of one version and encourage the interested reader to consult Hammel's full analysis for a rewarding discussion and example of structural methodology. I quote in full:

> Papa Bear, Mama Bear, and Baby Bear were eating breakfast. Papa Bear said "My porridge is too hot." Mama Bear said, "My porridge is too hot, too." Baby Bear said, "My porridge is too hot, and I burned my tongue." So they went into the woods to look for some honey and to let the porridge cool. Meanwhile, Goldilocks had been walking in the woods and found their house. She went in and saw the porridge and tasted it. Papa Bear's porridge was too hot. Mama Bear's porridge was too cold. Baby Bear's porridge was just right and she ate it all up. Then Goldilocks sat in Papa Bear's chair, but it was too hard. Then she sat in Mama Bear's chair, but it was too soft. Then she sat in Baby Bear's chair, and it was just right, but she broke it. Then Goldilocks was tired and wanted to rest. She tried Papa Bear's bed, but it was too hard. She tried Mama Bear's bed, but it was too soft. Then she tried Baby Bear's bed, and it was just right, and she fell fast asleep. When the three bears came home with the golden honey, Papa Bear said, "Someone has been eating my porridge." Mama Bear said, "Someone has been eating *my* porridge." Baby Bear said, "Someone ate my porridge all up." Then Papa Bear said, "Someone has been sitting in my chair." Mama Bear said, "Someone has been sitting in *my* chair." And Baby Bear said, "Someone sat in my chair and broke it." Than Papa Bear said, "Someone has been sleeping in my bed." Mama Bear said, "Someone has been sleeping in *my* bed." And Baby Bear said, "Someone *is* sleeping in my bed." The three bears looked at Goldilocks. Goldilocks woke up and

saw the bears and ran away home. The bears went back to their breakfast of porridge, milk and honey. (Hammel, (1972: 8-9)

Mytheme, the meaningful unit Lévi-Strauss first identified in myth, is like a sememe, the unit of meaning in ordinary speech. Just as semanticists talk of different types of meaning in ordinary speech (Leech, 1974), we may recognize different types of meaning in myths. At one level, we may analyze the equivalent of the semanticist's "conceptual meaning" by looking for contrastiveness and constituent structures:

man=	+ human	woman=	+ human	boy=	+ human
	+ adult		+ adult		- adult
	+ male		- male		+ male

At other levels we can look at "connotative meaning": woman implies a list of associative properties, such as housewife, mother, gregariousness, etc. "Collocative meaning" is implied by the words associated with the term: woman is pretty, man is handsome; and so on until every last aspect of meaning is accounted for. Detailed analysis of even a simple myth along these lines, using the Lévi-Straussian methods at each level and then for the whole has an effect similar to using a centrifuge to separate the constituents of a complex liquid such as milk. However, the whole process is extremely elaborate and complicated, so in analyzing this preliminary example, and even in dealing with "Star Trek," we merely skim off the cream in a rather crude fashion.

The first step in a structural analysis is to identify the mythemes and arrange them in groups, but at the same time to try to preserve as much of the narrative sequence as possible. The simplest way is as displayed below.

20

A_{fx}	Bf_y	Bf_x	$Y_{a\text{-}1}$
family of bears tries to eat breakfast of porridge: a) Papa Bear: "too hot" b) Mama Bear: "too hot" c) Baby Bear: burns tongue			bears go into woods to gather honey
	Goldilocks walking through woods intrudes on bear's domain: a) tries to eat porridge, twice unsuccessfully b) tries to sit on chair, twice unsuccessfully c) tries to sleep on bed, twice unsuccessfully	Goldilocks consumes or destroys the bears' property: a) eats all of Baby Bear's porridge b) comfortable on Baby Bear's chair but breaks it c) falls asleep on Baby Bear's bed	
family of bears return to home with honey to find their property tampered with: a) "someone eating my porridge" b) "someone sitting on my chair" c) "someone sleeping on my bed"			bears find their property consumed or destroyed: a) "someone ate my porridge all up" b) "someone sat on my chair and broke it." c) "someone *is* sleeping in my bed"
	Goldilocks wakes up, runs from bears	Goldilocks returns to her home	

The mythemes thus abstracted are grouped in columns. Throughout the narrative, abridged in the table but running from left to right, the mythemes are contrasted and repeated at another level of contrast to express their relationships. Myths are often cryptic; despite their repetitiveness, they often express different kinds of meaningful relationships simultaneously. Hence, the appreciation of a myth is usually at an "impressionistic," symbolic level, and the analysis is dependent upon scant clues and subtle nuances of usage. In my present analysis I shall deal only with the summary relationships expressed on the bottom of the table.

As Hammel notes, "Philosophically or interpretively speaking, Goldilocks' adventure consists of the introduction, playing out, and resolution of a conflict between Nature and Culture" (1972: 9). The summary logic of the narrative places the conflict in a well-defined metaphoric structure that dynamically reconciles the opposed elements by both interparticipation of their qualities or functions (e.g., B_{fx} becomes B_{fy}) and reduction of their opposed qualities or inversion of them (e.g., fy becomes Y_{a-1}). This reconciliation of the conflict, then, is through a process of *mediation* in the terms and functions of the characters. Thus the culturalized Bear family is unable to partake in human activities (eating porridge, sitting in chairs, sleeping in beds) and goes to the woods to collect honey, activities associated with nature. The intruding girl, Goldilocks, succeeds where the bears fail; she ultimately returns to her home. The bears are left with a lifestyle less complete than before the intrusion: The Baby Bear's porridge, chair, and bed have been destroyed by her actions. Hammel carries the analysis to several other levels, which I shall let him summarize.

> The major dimensions of contrast are those of 1) Nature versus Culture, 2) object versus being, and 3) active/large versus active/small. The dimensions of similarity, which bridge and mediate the oppositions just stated, are 1) color and sweetness, which link Goldilocks and honey, 2) utilization, which places the bears and the honey in the same functional relationship as Goldilocks and the bed and the por-

ridge, and 3) goodness to fit to an opposite, which unites the honey to the porridge and Goldilocks to the Baby Bear. (Hammel, 1972: 14)

However, while I agree with his conclusion that the moral of the story is simply "people are not animals, Culture is not Nature," I would prefer to emphasize that the moral is expressed more exactly as:

cultural bears : natural girl : : cultural girl : nature inverted

or,

$$Af_x : Bfy : : Bf_x : Y_{a-1}$$

The opposition of Nature and Culture, despite the recounter's attempts at reconciliation, is indeed irreconcilable. Although culture and nature are homologous in some ways, they are different in others. Even in the juxtaposition of cultural bears and natural girls we must recognize a lack in culture. So, "cultural bears are to natural girls as cultural girls are to Nature incompleted (less than whole, a-1)," says the myth.

In his expeditions through the mythological traditions of many cultures, Lévi-Strauss has come to the conclusion that mythic reality expresses a realization of man's place in the universe that is both hopeful and pathetic. It is hopeful in that it regards the achievements of man (culture) as superior to those of the universe around him (nature)—he is created in the image of God; it is pathetic in that it regards the achievements of man (culture) as a tenuous delusion—merely an artificial reality incapable of even self perpetuity and maintenance without the aid of nature. Human nature (culture) is a nature less than complete. Sex, eating, death, and so forth are facts of life no matter how nicely we dress them in cultural trappings (for a structural look at the cultural trappings of an American meal, see Douglas, 1971).

We will now return to our discussion of "Star Trek." Careful recording and analysis of television serial episodes such as "Star Trek" reveal the same structural features and mythic logic as those found by Lévi-Strauss, Hammel, and others in diverse

23

non-Western mythic traditions and children's fairy tales. Television, of course, has an additional visual dimension—a complex product of choreography, actors, and camera shots—but all this is governed by the same principles that underlie the verbal dimensions of oral myth. To the extent that a television serial is considered a single program, each episode may be treated as a different version of one myth with the same basic mythemic relationships—set in different external contexts. While a viewer can comprehend the meaning of a single episode in isolation, additional episodes elaborate on the basic relationships and add different dimensions. Thus a broader, yet more fundamental, understanding of the structures can be obtained by comparing the different episodes.

Levels of Reality Represented and Linked by Myth

Myth, as Lévi-Strauss has demonstrated over the years since his analysis of the Zuni material (1963c: 219-227), not only has a "horizontal" structure of relations between mytheme bundles, but a "vertical" relation between different levels of reality (economic, ecological, cosmological, etc.). Further, myth stands in a dialectical relationship to society, the "lived-in structure." Again, let me elaborate, for Lévi-Strauss is referring here not to the types of meaning discussed earlier but rather almost to their opposite, the kinds of deception in myth.

Myth somehow gets away with convincing one—even if only for the moment—that its message contains a truth in the face of a nonsensical circumstance. We accept its argument in part because a certain internal symmetry in its different levels of reality replaces that of the real world. For those who do not recognize this symmetry, the myth, no matter how well translated, is mere falsehood. In this sense we can say that one culture's bible is another culture's myth, for the dialectical relationship between mythic reality and the real world is not significant for the believer. Or, to be more accurate, the symmetry of the mythic reality could be said to be more perfect and more workable and therefore has instructional or inspirational value.

24

One of the major functions of myth is to resolve elementary dilemmas of existence. As E. R. Leach puts it, "Lévi-Strauss has argued that when we are considering the universalist aspect of primitive mythology we shall repeatedly discover that the hidden message is concerned with the resolution of unwelcome contradictions. ... The repetitions and prevarications of mythology so fog the issue that irresolvable logical inconsistencies are lost sight of even when they are logically expressed" (1970: 58).

Myth represents those dilemmas in sets of imagery that are homologous to reality. In complex myths, or in myths represented in widely varying forms (as is often the case in non-Western traditions), many such sets occur in the same myth. The sets are arranged in an order to progressively reduce the initial opposites, sometimes through scenes that have no overt relationship but that still retain common structural properties. Often the dilemmas are pervasive enough in a culture's activities that the scene shifts (or is possibly simultaneously represented) from warfare to family life, from institutions of social control to those of daily livelihood, from the community to the individual, and so on. At each level, between each level, and through each level the major dimensions of the problems are posed, reduced, and resolved at what Lévi-Strauss has identified as a structural level.

In "Star Trek" the metaphor of the spaceship, its crew, and the various extraterrestrial phenomena they encounter constitute a highly complex and multidimensional reality subtly juxtaposed to the lived-in existence of American society.

Since "Star Trek" is shown as a series of episodes, to understand a given episode fully we must compare its structure to that of past ones. What in one episode is elaborate and exaggerated is tacitly presented in subsequent episodes. The development of the characters and their relationships to one another and to foreign beings is a process continued through the entire series.[2] The analytically active mind has no trouble seeing that the spaceship and its crew represent a number of contemporary organizations and institutions. That the metaphor has its origins in the common denominator of our culture's organizational categories and structures is clear. Transformations linking different episodes

25

are simple and obvious. In one program, the organization is (1) *the military*, with a commander (Captain Kirk), lieutenants, corporals, and civilian advisors. In another, the metaphor is (2) *a nation*, with its president (Kirk) and a cabinet representing specialist functions such as scientific, technological, medical, sociological, etc. Equally obvious is (3) *a corporation*—the ship is named the *Enterprise*—with its chairman of the board, a scientific research division, industrial psychologist, public relations divisions, etc. A constant but only occasionally central metaphorical representation is that of (4) *humanity*—"spaceship Earth"—with each of the races and nationalities represented in stereotypic role relations. It is not hard to find the metaphor of (5) *the human body*, contained by an outer skin (the ship) and including counterparts to the various organs of food distribution, locomotion, emotions, intellect, and drives.

In any given episode, one or more of these metaphors, along with others, is overtly featured. The metaphorical representation, organized man, is presented in an adventurous situation, always in confrontation with that which seeks to destroy it. The confrontations take the form of clearcut dichotomies which are portrayed verbally and visually on many planes.

	Realm	*vs.*	*Opposition*
Nation:	The *Enterprise* crew is a good power protecting the weak and innocent		The evil Klingan Empire, which exploits the weak and innocent
Military:	The *Enterprise* crew of reasonable officers and devoted ranks		The Klingan crew of brutal officers and self-serving ranks
Military:	The *Enterprise* crew of orderly command		The primitive and rebellious band
Humanity:	Human free will and compassion		The computer being and robot-populated worlds
Humanity:	Intellect combined with corporal desires		The mind-only beings and spiritual worlds
Ideology:	The man of action		Pacifists and idealists

Inevitably, the *Enterprise* crew overcomes the adversary in a complex process of mediating the opposition and demonstrating the superiority of the *Enterprise* crew. The sequence involves a series of partial oppositions and partial mediators in a typically nonlineal progression. Each episode, for that matter, is clearly meant to be merely a part of a longer series of confrontations that serve to define human morality in the future.

To effect mediation, the program incorporates a wide variety of inherently medial beings, the most important of whom is Spock, the half-human, half-Vulcan being who is second in command of the ship. Others are encountered in different worlds; they vary from animated rocks to minimally materialized bundles of energy; from emotional robots to mechanized humans. But even Captain Kirk, the stereotyped ideal of American normalcy, can function as a mediator when the opposing ideals of our own society confront one another.

We have seen that the program is based on moral problems, stated in the form of conflict between opposites, and the resolution of these problems involves mediation. An altogether too brief synopsis and analysis of a single episode will help to establish the characteristic structure of the program and the role of the mediators in more detail. Again, I shall only have time to "skim the cream."

In this episode,[3] the *Enterprise* is engaged to bring a mineral from one planet (B) to save another planet (A) from an epidemic disease. One minute into the program we encounter multidimensional dialectic involving planet of disease (organic)–planet of medicine (mineral), *Enterprise* as mediator (technological). Rushing to planet B the crew discovers a revolution between the Dionysian miners who live on the surface of the planet and the planet's commercial rulers, who live an Apollonian existence in a cloud city. The social revolution is holding up the shipment of the mineral. When Captain Kirk forcibly and physically conquers the female (dark hair and complexion, ill-clad) leader of the miners and the intellectual Spock rejects the affections of the daughter (blonde, toga-clad) of the leader of the sky people, the classical dichotomy is partially mediated by the more extreme dichotomies inherent in the interstellar

27

crew. Halfway through the program we see the sophisticated discipline of the sky people crumble and their aggressive tendencies surface. Meanwhile, the miners are shown to be capable of reason and feelings.

Together, Kirk and Spock reason that the apparently opposed races (or civilizations) are merely the result of the miners' continual exposure to the mineral-medicine, which accentuates their aggressive tendencies. After a sequence in which the miners are removed from the mineral's influence and the skyleader is exposed to it (thus each part fully takes on the character of the other) the two races recognize their common nature. In the end the *Enterprise* crew agrees to mediate a just settlement of reciprocal duties between the two peoples and finally leave to bring the medicine to avert the epidemic on planet A.

Interestingly, the internal dichotomy of the one planet (B) is not completely resolved, but is qualitatively altered from that of a natural one to a cultural one. The physical differences are the product of the invisible emissions of an inert environmental agent that is the backbone of the planet's economy. The physically based division of labor is changed qualitatively into a cultural one when the damaging effects of the mineral can be controlled by technology. The passage from nature to culture is apparently one of the concerns of our culture, and one of our methods of comprehending it (i.e., through myth) is the same as that in primitive societies.

The structure of "Star Trek" appears to adhere closely to the "law of myth" as expressed by Lévi-Strauss's formula (f_xA: $f_yB::f_xB:f_{a-1}A$). Dichotomies expressed as oppositions between the terms and functions of A and B are equated with a situation in which B is given the starting function of A and is opposed to the inverted character of A serving as a function of the earlier function of B. Hence, planet B is capable of providing the cure for planet A, but is itself diseased—socially—and the curative function of medicine is withheld because of internal opposition and conflict. The episode utilizes the formula again and again in relation to the oppositions inherent in planet B—repeatedly at various levels in the complex opposition between Apollonian and Dionysian imagery. Analytically this process may be treated somewhat like embedding in transformational linguistic analysis. Eventually the oppositions are mediated, though not eliminated, since a division of labor remains. Yet the transformation from nature to culture is complete.

Oppositions abound throughout the episode at all levels as expressed via ideology, materials, emotions, actions, and appearances.

Planet A	*Planet B*
sickness, needs medicine	has medicine
	sky people earth people
	Apollonian rulers Dionysian workers
	beauty toil
	distribution production

The opposed elements undergo a series of operations that alter their oppositions. This process itself involves two types of mediators and mediating actions: (1) confrontation with a character (or character set) who shares the qualities of both poles, but is superior to each in its own way, and (2) the inversion of the characteristics of the opposed characters until their common nature is established.

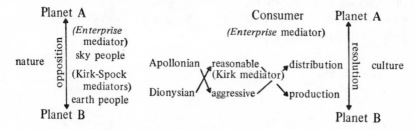

The use of mediation and mediators is of fundamental importance to an understanding of the significance of "Star Trek" to its ardent followers. The initial and continual opposition of a planet in need of a curative mineral and a planet that possesses this mineral is mediated not only by the *Enterprise* but also by the entire play on contradiction, which occupies the body of the episode. The internal contradiction among the people of planet B is shifted from an irreconcilable natural one to an "understandable" cultural one based only on the arbitrary but necessary division of labor in a system of exchange.

Mediation, a logical process, may use medial beings, such as Spock, but need not. Actually, mediation is, in this episode at least, accomplished more frequently by balancing extremes with the "super-normal" hero Captain Kirk (he may be simply a "well-balanced" person), or by inversion of the characters' behavior as a reaction to the catalytic agent or element, the "medicine," which is not itself medial.

Thus the resolution of the conflict, felt to be a revelation or conquest of sorts, is transformed by the media into a logical encounter. What reason would the American public give for the popularity of such logical games? I suspect that the answer is analogous to the reply that any member of a nonliterate, nonindustrial society might give. Myth and "Star Trek" provide a model of real society in which the conflicts of life can reasonably be resolved precisely by adhering to values transcending nature, those same values that are so frail and elusive in the factual world.

Finding not only the same laws but the same significance in myth of television affirms Lévi-Strauss's expectations that "man has always been thinking equally well; the improvements lie not in the alleged progress of man's mind, but in the discovery of new areas to which it may apply its unchanged and unchanging powers" (1963c: 230).

NOTES

This paper was first read in the symposium, "Form and Formative in the Symbolic Process," held at the American Anthropological Association Annual Convention, 1974, Mexico City. I wish to thank the members of that symposium for their helpful suggestions and their critical comments.

1. Particularly noteworthy contributions available in English are: Leach, 1962a, 1966, and Köngäs-Maranda and Maranda, 1971.

2. Although different episodes have different authors, a group of editors assures consistency from episode to episode. The overriding criterion, though, is public appeal—that the story encapsulate the collective fantasy of the audience. The potential objection (cf. Hammel, 1972) is that because each "Star Trek" episode has a known author, structural methodology, which is geared to collective representations does not apply. Even if it did, the question of authorship is, I think, a red herring.

3. I purposely omit the title and the details from the episode in order to divorce my analysis from a "literary" analysis of the episode. The analysis I give emphasizes the gross structural features. I expect that this type of analysis will draw criticism from certain elements of the large crowd of devoted fans, called "Trekkies," whose attention—as is true of Biblical scholars—is on the accuracy of the details.

References

Douglas, M., 1971, "Deciphering a Meal." In C. Geertz, ed. *Myth, Symbol, and Culture.* New York: Norton.

Hammel, E., 1972, "The Myth of Structural Analysis: Lévi-Strauss and the Three Bears." Addison-Wesley Module in Anthropology, No. 25.

Köngäs-Maranda, E. and P. Maranda, 1971, *Structural Models in Folklore and Transformational Essays.* The Hague: Mouton.

Leach, E. R., 1961, "Lévi-Strauss in the Garden of Eden: An Examination of Some Recent developments in the Analysis of Myth." *Transactions* of the New York Academy of Sciences, Ser. II, vol. 23, no. 4.

   −1962a, "Genesis as Myth." *Discovery,* May 1962:30-35. (Also reprinted in *myth and cosmos*

   −1962b, "Pulleyar and Lord Buddha." *Psychoanalysis and Psychoanalytic Review* 49, no. 2: 81-102

   −1966, "The Legitimacy of Solomon: Some Structural Aspects of Old Testament History." *Archives of European Sociology* 7: 58-101.

Leech, G., 1974, *Semantics.* Baltimore: Penguin.

Lévi-Strauss, C., 1955, "The Structural Study of Myth." In *Myth, a Symposium. Journal of American Folklore* 78, no. 270: 428-444.

   −1960, "Four Winnebago Myths: A Structural Sketch." In S. Diamond, ed. *Culture in History, Essays in Honor of Paul Radin.* Published for Brandeis University Press by Columbia University Press, New York.

   −1963a, *Totemism.* London: Merlin Press. (English translation of *Le Totemisme aujourd'hui,* Paris.)

   −1963b, *La Pensée Sauvage.* (English translation, *The Savage Mind.* Chicago: University of Chicago Press.)

   −1963c, *Structural Anthropology.* New York: Basic Books.

   −1964, *Mythologiques I: Le Cru et le Cuit.* Paris: Plon. (English translation, *The Raw and the Cooked.* New York: Harper & Row, 1969.)

   −1967, *Mythologiques II: Du Mel aux Cendres.* Paris: Plon. (English translation, *From Honey to Ashes.* New York: Harper & Row.)

   −1968, *Mythologiques III: L'Origine des manières detable.* Paris: Plon.

   −1971, *Mythologiques IV: L'Homme Nu.* Paris: Plon.

FOOTBALL GAMES AND ROCK CONCERTS

The Ritual Enactment of American Success Models

SUSAN P. MONTAGUE

and

ROBERT MORAIS

This paper stems from a particularly insightful comment made by anthropologist Clifford Geertz about ritual. He writes that rituals are "not only models *of* what ... [men] ... believe, but also models for the believing of it. In these plastic dramas men attain their faith as they portray it" (1966: 29). Anthropologists have long recognized that myth and ritual function as vehicles to remind people of the basic ideology that underlies society's organization. Geertz touches on the still remaining question of faith: How is it that people become convinced that the ideology presented to them is actually truthful and correct? This question has remained unexplored, largely due to the anthropological conception of "primitives" as people who live in an ideologically monolithic universe. It is assumed that in the absence of alternative ideologies the question of faith does not arise. But this conceptualization is too naive, and certainly cannot handle questions of how faith in the existing social system is generated in societies (such as our own) that offer a variety of alternative ideologies.

Geertz does not elaborate on his idea, but his comment provides a starting point for exploring the question of why Americans find such disparate performances as football games and rock concerts so emotionally compelling. Unfortunately, informants cannot provide an adequate explanation to account for their attraction to these phenomena. This has left scholars with the task of coming up with indirect explanations, which most often are psychological, and focus on the American predilection toward violence. Various writers differ on just why Americans find violence so stimulating and desirable, but they agree that this factor does attract Americans. However, these explanations are inadequate because they fail to account for why certain standardized expressions of violence are so much more popular than others.

More importantly, the explanations miss the point. Football games and rock concerts are standardized cultural performances. Viewers find them compelling insofar as they embody significant messages. From this perspective, it is striking that the symbolic content of both these entertainment forms is heavily oriented toward the definition of success in our society. In this paper, we argue that it is impossible to directly verify in everyday life that the tenets of American success models are correct. Actors cannot readily prove to themselves that application of the models will in fact result in success. Consequently, faith in these models must be generated in some other way. This is done through symbolic validation, which is embodied in, among other things, ritual performances including football games and rock concerts. We will examine how these performance modes provide validation of American success models.

To begin it is necessary to examine the concept of success. Success is an articulating concept bridging the gap between, on the one hand, the American cosmological model of the social universe and, on the other, actor-grounded behavioral models. The cosmological model, based on traditional Christian theology, portrays a perfect universe created by God, functioning according to His laws. Man, however, violated these laws out of greed; therefore, he must wage a never-ceasing battle against his human failing. Due to his flawed character, he can never achieve God's perfection, but the price of relaxed vigilance is personal and social disaster. This model underwent gradual modification, which culminated in the late nineteenth century in the scientific-physicalist revolution wherein the laws of nature competed with and partially replaced the laws of God. However, the scientific-physicalist model of the cosmos compounded man's difficult situation, since the laws of God manifest two useful properties missing in the laws of nature. First, they are directly revealed and written down in wholly legitimized sacred books. Second, they are moral laws, which provide direct guidelines for man's behavior. The laws of nature are neither directly revealed nor moral, but instead must be discovered through an indirect process of experimentation. Further, since they are physical and not moral laws, men must also find a means for deriving behavioral guidelines from them.

The more pertinent problem for the individual is to translate universal behavioral guidelines, however formulated, into specific actions. In contemporary American culture, the concept of success constitutes one bridge between these two levels, facilitating the conversion of the general into the specific and vice versa. It does this in two ways, first by stating criteria by which the two levels are to be articulated, and second by defining a social feedback system that provides the actor with a means for monitoring the adequacy or inadequacy of his behavior. The feedback system demands our attention first.

Until the late Middle Ages, this mediation between the individual and the universal was the monopoly of Catholicism's monolithic institutional structure, and was expressed through the concepts of grace and salvation. The mediating ability was embodied in annointed individuals who participated in rituals of direct spiritual communion with God. This relationship also legitimized their role as moral arbiters of people's behavior. However, with the rise of Protestantism, the mediating role of the priest was greatly diminished, and in theory each individual was left to confront God directly and alone. This in fact meant that behavioral monitoring gradually moved outside any one given institution and was taken over by society at large. However, the result, which is still with us, is a nebulous feedback system that is both impersonal and indirect. If there is no oracle to consult, there can be no one person the actor can turn to for authoritative interpretation. Instead, feedback is provided by an intricate system of social rewards, anonymously conferred. The actor himself must attempt to monitor his behavior by examining how well he is doing in the process. This means that there must be a reward currency, and indeed there is—the so-called status symbol.

Because the reward system is indirect and impersonal, it is difficult for any given actor to verify that it actually works. According to the ideology, the system functions automatically. But how can the individual be assured that he is actually receiving his just and due reward? Further, while the rewards are conceived of as coming from society at large, they are actually conferred by a number of independent institutions. This raises the problem of standardization, since again it is difficult for the actor to determine whether or not he would receive the same reward if he worked for a different institution. Thus, in order for the system to be accepted by society's members as suitable and just, two directly unverifiable points must somehow be verified: first, that it works, and second, that it works uniformly across the board.

The other feature of the success concept is that it functions to bridge the ideological gap between universal law and the individual's behavioral guidelines in such a way as to facilitate the construction of behavioral rules that are consonant with cosmological law. This is accomplished by avoiding the question of the actual content of the universal law, and focusing instead on the motivation that underlies that content. The motivation is love. Just as the universe was created out of God's love, so the individual who acts with love can assume that he is behaving properly. Ironically, this device, which is appropriate to the Christian model of the universe, is even more important for the formulation of behavioral guidelines under the scientific-physicalist model, which does not actually contain any motivational component. Since scientific-physicalist laws are not social laws, it is difficult to derive behavioral interpretations directly from them. This difficulty enhances the value of a cultural mechanism that avoids the direct confrontation of universal law and individual behavior. Thus our culture fosters and reinforces the nature-love equation, even though that equation is not necessarily valid.

The concept of success shifts the problem of formulating behavioral guidelines from correct interpretation of universal law to correct application of universal motivation. This means that the actor and society must define which behaviors are loving. This type of definition constitutes the subject matter of success models.[1] Let us look at how the two success models embodied in football and rock define loving behavior.

Within the traditional American success model, love is defined as altruistic self-sacrifice. The properly oriented actor dedicates his life to working to improve the lives of others. In its more general form, this means that men hold jobs in the world of commerce, and women run the home and raise children. Success is defined in terms of men's work accomplishments. Women do not participate directly in the success system, but measure their status in terms of that of their husbands' accomplishments. The success system rewards moral character, which is manifested for men through work, and for women by domestic performance. A proper marriage is one that matches the moral character of the partners. Given such a union, the reward to the man can validly extend to cover the woman.

This model not only defines proper behavior, but also improper. A popular "success" author informs us that: "In time I came to recognize four basic causes for failure among salesmen; they apply equally, of course, to the pursuit of success in any line of endeavor. They are: illicit sex, alcohol, deception, and stealing (Stone, 1962: 133). Other writers on contemporary morality and success go further, and condemn smoking and gambling. Such acts are seen as indulgences that deter the individual from the path of altruistic self-sacrifice, and thus lead to failure.

The second success model, which we call the creative model, is the converse of the first. It argues that love is manifested through self-expression, rather than altruistic self-denial. Each individual possesses unique talents, and by allowing these to flower, he makes his contribution to the world. In this system, creativity replaces altruism as the valued personal commodity. This model is directly in line with scientific-physicalism, and its earliest manifestations in American pulp literature convert the ideal worker from the dedicated drudge (Alger's bank clerks and busboys) to the explorer, inventor, and scientist (Stratemeyer's Tom Swift and Don Sturdy): actors bent on discovery of the laws of the physical world. The traditional model is a straight-forward application of the Protestant Ethic, and the creative model is a response to the adoption of scientific-physicalism.

The creative model raises the same sort of difficulties that plague scientific-physicalism itself. If natural laws are difficult to discover and verify, it is also difficult to specify how to socialize individuals capable of discovering and verifying them. The valued, but routine, tasks under the traditional model can be accomplished by virtually anyone who works at them hard enough. However, creativity is more than a matter of hard work. It involves personal inventiveness, based on a recombination of elements drawn from the actor's past experiences that gives him insight into a hitherto unsolved problem. It is impossible to predict precisely which elements the creative actor will draw together to obtain his fruitful insight, which means that any and all personal experiences are appropriate, whether or not society has previously defined them as moral or immoral. Further, creativity is not amenable to a rigid timetable, and it is difficult to argue that the actor should do any specific thing at any given time. Both these facts are socially unpalatable. As a result, although the creative model appeared in America in the early twentieth century, it was not until the late 1960s that its logic was pushed to completion with the argument that the truly moral member of society is the one who orients his behavior toward "doing his own thing."

With this background, let us look at how the success models are presented and validated in football games and rock concerts. In another essay in this collection, Arens has examined football as ritual, and we shall draw on some of the points he makes. He notes that football is a uniquely American game, but more than that, a cultural feature that distinguishes us from other peoples with whom we share a good many cultural traits, including language. In the United States, football is an extraordinarily popular phenomenon. Arens suggests that this is because football reflects characteristics that have a high priority in American culture: technological complexity, coordination, and specialization. He points out that the tendency to violence, which native informants stress as a captivating feature of football, is not unique to the sport. What is unique is that the violence is "expressed within the framework of teamwork, specialization, mechanization, and variation." In short, to push Arens' observations a bit further, the football team looks very much like a small-scale model of the American corporation: compartmentalized, highly sophisticated in the coordinated application of a differentiated, specialized technology, turning out a winning product in a competitive market. Football ideology bears out this analogy. Successful football coaches frequently function during the off-season as business-management consultants. Some, such as Phil Krueger, a coach at U.S.C., preach that the value of football lies not in the game itself, but in its effectiveness as a vehicle that prepares men for successful business careers (Fiske, 1975: 66). Indeed, the late Vince Lombardi, coach of the perennial champion Green Bay Packers, spent a good portion of his off-season delivering inspirational lectures to middle-management on how to be a winner and rise to the top.

If there is good reason to conclude that Americans watching football are watching a model of their own work world, the question that confronts us is why Americans should actually choose to spend leisure time in this pursuit. The function of leisure as we ordinarily think of it is to get away from work. We argue that at least two factors account for this seemingly peculiar phenomenon. First, football, as a small-scale enactment of the commercial structure and process, renders visible and directly comprehensible a system that is far too large and complex to be directly comprehended by any individual. Even economists, specialists who devote themselves to attempting to obtain an overview of the structure and processes of the American economy, find the task impossible. The ordinary individual is of course at a loss as to how to begin. It is likely that he finds it difficult even to comprehend the internal structure of the company that employs him. This difficulty is a concomitant of the size and complexity of corporations in contemporary America. Football, through a reduction of scale and visual presentation, solves these dilemmas through concrete expression. The viewer, following the progress of teams within a league, can comprehend the functioning of the entire system. In addition he can watch a single team, his team, and observe its organization and performance as an internally coherent entity. Insofar as football is directly equated with the business world, the invisible and incomprehensible is rendered visible and comprehensible. It is inferred by the viewers that the processes that are seen to work in one system also operate in the other.

The second reason Americans spend leisure time watching their symbolic work world is an extension of the first. If the structure and processes that govern the world of football are equated with those of the world of commerce, then the principles that govern the actor's success on the football field must also apply in the world of work. As indicated above, Krueger feels that football is invaluable precisely because it trains men for success in business. But, as Fiske notes, the players are objects of respect and admiration, and "the values which they represent are emulated by their male peers" (1975: 65). The audience, too, learns by watching the players. "Peers" in this instance include a widely heterogeneous population of American men. As Arens comments, "Personally, I can think of precious little else that I have in common with our former or current president, with a rural Texan, or an urban black other than a mutual passion for this game. Football represents not only 'Middle America,' . . . but the whole of America." The values that are held up to this widely diversified audience are strikingly similar to the values of the traditional success model. The greatest football coaches are not seen to work with talent significantly superior to that on other teams. Rather, fine coaches inspire their men on to greater heights of dedication, hard work, and self-sacrifice. The televised game commentary (often provided by former idols) and the press reports focus largely on the teams' training. As Arens points out, it is here that football becomes extremely ritualistic, in the sense that the elements selected for positive comment actually have little to do directly with improving the athletic skills of the players. Instead, they are elements symbolic of dedication, hard work, and most of all, self-sacrifice for the good of the team. Let us see how this works.

Football players are required to report to summer training

camps each year to prepare for the fall playing season. The purpose of the camp is to improve player skills, develop team coordination, and get the players into condition to undergo the rigors of game combat. While team coordination is probably the most significant rational activity, both the camp schedule and the publicity place equally, if not greater, emphasis on the development of physical toughness. "Hitting," or physical collision with an adversary, is an emphasized activity. At the same time, while it is clear that hitting is an important component of the game, players express fears of suffering injuries that might sideline them during the playing season or end their careers. However, they remain, despite the validity of their fears, under heavy pressure to hit during training. Refusal to do so is taken as a sign of cowardice, lack of dedication, refusal to be self-sacrificing for the team. Actual signs of physical incapacity are interpreted in the same manner. Players shun their injured comrades, and one insider reports that his college coach accused him of cowardice for refusing to compete after sustaining a broken neck. The epitome of the truly great player, held up for others to emulate, is Joe Namath, who supposedly quarterbacked the underdog Jets to a Super Bowl victory when he was sleeping in the living room of his parents' house because his knees were so bad he could not climb the stairs to his second-floor bedroom. His personal pain did not deter him from accomplishing the almost impossible on behalf of his team.

In addition, great emphasis is placed on forms of self-denial. During the training period players are prohibited from indulging not only in illicit sex, but also licit sex, by being segregated from their wives. Also, the players must not smoke or drink. A movie version of training camp shows team members sneaking out after bed check for a few beers at a local tavern like naughty boys on an adventurous escapade. Gambling is also taboo at all times. The football commissioner went so far as to threaten to ban Joe Namath from competition until he sold his interest in a New York bar and restaurant, which numbered among its clientele several suspected syndicate gamblers.

All of these self-sacrificing, self-denying behaviors are utilized as indices of player and team worthiness. The audience is told repeatedly that winning teams deserve to win, and do win, because their players are dedicated, hard-working, and self-sacrificing. These attributes are stressed even though the true problem of the game lies in the effective application of a complex division of labor. While this is recognized in football commentary, it is not stressed to the extent that the attributes of the success model are. Players often complain that the public, which eats up their self-sacrifices, is not as interested in the content of the various different highly skilled roles required to play the game. This makes sense because the viewer can directly comprehend specialization: he too works at a specialized job. What he cannot comprehend as easily, but what is of greater personal interest, is how the traditional success model actually works. The discrepancy here is between the problem of the game, coordination, and the problem of the viewer's life, behavioral guidelines. Football's popularity rests to a large part on the demonstration of the components of the success model at work, rather than on the concrete realities of the game itself.

Football validates the success model by staging a real event in which the principles of success are shown to work as promised by society. The contest actually happens before the viewer's eyes. The reality of the event is then transferred to the ideology of the success model, which is presented as accounting for the winning team's superior performance. Of course, there is a sleight of hand going on here, because "the best team always wins." The team that wins is not necessarily best; it is best because it wins. In order to set the stage for the legitimacy of the assertion that the best team does indeed win, the teams must rigidly and publicly adhere to behaviors symbolic of the success model during their training. It can then be argued that a team's superior performance is consonant with the expectations of the success model. The burden of proof switches to the losers: If the team that abided by the rules wins, then the team that loses must have failed to dedicate itself seriously enough.

Football not only provides the viewer with a working demonstration of the traditional success model, but also of the accompanying monitor-reward system. Again, the actor who cannot directly comprehend the structure of the business world, or even that of his own company, where he must compete for success, cannot directly verify that this system works. This explains why a good deal of football commentary is devoted to a careful statistical monitoring of each player's performance. Players' accomplishments are compared and contrasted with those of fellow team members and competitors. Rewards in the form of salary and recognition are then extended as a result of this evaluation. Again, insofar as the equation is drawn between football and business, the viewer is reassured that the system really works, for he sees actors being dispassionately and accurately monitored and rewarded according to the merits of their performance. He can also appreciate that the monitor-reward system is standardized and thus equitable.

Rock as a performance mode shares many of the basic characteristics of football. Although rock is not a uniquely American phenomenon (it has been enthusiastically received in other countries), it began here. The book *Rock Dreams* portrays the five kings of rock on its cover. Two are Americans: Elvis Presley and Bob Dylan. The other three are English: John Lennon, Mick Jagger, and David Bowie. Contemporary rock may be dominated by the English, but it grew from roots in American blues, and has, even in the hands of foreigners, retained its preoccupation with American culture. Rock, like football, thus is essentially an American phenomenon.

The recording industry is one of America's largest businesses, and its profits are anchored solidly in rock music. The avid buyers and listeners are just as inarticulate about their fascination with rock as are football fans about their sport. The release of power is also a common feature, although in rock it is accomplished through complex coordinated sounds rather than by physical violence. Armed with instruments, voices, and microphones, the Rolling Stones become the power equivalent of the Pittsburgh Steelers.

Although it is more difficult to sharply differentiate rock from other types of music than football from other sports, this is consonant with the creative success model. Rock bands face the problem of putting out a product that is qualitatively, not quantitatively, unique. There is only so much room for origi-

43

nality within the framework of straight rock. Performers solve this problem by amalgamating elements from other musical modes into their presentations. However, the wholly impregnable kings are the purists: Elvis, Lennon, and Jagger. Significantly, artistic success within the rock world can be measured by getting one's picture on the cover of *The Rolling Stone,* the rock newspaper, named after the purest of the pure.

Just as football preaches the traditional success model, rock preaches its opposite, the creative success model. An analysis of the ideology of rock as presented by the five superstars illustrates this point. The idols epitomize creativity derived from self-indulgence. The rock press focuses on how the stars satiate themselves, in contrast to the football press, which focuses on how players deny themselves. *Shooting Stars,* a book of rock star portraits, shows no one practicing or rehearsing. The entire book contains only ten or eleven pictures of stars performing or recording. The rest of the pictures are devoted to leisure activities: sleeping, lounging, drinking, traveling, partying, and picnicking. Performer interviews also generally fail to consider the work that goes into actually producing rock music. The image of the rock band is that of a collection of individually talented players who simply get it together musically. The frequent dissolution of rock groups is presented as an inevitable concomitant of the difficulties inherent in the continued association of individually creative people, each bent on "doing his own thing."

Self-indulgence is expressed through overt participation in activities that are taboo under the traditional success model. Performers both drink and smoke, often onstage, and make no secret of drug use. The most significant departure from the self-denial tenets of the traditional success model is in the area of sex. Football players are restricted from sexual activity during training and before a game. The converse is true for rock stars. The asexual rock star is a contradiction in terms because sexuality is the idiom of power in rock music. The star is expected to behave in an overtly sexual manner, suggestive onstage and promiscuous offstage. While the congratulatory crowd may go so far as to carry their favorite football players off the field after a dramatic victory, rock stars are physically attacked by hordes of would-be lovers, each bent on securing some token of intimate physical contact—a kiss if possible, a piece of hair or clothing, if not. The freshly scrubbed, girl next door cheerleader, whose formal role is to rally the team on to victory during the game, is replaced in the rock world by the whorelike groupie, whose formal role is to sleep with the star after the performance. Groupies have no place in the performance itself, because the star onstage is expected to direct his sexuality toward the audience. Elvis led the way in the 1950s with his pelvic contortions, but his gyrations were mild compared to Jagger and Bowie, the current kings. There is a telling scene in the movie *Gimme Shelter,* of Jagger watching the warm-up band, Ike and Tina Turner, on the backstage video monitor. He becomes annoyed when Tina begins to powerfully pantomime oral sex with her microphone. To the star, a warm-up band should build up the audience, not bring it to a climax.

Though rock lyrics also treat other topics, they are often blatantly sexual. To a fan any Stones song is great, but "Satisfaction," "Let's Spend the Night Together," "Brown Sugar," and "Honky Tonk Woman" are the real classics. Similarly, Dylan's most frequently played "oldie" on A.M. radio is "Lay Lady Lay." "Suffragette City," a song about a man being interrupted by a friend during intercourse, is one of Bowie's most popular audience numbers.

Obviously, the validation problem facing rock is different from that facing football. The traditional success model is fully consonant with the tenets of the success concept. However, the monitor-reward system is not really geared to handling creativity. Creativity is not amenable to precise statistical measurement, since it is a qualitative phenomenon. It can be measured only on some scale of social importance, but even this presents problems, because any given creation may or may not have much relevance at the time of its inception. The actor's contribution may thus go unheralded for years, perhapd forever. Further, the monitor-reward system is wholly ungeared to monitoring and rewarding the self-indulgence held to be a prerequisite of the creative act. These difficulties cast a doubt on the merits of the creative success model, for it would seem less consonant with the concept of success than the traditional model. However, the dual-component feature of the success concept supplies a way out. Remember that the concept contains both the monitor-reward system and the behavior motivation component. Rock argues that the traditional success model may be consonant with the monitor-reward system, but that it is not, and by definition cannot be, consonant with the behavior motivation component, love. This is because the traditional success model is competitive.[2] For every football team that wins, another goes down to defeat. Rock makes explicit this fact that in the real world the few win, the many lose—hence the prevalence of wars, famine, poverty, and social injustice. In the rock world, competition, a virtue under the traditional success model, is transformed into the scourge of mankind, the essence of evil. This means that those who achieve "success" by adhering to the tenets of the traditional model are not really successful. Theirs is a hollow accomplishment. Further, traditionally successful individuals who tout their own virtues are either hypocrites or naive fools. Jagger presents the devil as a far more sympathetic character than the powerful people who would shun him while piously espousing traditional goodness; unlike them, the devil is straightforward about the damage he does. The unhypocritical idealist is, according to Bowie, the person who would "Kill for the Good of the Fight for the Right to be Right." He would not only slaughter his enemies who, fools themselves, are only fighting for the same thing, but also make unnecessary grief for those who love him: "she kneels before the grave. A brave son—who gave his life to save the slogan."

Rock lyrics not only point up the negative consequences of competition for mankind, but also for the competing individual himself. The most the traditionally successful actor can hope for is retaliation. As Jagger puts it, "Under my thumb, the girl who once had me down." If he commands admiration, he also inspires jealousy. Bowie writes of band members eying their guitarist-lead singer, Ziggy Stardust: "And so we bitched about his fans, and should we crush his sweet hands." More commonly, the person who achieves success is portrayed as living a hollow, lonely life, isolated from love because he has devoted himself to excelling over his fellows, rather than helping them. Probably the most powerful indictment is contained in Dylan's "Ballad of a Thin Man," in which a conscientious, hard-working, successful man winds up totally lost and disoriented in the hostile environment of his own making, and is sneeringly taunted with the fact that he knows something is happening but he doesn't know what it is. Hell has rarely been more powerfully portrayed in any medium.

Rock begins validating the creative success model by discrediting the traditional model as not really loving. However, this is only the stage setting for the more important validation, a dramatic demonstration that the creative model does itself meet the love criterion. This demonstration is of a different sort from that found in football, where the audience watches the model being acted out by the two teams in competition. In contrast, with a rock concert the audience itself participates in the drama. Performers address the audience, and with its responses it becomes part of the performance. The rock star attempts to wed himself and the audience into an experience of love. Instead of merely seeing others and generalizing from them to himself, the audience member is encouraged to join with others and experience with them.

Loneliness, caused by isolation from others, is defined in the world of rock as the essence of nonlove, and it is by breaking down the barrier of isolation that the performer creates the emotional experience of love. The audience expects this breakdown and takes steps to initiate it even before the performer comes onstage. People talk with those sitting near them, and often smoke the same "joint," which is passed among total strangers. The first task of the performer, then, is to establish some sort of personal bond with the audience. A typical example is Jagger coming onstage after several warmup bands. He apologizes for the long delay, and explains that he has been chafing to get onstage, just as the audience has been yearning for him to appear. Rock performers not only allude to feelings that they and the audience share, they also talk in language heavy with the symbolism of interpersonal bonds. Audience members are not strangers, they are brothers and sisters, friends, fellow dope smokers.

The order of material in the concert is aimed at gradually heightening the performer-audience bond. Bowie, noted for his masterful stage performances, begins with songs of alienation and gradually intersperses sexual songs, building toward the salvation climax, "Rock and Roll Suicide." This song in turn encapsulates all that has gone before, beginning with a portrayal of the anguishing loneliness of everyday existence, and winding up with the ringing affirmation: "You're *not* alone, gimme your hand! And you're *wonderful*, gimme your hand!" On a typical night, throngs surge forward, their hands outstretched, and as he takes them, one after another, each audience member can share in belonging, being valued, being loved. The audience leaves the warm, intimate satisfaction of the theater to confront the cold, competitive, lonely world outside, yet is reassured that love can be realized, for it has just happened.

The rock audience, like the football crowd, is asked to generalize from one set of experiences to another, from the professional performance to his own life. However, the two generalizations differ radically. The football fan is encouraged first to equate two separate systems, and then how individuals function within them. The key relationship is between the individual and the system. Rock, though, does not ask the audience to equate systems since it is ideologically antisystem. Instead, the rock fan is encouraged to equate one actor, the star, with another, himself. The key relationship is individual to individual. On the contrary, the football fan can watch the contest without ever identifying with any given player. However, there is no rock without the star, no fan without his personal favorite performer or performers. Indeed, as opposed to a football contest, the rock concert lacks a broader organizational context because it stands apart from the system. The concert is simply an event without meaning beyond the "happening," whereas a football game has meaning for the future actions of a whole host of teams in the larger context of league competition. The lack of context that characterizes rock concerts is itself an important part of the message encouraging individuals to relate to one another. Rock implies that context should always be subordinated to people. The rock performer takes a collection of individuals who have no particular reason beyond their common humanity for wanting to relate to one another, and tries to turn them into a community of love. It matters little that the community is highly transitory. The argument is that all people are the same but unable to perceive this fact, because so much of their time is spent participating in various competing systems. The star, freed from systemic context, demonstrates both that love can be realized, and how to go about experiencing it. The members of the audience need only keep their sights set firmly on this goal and emulate the rock star, and they too will be able to create and enjoy love as he does, which is the essence of true success.

In this paper we have outlined the content of two mutually contradictory success models. While we have not traced the historical development of each in detail, we have noted that the creative model has gradually developed as an increasingly complete inversion of the traditional model. However, the complete development of the creative model has not caused the traditional model to become outmoded or to fall into disuse. The question then is, why does our society possess and utilize two contradictory success models? We argue that this is the case because neither strikes a workable mean between the individual's and society's needs, and that they err in opposite directions.

The traditional model (which ironically is associated with a personalized, Christian, model of the universe) sacrifices the individual and his emotional satisfaction to society. The creative model (associated with an impersonalized, scientific-physicalist model of the universe) sacrifices society for the sake of the individual. These points are illustrated with reference to rock and football, which expect the performers to adhere rigidly to only one of the two models.

The problem with the traditional model is the degree to which the individual is expected to deny himself pleasure and emotional fulfillment and still lead a personally rewarding life. Football exposés point out that far from building character, the game produces sadomasochistic brutes. Players are transformed into so many hunks of moving meat to be exploited and then discarded when their self-sacrifice has rendered them physically useless. No consideration is given to their needs as people (i.e., to their feelings). They become human machines that are expected to tolerate and mete out punishment. Participants turned writers argue that football players face a choice: to reject the ideology of the game, or to reject their own humanity. The most common solution is a compromise. When players appear in public they adhere to the game's ideology, and in private consciously violate it by indulging in the taboo behaviors often characteristic of the creative success model.

In contrast, the weakness of the creative model is the extent to which it encourages each individual to "do his own thing," rather than perform routine, but socially necessary, tasks. Any society can contain only so much freedom and anarchy. Rock performers find themselves in a double bind. Ironically, while they publicly epitomize the creative success model, their work demands that they succumb to the tenets of the traditional success model. They must practice regularly, make frequent public appearances, show up for concerts and play the same songs over and over again. In general, they have to subordinate their individual or even collective desires to those of their manager, recording company, and ever-demanding audience. Their work is largely routinized, so that what they preach and what they actually do are two separate things.

In addition, they too confront the question of meaning. If, for football players, meaning is impersonalized and lies outside the system, for the rock star, it is personalized and lies within the individual. However, the result is the same—a sense of personal loss. For as *every* conceivable personal experience becomes meaningful, *no* individual experience remains very meaningful. As a result, the lives of rock stars are often characterized by a constant search for meaning derived from novel or more intense experiences. Rock performers are noted for dying from overdoses of drugs, which are taken either to produce heightened states of consciousness, or at least to provide a temporary escape from the intolerability of what becomes a meaningless everyday existence.

The difficulties that beset both football players and rock stars as they try to act out only one of the two models are largely related to lack of flexibility. There are times when social needs are paramount, and times when the individual must act on his own needs. Further, meaning is located neither wholly within an external system nor wholly within the individual, but in the interplay between the two. Taken together, the two models provide the actor with flexible guidelines. Further, because the two models share legitimacy under the same success umbrella, the individual need never feel he is acting inconsistently as he switches back and forth between them. And because the concept of success is articulated with universal law, both the individual and society recognize that his actions are at all times consonant (unless he applies the wrong success model to the situation) with the higher goal, the management of human affairs according to the rules of the universe. That indeed is success.

In this paper, we have attempted to describe how two success models, the traditional and the creative, are enacted and grounded as truth in two performance modes, football games and rock concerts. We have also examined the question of why American culture contains two radically different success models. However, we have barely scratched the surface, and have left untouched a host of questions, among the most important of which is: What are the criteria individuals use in deciding which success model to apply to which life situation? At this point, we simply do not know.

Notes

We wish to thank the many American informants who patiently discussed football, rock, and success with us. We are also grateful to W. Arens, Richard Feinberg, Julia Hecht, and Michael Moffatt for their thoughtful comments on an earlier draft of the paper.

1. Success models thus propose behavioral guidelines that are only indirectly linked to the universal laws. However, the symbolism of love maintains the illusion of a direct linkage.

2. Huber notes that competition has been a continual problem for traditional success-model writers. They play down interpersonal competition, preferring the view that the actor competes with himself (i.e., with his baser desires) to achieve. He also notes that Social Darwinism has only rarely been advocated by traditional success-model writers precisely because its dog-eat-dog tenets conflict with the Christian love ethic (1971).

References

Cohn, Nik, 1974, *Rock Dreams*. New York: Popular Library

Fiske, Shirley, 1975, "Pigskin Review: An American Initiation." In Michael A. Rynkiewich and James R. Spradley, eds. *The Nacirema: Readings on American Culture*. Boston: Little, Brown.

Geertz, Clifford, 1966, "Religion as a Cultural System." In M. Banton, ed. *Anthropological Approaches to the Study of Religion*. London: Tavistock.

Huber, Richard M., 1971, *The American Idea of Success*. New York: McGraw Hill.

Leibovitz, Annie, ed., 1973, *Shooting Stars: The Rolling Stone Book of Portraits*. San Francisco: Straight Arrow Books.

Shaw, Bernard, 1961, *The Millionairess*. London: Penguin.

Shaw, Gary, 1972, *Meat on the Hoof.* New York: Dell.

Stone, W. Clement, 1962, *The Success System that Never Fails*. Englewood Cliffs, N.J.: Prentice Hall.

GOOD MARX FOR THE ANTHROPOLOGIST

Structure and Anti-Structure in "Duck Soup"

IVAN KARP

It might strike the reader as a dubious exercise but I intend to take some of the concepts developed in the study of ritual in non-Western societies and apply them to the movie *Duck Soup*. The intention is to make sense out of apparent nonsense. Ritual, in this sense, does not necessarily refer to religious action—behavior directed toward "non-empirical beings."[1] Thus I use a definition that regards ritual as an aspect of social behavior directed toward making statements about how the actor "thinks and feels about . . . [social] relationships and about the natural and social environments in which they occur" (Turner, 1969: 6). Some social behavior is more oriented to saying things than to getting things done, although there are elements of both in everything that people do. Social behavior that is predominantly expressive (oriented to saying things) and performed on special occasions is called "ritual" by anthropologists.[2] The analysis of the meaning of behavior on these occasions draws connections between what the ritual expresses and other dimensions of social life or other situations in which the actors might find themselves.

There is not always a direct relationship between what is expressed and what the ritual refers to. In fact, most anthropologists who are interested in understanding rituals agree that if something can be expressed directly, then there is little reason for it to be expressed in a ritual format. If there is one aspect

53

of ritual that may be referred to as the "function" of ritual, it is that it allows for the expression of what is otherwise inexpressible. This is why anthropologists often fail to obtain significant results from questioning people about their rituals. How can they explain what they are otherwise not allowed or cannot say except through ritual? Thus it is not so paradoxical that the best informants for anthropologists are often persons who are marginal to their own society and, as a consequence, are more involved in questioning the social conditions of their existence.[3]

One anthropologist whose work has been very influential in this regard is V. W. Turner, who in a series of essays and monographs on the Ndembu of Zambia has examined the relationship between what is expressed in ritual and the experiences of the actors—particularly to their social and personal conflicts (1967, 1968, 1969). In the course of his analysis, Turner has evolved the concept of "anti-structure," which he uses to examine the relationship of what is expressed in ritual to the structure of society, and also to explain why ritual helps to resolve or at least mediate conflicts in which participants are involved. My concern however is not with conflict resolution or mediation; instead I want to use the concept of anti-structure to describe *Duck Soup*. This is done in order to demonstrate that anti-structure is a useful analytical tool for examining the interrelations among roles played by actors (in the theatrical sense) on some expressive occasions, such as in movies, and the roles played by actors (in the social sense) on formal and public occasions during which the hierarchy of etiquette prevails. Thus, this is a modest attempt at academic imperialism since I am convinced that there are as yet no theoretical reasons for asserting that there are substantial differences between what is called a "primitive ritual" and an expressive occasion such as a movie.

Turner's conception of anti-structure derives from the theoretical position which views social structure as a system of constraints applied to social persons to coerce them to behave in ways antithetical to their immediate self-interests.[4] Structure is not the only aspect of society that merits description, however. For Turner, structure can only be effective as a system of constraints because the persons involved alternate their participation in structure with occasions that are anti-structural in nature and meaning. Turner views the alternation of structure and anti-structure as the major unanalyzed aspect in the study of society. I shall not be concerned here with the relation of anti-structure and structure to social stability and change. Rather, I want to use Turner's important insight that there are in many societies occasions reserved for the expression of attitudes, opinions, and feelings that are not tolerated in the etiquette of other, and especially public, occasions. The importance of these ritual expressions of anti-structure is that these publicly intolerable attitudes are positively valued on ritual occasions instead of being negatively sanctioned. Hence, the expression of anti-structure bears a dialectical relationship to the constraints imposed on other, more structural, occasions.

> Society (*societas*) seems to be a process rather than a thing—
> a dialectical process with successive phases of structure and
> communitas. There would seem to be—if one can use such
> a controversial term—a human "need" to participate in
> both modalities. Persons starved of one in their functional
> day-to-day activities seek it in ritual liminality. The struc-
> turally inferior aspire to symbolic structural superiority in
> ritual; the structurally superior aspire to symbolic communi-
> tas and undergo penance to achieve it. (1969: 203)

It might be added that Turner's "dialectics" differs from classical Hegelian-Marxian dialectics in that the alternation of structure and anti-structure does not imply a *transcendence* of one by the other. In Turner's formulation structure and anti-structure chase each other in a perpetual equilibrium.

In his most recent essay on this topic Turner (1974) distinguishes "liminality" and "communitas" as the two dimensions of anti-structure. Liminality is typically found during transition rituals, in which persons move from one identity to another. In these instances individuals are stripped of one identity and before they assume another, they exist in a state that is "betwixt and between." Their liminal state expresses a contravention of the structure without an assertion of other social possibilities. Communitas is expressed during liminal states. It is the ritual opposite of structure in that it unites persons whom structure separates in terms of social distance, and exists in continual tension with structure at all levels of organization (1974: 274-275). The form that communitas might take is related to but not determined by the structure of the society in which the ritual is embedded. Turner stresses the *dialectical* and *necessary* relationship between structure and communitas or, more generally, structure and anti-structure.

In what follows below I describe the relationships expressed by a set of characters in the Marx Brothers' classic film *Duck Soup* to the structural relationships expressed by the etiquette of public occasions. I trust that if the following analysis does not illuminate the reader's understanding of the Marx Brothers' movies, it will not lessen his enjoyment of them. It hasn't mine.

Duck Soup is an appropriate vehicle for analysis because it is generally acknowledged as the zenith of the Marx Brothers' art. However, it was not a commercial success and their contract with Paramount Studios was not renewed after this film. This initiated the Marx Brothers' sad artistic decline—guided initially by the capable but crass Irving Thalberg (Adamson, 1973). The film was created in order for the Marx Brothers to express their artistic personalities without the regard found in many of their earlier films for plot constraints or the conventions of the Broadway or vaudeville stage. Therefore, in *Duck Soup* we have the Marx Brothers at their best and in a vehicle that expresses what is most distinctive about them.

For those who may be unfamiliar with the film's plot, I will present a brief synopsis, which I preface with the warning that plots are the creatures of structure. Consequently, to pay too much attention to twists of plot in a vehicle of anti-structure such as *Duck Soup* is to refuse to enter into the spirit of the occasion. First, the title. Unsubstantiated rumor has it that the title refers to the Marx Brothers' opinion of the quality of the food at the Paramount dining room—Duck Soup! Groucho has another explanation: "Take two turkeys, one goose, four cabbages, but no duck, and mix them together. After one taste, you'll duck soup the rest of your life" (Adamson, 1973: 224). Back to the plot. The imaginary country of Fredonia is in the midst of a financial crisis. The crisis is resolved by Mrs. Teasdale (played by Margaret Dumont), the wealthy widow of a former prime minister. Her price is to have her candidate installed as chief of state. The new prime minister, Rufus T. Firefly (played by Groucho Marx) appears to be installed at a grand ball where his first words as prime minister are, "take a card." His first official act is to dictate a letter to his dentist. He then sings a song about the policies he will follow in office. The refrain goes: "If any form of pleasure is exhibited, report it to me and it will be prohibited." A recent commentary on the film tells us:

> the only difference between him and any other head of state is that coming from his mouth it sounds funny. Disrespect for crowned heads is what we're all set to see Groucho perform, but he executes the most ignoble sacrilege on the whole condition of sovereignty just by taking office.... He cheerfully proclaims he'll accept all the power due his office and none of the responsibility, and it gets a rise out of the people instead of an uprising. His conversation about Margaret Dumont's husband (who . . . [he says] died of a surfeit of Margaret Dumont) gets the same response out of her: Groucho is a bald-faced opportunist and makes no bones about it. He is the ideal ruler. (Adamson, 1973: 227).

While the plot gets far more complicated, it doesn't make any better sense. Groucho gets into a series of disputes with Ambassador Trentino of the neighboring country of Sylvania who is after Mrs. Teasdale's money. Somehow the fights lead to a declaration of war between the two countries. The manifest reason is a contest of honor between Groucho-Firefly and Trentino that would put the fiercest Mediterranean countryman to shame. Chico (under the nom de guerre of Chicolini) and Harpo (who doesn't have a name at all)[5] are spies for Trentino and, when not stealing plans of war, they are working for Groucho and vending peanuts. Finally the spies are caught, but their trial—made into a travesty by Chico and the worst puns anyone has ever heard—is interrupted by war with Sylvania, Ambassador Trentino's country. The events of this particular conflict are not reducible to mere words. Fredonia wins after Trentino is caught in the door of a house in which the Marx Brothers are blockaded. They pelt him with fruit until he surrenders. The victory stirs Mrs. Teasdale to break into the national anthem of Fredonia; so the Marx Brothers pelt *her* with fruit. We aren't allowed to stay around long enough to discover if she surrenders.

Plot takes us exactly where the movie intended—nowhere. In the world of anti-structure a logical, linear progression has no particular place. There must be a beginning and an end in order to leave and return to structure again, but it matters little if we begin at the middle and end before the beginning. If sense is not to be made of the film at the level of a sequence of events, it must be found at another level. Otherwise audiences would not still be overcome with hysteria by this film 40 years after it was made. I suggest that the level at which sense is to be found is in the logic of social relations and in the relationship of that logic to the audience's experience of the participation in social relationships having a similar structural pattern.[6] In pursuing this mode of analysis I am not departing in any way from the conventional anthropological analysis of ritual. Social anthropologists from Van Gennep (1960) on have examined the patterns of transformations that the normative content of social relationships undergo on ritual occasions. Studies of ritually privileged license and obscenity bear this out.

The pivot of most of the Marx Brothers' movies is the relationship between Groucho and those he victimizes. They are, by and large, persons in social positions that demand respect and deference, and are naturally offended when they receive less than what they require as their social due. Ambassador Trentino of *Duck Soup,* or Herman Gottlieb, the pompous and self-satisfied manager of the New York Opera from *A Night at the Opera,* are good examples of this type, but the ubiquitous Margaret Dumont, the archetype of the dowager matron, provides us with the purest representative of the kind. There is nothing especially mean or malicious or even particularly self-seeking about Mrs. Teasdale and the other dowagers that Margaret Dumont usually plays. She is merely a pompous woman (often a widow) who either represents or wants to represent the pinnacle of social prestige. She is always wealthy and willing to use her wealth for philanthropic purposes—as she understands them. Groucho, on the other hand, is willing to use her. She is destined to be Groucho's foil. His intention is to flatter her, seduce her, and marry her in order to enjoy her wealth. His exchanges with her start out with Groucho expressing admiration for her beauty, figure, intelligence, culture, or whatever else comes to mind. Groucho's trouble is that he can't keep *his* mind on the job at hand. His distaste for Dumont always gets the better of him, and he winds up expressing his genuine and very funny opinion of her. In *Duck Soup* he impugns her honor, insults her figure, portrays her as overcome by uncontrollable sexual desire, and implies she drove her husband to his death. Otherwise they get on fine.

We might conclude that Groucho is not polite to her. And that is precisely what strikes us as particularly funny about their relationship. Proper behavior in a given situation is very important to the characters that Margaret Dumont plays. She stresses both for herself and the people around her proper dress, proper demeanor, and proper etiquette. The formal garden party and the inaugural ball are her milieu in *Duck Soup*. Even in her boudoir she presents us with a formally and impeccably well dressed presence. Her major concern appears to be that the social forms are maintained; and she directs a sense of outrage at persons who do not defer to and recognize the importance of such socially eminent persons as ambassadors and cabinet ministers. She is the type of character who remains a stock figure in satires, from Gilbert and Sullivan's *The Mikado* (which has a good deal in common with *Duck Soup*) on to the present.

Because of her emphasis on the structural (i.e., public) characteristics of individuals rather than on their personal qualities, she is a stifling and constraining presence. The very existence of Groucho (not to mention what he says and does to her) liberates the audience from Margaret Dumont. In classical structuralist fashion the differences between Rufus T. Firefly as portrayed by Groucho and Mrs. Teasdale as portrayed by Margaret Dumont can be represented through a series of oppositions.

Where Teasdale is always impeccably tailored, Firefly is always dressed in an ill-fitting outfit. Both Mrs. Teasdale and Firefly are aware of the rules of etiquette but while she is concerned with upholding the rules of conventional morality, Firefly pokes fun at the people who live by the rules and respond emotionally to their violations. Thus, the net effect of the Groucho-Dumont opposition or the Firefly-Teasdale opposition (they amount to the same thing) is to provide the audience with a spectacular and ongoing relationship of continual status reversal. By victimizing her on the basis of publicly displaying her disconcerting (for her) personal characteristics, her claims to superiority are turned to a position of social inferiority. The relationship is based on Mrs. Teasdale's claims about her superior status vis-à-vis the rest of the world (including Firefly). Firefly exploits those claims by providing information and attitudes that poke fun, often cruel fun, at the pretensions of Teasdale and most of the people he is surrounded by. The audience participates in what becomes the disruption of claims to deference on public occasions. The audience is able, in fact willing, to participate because these claims are based on the assumption that the norms of social behavior express differences of quality between the actors. Firefly expresses what many of the audience will have felt many times but had been forced to repress—that their definition of the situation does not merit the assumption of inequality, which they see themselves as forced to acknowledge and legitimize on public occasions.

Firefly and Teasdale represent an important starting point for this analysis. Other dimensions are to be found in the characters played by Chico and Harpo. Chico's character is called, with startling originality, Chicolini while Harpo's character has no name, or at least it is not revealed to the audience.

Chicolini is, as with all the characters Chico plays, an immigrant. He wears funny clothes, talks with an accent, and works at what are almost archetypically immigrant occupations.

In *Duck Soup* he runs a combination peanut and hotdog stand and supplements his income with a little espionage on the side. If he were an organ grinder and had a monkey on a string, I don't think we would be surprised. But this is no immigrant made for poking fun at. Although he represents the image of the greenhorn so dear to vaudeville and later burlesque comedians, he is not the one who is taken in and fleeced. The fleecing, with an appropriately mixed metaphor, is on the other foot. Chico's major contribution to the Marx Brothers' movies in general, and *Duck Soup* in particular, is through a series of outrageous puns. His wit makes no more linear sense than Groucho's or Harpo's. The major difference is that, while Groucho's humor is aimed at deflating pomposity, Chico's humor is aimed at taking advantage of his victim's image of Chico as ignorant and gullible. In *Duck Soup* Chicolini plays with that image by perpetrating on us a series of puns and by taking advantage of the same people that Firefly mocks. Consider the following dialogue:

The Shadow

Trentino: Oh! Now, Chicolini, I want a full detailed report of your investigation.

Chico: All right, I tell you. Monday we watch-a Firefly's house, but he no come out. He wasn't home. Tuesday we go to the ball game, but he fool us. He no show up. Wednesday he go to the ball game, and we fool him. *We* no show up. Thursday was a doubleheader. Nobody show up. Friday it rained all day. There was no ball game, so we stayed home and we listened to it over the radio.

Trentino: Then you didn't shadow Firefly?

Chico: Oh, sure we shadow Firefly. We shadow him all day.

Trentino: But what day was that?

Chico: Shadowday! Hahaha. Atsa some joke, eh, Boss?
(Adamson, 1973: 227)

or again when Chicolini is on trial for espionage:

The Trial

Groucho: Chicolini, give me a number from one to ten.

Chico: Eleven.

Groucho: Right.

Chico: Now I ask you one. What is it has a trunk, but no key, weighs 2,000 pounds, and lives in the circus?

Prosecutor: That's irrelevant.

Chico: A relephant! Hey, that's the answer! There's a whole lotter elephants in the circus.

Minister: That sort of testimony we can eliminate.

Chico: Atsa fine. I'll take some.

Minister: You'll take *what?*

Chico: Eliminate. A nice cool glass eliminate.

* * * * * *

Minister of Finance: Something must be done! War would mean a prohibitive increase in our taxes.

Chico: Hey, I got an uncle lives in Taxes.

Minister of Finance: No, I'm talking about taxes—money, dollars.

Chico: Dollas! There's-a where my uncle lives. Dollas, Taxes!

Minister of Finance: Aww!

(Adamson, 1973: 242-243)

If Groucho inverts the norms and values of the social reality that is accepted by the Teasdales and Trentinos of his world, we may say that Chico has a *tangential* relationship to that same reality. He approaches reality from an oblique angle. Chico, however, does not usually act alone. He is accompanied by Harpo, who presents us with a persona entirely different from Chico and Groucho. *Duck Soup* is Harpo's finest hour. All the innate anarchy and formlessness of his character is expressed in this film. Perhaps his finest scene is during his and Chico's conference with Ambassador Trentino. His voluminous clothes produce an assortment of tools from scissors to a blowtorch used for lighting cigars. He consistently, persistently, and absolutely destroys every premise on which social action can be based until the scene can continue no longer. There is no way that the everyday rationality of the Trentino character can deal with the phenomenon of Harpo.

Even Harpo's appearance and manner deny the categories of everyday life. He is more than just a stock vaudeville clown figure as he is sometimes interpreted. Immediately, one recognizes that his appearance conveys a remarkable kind of sexual ambiguity. His hair, figure, and face cannot be placed in either of the two sexual categories. Perhaps this is because of his childlike manner. His systematic inarticulateness, his lack of social knowledge, his naiveté and polymorphous sexuality (in *Duck Soup* he winds up in bed with a horse after chasing a voluptuous blonde)[7] are all reminiscent of the condition of infancy, or at least the Freudian version of infancy.

For whatever the reason, Harpo is not easily placed into basic and perhaps even universal categories of the social world such as man-woman and child-adult. I suggest that this is because Harpo expresses an attitude to the world that is, to quote Turner, "betwixt and between" the world of structure. Harpo is preeminently a *liminal* figure and as such contradicts the most basic values and distinctions of his and our society. Thus, the figure of Harpo represents for the audience the inversion and obliteration of structure in its most elementary forms.

We have in the Marx Brothers' personae three stock figures from drama and comedy, the flimflammer or con man, the immigrant, and the clown. None is admirable by the standards of our society; they are all marginal to the central concerns of anyone trying to get on in life. What these characters have in common, and what the audience responds to, is that they say *NO* to the application of constraints on behavior to which the rest of their world unthinkingly acquiesces. Of course, their very marginality makes them less liable to the imposition of sanctions. They aren't likely to receive the rewards that everyone else is striving so hard to get. Therefore, they are not obliged to accept the discrepancy between the personal perception of a situation and the acknowledgment of a social norm that is part of the audience's experience of the social world. In the case of Harpo, the audience is given an example of freedom from the constraints imposed on action as a result of being placed by other people into basic social categories such as man-woman or child-adult. With Groucho and Chico, the audience is given an example of freedom from constraints (such as being "nice" or "polite" or "paying attention") that are the necessary baggage that accompanies the achievement of social goals through other people.

In fact, I think this is a major aspect of the appeal of the Marx Brothers. Their characters *express* attitudes to the social world that are coterminous with unexpressed attitudes experienced by large portions of the audiences that have appreciated *Duck Soup* and other Marx Brothers films over the years. This is why so many of the Marx Brothers' best scenes are concerned with public occasions such as balls, parties, trials, and operas. On these occasions the presentation of self is limited to the expression of social rather than personal attributes to a far greater degree than on more intimate occasions. In the Marx Brothers films this ritual separation of persons is stood on its head and the brothers and their audience form an unstructured community united through laughter at the structure. Communitas is to be found in the interaction between the audience and the Marx Brothers. In this sense, anyone who attends a performance of *Duck Soup* is engaging in an action akin to taking part in a ritual. How the person responds is, of course, a matter of personal history and temperament. I cannot help but think, however, that the continuing popularity of this movie is based on its ability to strike deep and responsive chords in the experience of the audience.[8]

I have tried, through the use of the concept of anti-structure, to discover within *Duck Soup* elements that correspond to the experiences of the audience that enable it to respond to the movie. I have tried to show that the social world of the Marx Brothers has structural features in common with that of the audience. Instead of viewing *Duck Soup* as an entity in itself, I have stressed a relationship between what is expressed in the film and the social experience of the actors. This relationship demonstrates that anti-structure is not chaotic and formless: It derives its form and meaning from structure.[9] In the case, for example, of Groucho and Margaret Dumont the form of anti-structure is derived from an antithetical relationship of deference expressed in the etiquette of hierarchy. In this sense, anti-structure is like Monica Wilson's (1951) definition of witchcraft as "standardized nightmares" that derive their meaning from tensions found in social relationships (Middleton and Winter, 1963). The difference is that in witchcraft beliefs, the uncertainties that are elements in social action are developed into a moral theory of causation. In Marx Brothers' films the irritants that accompany social action are expressed.

But what happens as a result of the expression of these irritants? Surely, the audience's interpretation of similar experiences has been altered after seeing *Duck Soup,* just as it would have been altered after seeing any movie—no matter how banal. Since this paper has treated *Duck Soup* as a ritual it should conclude with at least some comments on the consequences for the actors of participation in the affair. Although rituals obviously serve to ease social tensions, in each society a ritual must be examined anew before such general conclusions can be reaffirmed. In the case of *Duck Soup* it would be easy but incorrect to suggest that after having seen this movie the audience can rest easier in the face of social inequities. If I did suggest that, the analysis would be dialectical in the sense that Turner uses the notion of dialectics. Instead, I wish to suggest that I find it difficult to imagine how anyone can take *Duck Soup* seriously, in the sense of laughing at what it laughs at, and return to the world of structure and accept with reverence and equanimity the received wisdom of public occasions. The consequence of joining with the Marx Brothers in laughing at structure is to formulate and verify for the moviegoer his private and inchoate experience of the structure, and thus to make that experience an objective, social fact.

In this sense the title of the paper plays on the historical accident of the identicalness of the surnames of Karl Marx and the Marx Brothers. The young Karl Marx called for "*a ruthless criticism of everything existing* . . . ruthless in two senses: The criticism must not be afraid of its own conclusions, nor of conflict with the powers that be" (Tucker, 1972: 9, emphasis in original). The Marx Brothers similarly ask us to take nothing for granted, nor to be afraid of our conclusions. Remember Chico's famous line in *Duck Soup*. Groucho has just left Mrs. Teasdale's boudoir. Chico, dressed as Groucho, crawls out from under the bed. Mrs. Teasdale says, "Why, I can't believe my own eyes." "Lady," replies Chico, "Who you gonna believe? Me or your own eyes?"

Notes

I would like to thank Nigel Bolland, Mary Bufwack, David Jacobson, Patricia Karp, and Warren Ramshaw for their penetrating comments on earlier versions of this paper.

1. See Tyler's famous minimal definition of religion, which does not even refer to religion as expressing "ultimate concerns" (Evans-Pritchard, (1965: 25).

2. This approach is illustrated by Leach (1954) and Harris (1957), among others.

3. See Turner's fascinating essay (1967) on just such a person, Muchona, the Hornet.

4. Durkheim's own position on self and society is actually far more radical. For him the self is socially derived and there can be no distinction between self-interests and societal interests. For a discussion of this see Thomas Luckmann's analysis of Durkheim's concept of the self in relation to a sociology of religion (1967).

5. Zimmerman and Goldblatt assert that Harpo is called "Pinky" in *Duck Soup* (1968: 84). I have no such recollection.

6. In a series of works beginning with *The Presentation of Self in Everyday Life,* Erving Goffman has documented the assertion that the private and personal self is allowed little scope for expression on public and formal occasions. See also Meyer Fortes' "Ritual and Office in Tribal Society" in Max Gluckman (1962). In this paper I am taking this portion of the analysis as given. Clearly, I am making a number of assertions about the social experience and state of consciousness of the audience. These are derived partly from my reading of social scientists, such as Goffman, and partly from my own experience. In the absence of empirical evidence that could confirm or deny these assertions, this analysis must be taken as partial and tentative.

7. Is this the same horse whose picture he carried next to his heart in *Animal Crackers?*

8. Here again we confront the problem of assertion about the audience. One reader suggested, for example, that an audience composed largely of college students (as seems to be the case for Marx Brothers fans currently) cannot be analyzed in the same fashion as the earlier, predominantly lower-class audiences of *Duck Soup.* I suggest that the continuing popularity of the Marx Brothers can be analyzed in terms of continuities in the experience of the audiences. One such continuity might be the mar-

ginal relationship to sources of power in our society of both contemporary college students and the 1930s audiences of the Marx Brothers.

9. It only *seems* chaotic and formless to the participants. Anti-structure derives its form through inverting and contravening the structure.

References

Adamson, Joe, 1973, *Groucho, Harpo, Chico and Sometimes Zeppo.* New York: Simon & Schuster.

Evans-Pritchard, E. E., 1965, *Theories of Primitive Religion.* London: Oxford University Press.

Gluckman, Max, 1962, *Essays on the Ritual of Social Relations.* Manchester: Manchester University Press.

Goffman, Erving, 1959, *Presentation of Self in Everyday Life.* New York: Anchor.

Harris, Grace, 1957, "Possession 'Hysteria' in a Kenya Tribe." *American Anthropologist* 59: 1046-1066.

Leach, E. R., 1954, *Political Systems of Highland Burma.* London: Athlone Press.

Luckmann, Thomas, 1967, *The Invisible Religion.* New York: Macmillan.

Middleton, J. and E. H. Winter, eds., 1963, *Witchcraft and Sorcery in East Africa.* London; Routledge & Kegan Paul.

Tucker, R. C., 1972, *The Marx-Engels Reader.* New York: Norton.

Turner, V. W., 1967, *The Forest of Symbols.* Ithaca: Cornell University Press.

    —1968, *The Drums of Affliction.* London: Oxford University Press.

    —1969, *The Ritual Process.* Chicago: Aldine.

    —1974, *Dramas, Fields, and Metaphors.* Ithaca: Cornell University Press.

Van Gennep, A., 1960, *The Rites of Passage.* London: Routledge & Kegan Paul.

Wilson, Monica, 1951, "Witch Beliefs and Social Structure." *American Journal of Sociology* 56: 307-313.

Zimmerman, Paul and Burt Goldblatt, 1968, *The Marx Brothers at the Movies.* New York: New American Library

HOMES
AND
HOMEMAKERS
ON AMERICAN TV

JOHN T. KIRKPATRICK

Advertisements and situation comedies are viewed daily by millions of Americans. This paper assumes that these dramatic forms offer valuable insights into contemporary definitions of proper behavior and especially with reference to the role of the "homemaker." The materials studied were initially sorted according to their settings, but it became clear that most kitchen ads, for instance, shared a single organization with laundry room ads, and that the remainder of kitchen ads could be divided into two sets, each having common features with types of ads in other settings. A definitive study of the interaction of setting, characterization, action, and outcome of these ads is beyond the limits of this paper. Rather, the contrast between one type of ad and the situation comedies is stressed in order to bring out features of the dramas found in each.

The evidence from situation comedies comes from a small sample, in which the Norman Lear shows—"All in the Family" and its offspring—are overrepresented. The discussion is not, however, limited to the Lear formula, or even to the fads of the last two years: Such changes as the successive popularity of suburban WASP homes, ethnic homes, and Depression homes for comedy settings should not affect the analysis. The discussion does not, however, account for shows set outside of *family* homes, such as "The Mary Tyler Moore Show."[1]

The data considered here are all presented to an audience of both women and men: Although the ads may be intended to convince women, they are comprehended by far more people than the upwardly mobile young marrieds who are portrayed.

There is a highly general advertising scenario that may be termed the drama of competence. The minimal constituents are a woman, a doubt whether she can handle a problem in homemaking, and a solution to her problem, usually one available in the supermarket. The problem may seem to be a limited, technical one, but we learn that more than the mechanics of, for instance, washing dishes, are involved. A problem of homemaking may threaten the health and identity of the family and raises the issue of whether the woman is "really" a competent homemaker, wife, and mother. Hence when a floor wax protects against scuff marks or when a cereal contains vitamins, these products assert that the woman is truly what she claims to be, mother and homemaker. As the Pillsbury people put it: "Nothin' says lovin' like somethin' from the oven."

The action of the supporting cast is simple. People depend on the heroine's competence, unveil her lack of such, or show her how to gain competence. Each element of the drama may be portrayed in various ways, but there is hardly total free play in the realization of various elements. Some, however, are more amenable to variant forms than others. The product is typically a food or cleansing agent; carpet or bathroom products are inserted into different dramas. The action of cleansing does not determine the drama, for food storage wrappers are advertised just as cleansers are. Mr. Clean, the Man from Glad and others intervene to chase filth and decay from the kitchen and distress from the homemaker.

A rough distinction between dependents and invaders may be drawn on the basis of the threat that characters pose to a homemaker. Dependents include husbands, children, pets and guests. These characters need not simply personify one action of the scenario, and often manifest both dependence and a challenge to competence at the same time. This is obvious, for example, when a child runs into the house, screaming "Mommy!" and tracking mud all over the linoleum. It is obvious that a child is both a dependent and the source of problems of competence.

As a result the threat does not need to be realized on the screen. In one floor wax ad the boy doesn't dirty the floor but glides on a translucent surfboard provided by the wax. The problem of competence in this example is voiced by a neighbor, who fails to obtain such splashy effects with her floor wax.

A recent ad for Total cereal concentrates the entire drama in one line. The husband and children have no time to eat more than a bite of breakfast. Mother knows that they need breakfast to do well all day but, as she says, "What's a mother to do?" It is her duty to keep her dependents healthy, and the implication of the ad seems to be that if they do not need breakfast in order to do well at work and school, they may not need the mother at all. With Total as their breakfast, eaten as dependents, they can be better students and workers. The ad upholds mother and home as necessary for the other characters' separate lives elsewhere.

In a dog food commercial, a young husband stops his wife from feeding the dog an inferior product. He knows that dogs need meat and demonstrates to his wife that she has been depriving their dog of the stuff the animal wants and needs. The wife learns her lesson and promises to feed the dog the right product in the future. Note that it is appropriate for the husband to have the secret knowledge that meat is what dogs need, but nourishing remains a mother's task.

A series of ads for a cleanser shows the ease with which a question concerning one woman's competence may be generalized to other, or all, women. Three women are leaving another's home, and two nastily agree that their hostess's home is secretly unclean: "Those pine cleaners must be covering up *something.*" In one ad, the hostess overhears; in another, the third guest goes home to her own kitchen and reacts with shock—could others suspect *her* home of having hidden dirt? The drama of competence is made painfully clear, although such familiar elements as children and location in a kitchen may be absent.

The homemaker's role may be precisely specified. She transforms products into food and meals—even cereals are made into "breakfast" or "a balanced diet" for the family—and she employs products that "do the job for her." The job is that of

71

warding off invisible substances, including dirt, germs, decay, and odors.

Other characters have a curious sort of identity. The reason they are present—as child, pet, neighbor, and so on—is immediately apparent. They are not fully under the homemaker's control, but the successful completion of the drama of competence neutralizes whatever identity, knowledge, or competence they have outside the relationship. Thus, children are thwarted in their role as carriers of dirt; the finicky personality of a cat who won't eat is overcome; and neighbors are successfully brought into the home and entertained. The world outside home exists only as a problem for the homemaker as nourisher and cleaner as in the Total ad in which the mother's gift of breakfast makes possible all the outside activities of her family.

One reason for isolating the drama of competence is that it appears to exist in abbreviated or implied form in other ads, as when an older woman tells a young homemaker of her difficulties before discovering some cleansing secret. It would be tempting to understand the drama of competence as simply the American way of representing cakes and cleansers, but this does not explain its presence in one of a series of ads for Sears paints. The announcer explains that in the early days in America gracious living was to be found, and women such as George Washington's mother had to be ready to serve a fine meal. While the camera shows the interior of an old house, the announcer speaks of a cake recipe of Mrs. Washington's and intimates that the cake was served to Lafayette and other such dignitaries who had, we presume, discerning palates. Finally, we learn that we have been viewing her house, which is a historic site, and that its interior is *now* painted with the superior Sears product. Mrs. Washington's secret of competence was invoked only to lead into the topic of the ad and to argue that there is some relevant connection between historic houses and the homes of everyday folk.

These illustrations show that concepts of home and homemaking are closely bound up with the advertising scenario. The categories reappear in situation comedies, although they are differently constrained. We are concerned, in dealing with both ads and situation comedies, with general features around which particular episodes or developments are organized. Since the shows are far more intricate than the ads, I must skim briefly over a highly complex topic at this point.

One of the most apparent differences in comedy homes is the relative flexibility of settings. The advertising drama of competence is typically staged in a kitchen. On the other hand, action in a situation comedy most often occurs in the living room, where we may find Dad's chair or other signs that it is not Mom's domain. In some comedies, the living and cooking areas are not separate rooms, in contrast to all the ads examined.

In the comedies, problems recurrently arise for the homemaker, but they are usually in connection with the interests of other characters, on whom attention is focused. Children appear as distinct personalities with their own problems, not just as carriers of dirt. Pets rarely appear because they cannot be treated as more than dependents. (Such animals as Lassie are, of course, a good deal more than dependents, but their magical qualities may fit in poorly with the verisimilitude of the situation comedy home.) Outsiders take on identities as complex as those of family members, as with Mrs. DiLorenzo, the feminist in "All in the Family " or the hero's coworkers in "The Dick Van Dyke Show."

The homemaker takes a smaller, but still important role in the comedies: Often the concept of a show is that the characters can maintain a home without a woman homemaker only with great effort. "Bachelor Father," "My Three Sons," "Family Affair," and "Sanford and Son" deal repeatedly with the problems that arise when no woman is available as homemaker and mother. Their continuity and popularity stands as an argument that the woman homemaker is replaceable, although all others in the home must labor and love intensely to do without her.

There are also shows that deal with the problem of a woman being jobholder and homemaker concurrently. The argument here parallels that of the above mentioned shows: with love, a family does not need a full-time homemaker. Even with a full complement of parents and children, problems do arise, problems that are often phrased in terms of ethics. Accordingly, the shows contain lengthy disquisitions on right and wrong behavior, and all family members contribute their particular bit. "Father Knows Best" brings the scenario into full bloom. Conflicts arise within characters' minds and experience, bringing about discussion in the home; Father knows best; he can probe into difficulties that the children face and he can also act independently outside the home. But Mother has the last word.

In "Good Times," the father and children are consistently tempted to abandon what they all know to be the path of righteousness. Their erring ways—whether in search of money, fame, an exciting boyfriend or the cause of black nationalism—provide most of the plot development. Within a half hour the characters are brought back into line, admitting that the way of life that Florida, the wife and mother, has upheld through the show is the right way. She stands for love, religion, and respect for law, but she does not articulate her stance as a viewpoint. Instead, others present intricate arguments in favor of temptation, detailing all its advantages, until certain home virtues, made explicit only by way of contrast, win out.

All these shows take as an underlying problematic a tension between the maintenance of home as the center of loving relationships, from which people gain strength to act in the world, and the outside world, in which some characters take their place as independent entities. While some situation comedy homes are deviant from the WASP *Father Knows Best* standard (e.g., lacking a mother, ethnic), any home situation is seen as involving enough difficulties to provide plot material for a comedy. While the ads discussed previously focused on the homemaker's ability to do the jobs assigned, the comedies stress the problem of being both a family member and an individual elsewhere: a worker, pal, student, or keen teen. Instead of a drama of competence we find a drama of loyalties. Difficult decisions about action elsewhere are faced in the domestic context; home is the locus of a practical, sensible, just, and loving morality, even on "All in the Family," where practical and just viewpoints are expressed separately, to the detriment of both.

In order to achieve the drama of loyalties, the home is established as both the field of action and as an option. The household emerges as an object of loyalty as well as the scene of shifting loyalties. This is achieved by equating mother and home. The mother becomes a summarizing symbol (Ortner, 1973) whose presence conjures up the entire complex of love, food, security and morality. In contrast to other characters the mother summarizes and elaborates on what is proper and what is not.

The mother's arena of action and her loyalties are overwhelmingly in the home: Maude, the would-be feminist, gives up her hopes of a job so that her husband can count on her being at home, can do well in his store, certain that all is well and his dinner will be on the table on time at home. Maude's yearning for independence is translated into a style of homemaking. She is portrayed in the show as a "real estate person," a label which, after a single episode, implies no commitment or activity outside the home.

The mother, it seems is constrained to summarize. This is most notable when we compare the role of Florida, first as the maid on "Maude" and then as mother and homemaker in her own "Good Times." As a maid, she is the most articulate character, exposing quite clearly the pretentions of all around her; but as a mother she can only protest vaguely against immorality. The character who inspired "Good Times," then, is muzzled by her role in it. As a homemaker, she must choose between respect for the individuality of her dependents and the general task of homemaking. Her problems now depend on the fact that others mediate between home and the outside.

Although much more remains to be said, it should be clear that common assumptions about settings, actions, and personnel are to be found in situation comedies. The contrast between these assumptions and those of the ads emerges under four headings:

1. The mother and homemaker is central to both, yet in the comedies she is the center around which others act and express themselves. In the ads, she may restrain their self-expression, if it threatens the home, or act so that their contribution is, in the end, only to praise her homemaking.

2. Persons have individuated biographies, interests, skills,

and other characteristics in the comedies and, as a consequence, problems of ethical action and conflicts of loyalties inevitably arise. In the ads, however, persons pose problems of homemaking, which can be solved simply through the use of certain products.

3. The comedy home and family are opposed explicitly to other zones—work, school, and the like—which have their own personnel, activities, and, most importantly, special, specific claims on family members. In the ads, such zones lack definition, and actors from different zones are equivalent in precipitating and witnessing the same situation—the homemaker's drama of competence.

4. The difference between acceptable outcomes in the two forms is striking. In the ads, a specific technical problem is solved. As a consequence, dependents may hug homemakers, or guests may admire the clean home, yet these are not the confirmation that the task has been accomplished. Rather, they are the *result* of its successful accomplishment. In the situation comedies, the tasks may be far more diffuse—"being honest," for instance—but whatever their specificity, people's reactions *confirm* successful performance. The characters may show shared knowledge of homemaking and related standards, but the proof of correct action lies in manifestations of love, not in a well-baked cake. One implication of this is that the ads may suggest that a cereal will solve most of a homemaker's problems and worries for all time, that is, they assume that all problems in the home have satisfactory technical solutions. Comedy resolutions, however, are provisional. The momentarily happy comedy home will be upset by a new problem next week and the characters will muster their individual resources to contain it.

These contrasts are not random. The two dramas may be seen as alternate solutions to a single, familiar contradiction in American culture. The contradiction lies in the fact that, for Americans, people are seen as both unique individuals and also in terms of the roles they play. Archie Bunker is both himself and, like many others, a father and worker. Obviously, roles and associated activities cannot be delimited if they depend on satisfying unique individuals with unique motives and needs. To put the matter bluntly, the ads stress that problems of role performance can be overcome or neutralized as a result of proper technique; the comedies assert that individuals, acting in their own unique ways, may accomplish adequate performance despite their deviation from general standards. We may note this both in the posing and the resolution of dramatic problems. Thus, Maude does not say, "What's a mother to do?" when her daughter has no time for breakfast, but instead yells, "Do you have to rub it in . . . the pretty young career girl goes off to work, leaving the tired housewife behind!" A moment later, Maude meets or surpasses housewifely standards in feeding her husband. It is quite clear that she is engaging in parody and wants to point out that she too is an individual. Later, her husband gives in to her, saying, "You gotta do your own thing and do it well to be happy." She kisses him; they agree that the matter over which they have quarreled is behind them, and Maude, with a knowledge granted to no advertising homemaker, says that it is "behind them, ahead of them, to the left, to the right. . . ." Her choice is correct because it is hers but it can be only a temporary solution.

This view of the dramas accounts for the variety of comedy families. In a drama of individuals, where love can affirm individual action as proper in a particular home, the individuals involved need not be all genealogically related, or a family may be precariously maintained without a mother. In contrast, the advertisements do not show sons-in-law, butlers, or others as residents of homes. The ads involve fulfillment of our expectations for the jobs of mothers, fathers, and children and hence show no marginal members in residence. Let me stress that both dramas depend on expectations for the proper activities of status holders. In the ads those expectations are met; in the comedies, individual action is deemed equivalent, in a particular home, to ideal role performance.

The preceding comments do not account for the constraints visible on situation comedy mothers. The problem may be posed a bit more clearly. Female homemakers are confined, in effect, to symbolizing the particularity of their homes. They set the scene in which individual acts are confirmed by love, and they do not move outside it. American notions of sexuality, however, do not explain why Edith Bunker is so vapid, why Maude cannot keep her job, and why other homemakers are more a backdrop than performers in comedies. Articulate and active women do exist in the comedies, but they are never homemakers.

We may note that while the advertising homemaker is the focal actor, constraining others to status positions by serving them, the comedy homemaker is the focal nonactor, around whom all others display their individuality. Neither drama is purely one of individuality or status; the contrast between female homemakers and all others in both dramas summarizes the presence of the contradiction and the possibility of its resolution.

Notes

I am indebted to Janet Dolgin, Nina Kammerer, David Kemnitzer, Richard Kurin, Susan Montague, and other readers for data, confirmation on the coding of particular episodes, and comments on earlier drafts.

1. Ideally, the selection of data and hence the demarcation of dramatic forms should be based on extensive analysis of the forms papearing on TV, the emissions in which form-marking characteristics are neutralized or otherwise ambiguous, and the possibility, within one emission, for a change of form. This paper lacks such an exhaustive basis, although advertisements other than those discussed were examined in order to demarcate the form under discussion. It should be noted that the analysis may not apply to comedies produced before about 1960. While the analysis might help in understanding "The Honeymooners" or the early "I Love Lucy" shows, it certainly would not have the same force in accounting for plotting and characterizations as it does with regard to later comedies. Further work on the stabilization of what is here termed the "drama of loyalties," clarifying the differences between it and the organization of both its predecessors and such nonfamily shows as "The Mary Tyler Moore Show" could well illumine how Americans perceive the family.

References

Ortner, Sherry, 1973, "On Key Symbols." *American Anthropologist* 75, no. 5, pp. 1338-1346.

Schneider, David M., 1968, *American Kinship*. Englewood Cliffs, N. J.: Prentice-Hall.

SOAP OPERAS

Sagas of American Kinship

SUSAN S. BEAN

Each weekday, more than 18 million people (Edmonson and Rounds, 1974: 184) tune in their television sets to watch a genre of drama known popularly as soap opera. Soap operas are known to most Americans by reputation, if not through direct exposure, as serial melodramas about doctors and adultery, shown on television during the day, and watched mostly by housewives. In New York City a viewer may select among fourteen half-hour shows aired between 11:30 in the morning and 5:00 in the evening.[1] The large number of soap operas produced and the large number of viewers they attract indicate the significant place they occupy in American life. This paper presents an analysis of the content of soap operas, which focuses on their major subject, one that is of central interest both to Americans and to anthropologists: the American family.

The story lines of·the fourteen soaps available in New York are repeated over and over. The numerous plots and subplots on the program "Days of Our Lives" (summer 1974), for example, are quite typical of soap operas in general. On "Days of Our Lives" (NBC) Bill and Laura are in love, but Laura is married to Mickey; Bob has divorced Phyllis to marry Julie, but Julie really loves another; Susan is married to Greg but his brother Eric is in love with her (will Susan fall in love with him?); Addie is married to Doug, but he and her daughter Julie used to be lovers (are they still really in love?). The triangle involving ties of love and marriage with various complications is the most frequently occurring plot. Each of the fourteen soap operas features at least one triangle, some as many as five.

Plots centered on conflicts between natural and social parentage are also common soap opera fare. Of these fourteen serials, only two programs have none (and one of these did in the recent past); some have as many as three. For example, on "Days of Our Lives," Laura's child is the natural child of Bill, but she is married to Mickey, who thinks the child is his and raises it as his own. The real father of Susan's child is Eric, but she is married to Greg, who is raising the child as his own. The natural father of Julie's child is long dead, and Julie's husband, who had raised the child as his own is recently dead. Julie feels that she should remarry because a son needs a father.

The people who get into these predicaments are very respectable Americans. The women, if married, are usually housewives. Some work as doctors, secretaries, nurses, and lawyers, but their professional activities remain well in the background. Women doctors, for example, are seldom seen practicing medicine. When a crucial operation is to be performed the doctor is male; female doctors may be shown observing from the operating room gallery. Occasionally, however, a woman's job occurs in the foreground of the drama, usually when it comes into competition with husband, home, and family. The men on the soap operas are doctors, lawyers, and businessmen with a representation of journalists, restaurateurs, and an occasional police officer, architect, or writer. No major, middle-aged, male character is a gas station attendant, a plumber, or a factory worker. Most are professionals, well-educated, and self-employed.

These people represent the achievement of the American dream: financial success, education, independence. They have "made it." (Although, of course, some occasionally falter, businesses collapse, failures lead to drink and so on.) They live in suburban America, in small cities and towns. Much of the action in soap operas takes place in the homes of these successful, well-established Americans. The kitchens are large and modern, the furnishings attractive and neat, and the inhabitants fashionably well dressed. The prestigious occupations of the

81

characters, and the middle- to upper-middle-class respectability of their homes is the backdrop against which the action takes place. The problems on which soap opera plots are based lie elsewhere.

Given the sameness of setting and plot, it would appear that the 18 million viewers are willing to watch the same thing over and over again each afternoon. Why? The repetition is certainly not an accident nor the result of poor program planning. Television programming is notoriously ratings oriented. Sponsors want viewers to see their commercials and buy their products, and programs are dropped if their ratings fall too low. In the case of soap operas, the attention to ratings is, if anything, even greater because of the direct participation of many of the sponsors who actually own and produce the programs. If the commercial sponsor participates in the production of the show, and if the sponsor's primary motivation is selling soap, it is obvious that he will provide in his programs what the ratings show the viewers are most interested in watching—the more viewers, the more potential customers. Given the number of viewers, something about the soap operas must be of tremendous interest. Rather than accident or poor planning accounting for the sameness in setting and substance, we have, on the contrary, successful formulas tried and true.

Soap operas are created and produced for American women: 70 to 80 percent of the viewers are women (Edmonson and Rounds, 1974: 184). Most are housewives, but many are working women. American women are (or are supposed to be) homemakers, even if they also hold jobs. One of the major duties of homemakers besides cooking and cleaning is the maintenance and management of family life. Women, as homemakers, take the greater responsibility in raising children, and in maintaining family ties. They remember birthdays and anniversaries with greeting cards, plan weddings, and arrange family dinners at Christmas and Thanksgiving. In America, women are the custodians of kinship.

The most common plots of soap operas, the triangles and problems of parentage, are about establishing and maintaining the family in America. If, in fact, this subject is one that vitally concerns the viewers (American women), it seems likely that the dramas are popular because they deal meaningfully with an area of great interest to American women, the family.[2] In the following pages the picture of the American family contained in the soap operas will be presented. The data on which the analysis is based were gathered from viewing and from monthly plot summaries available in *The Soap Opera Newsletter*.

THE TRIANGLE

On "Days of Our Lives," there are currently five triangles. One of them is the story of Bob, Phyllis and Julie.

> Bob and Phyllis were happily married for many years but now Bob has fallen in love with Julie. Bob decides he must leave Phyllis for he no longer loves her. Phyllis becomes distraught; she thinks about killing Julie. Bob proposes marriage to Julie and she eventually accepts, even though she does not love him, for he can provide her with social and financial security. Can their marriage be successful if Julie does not love Bob (and in fact is in love with another)?

The story begins with a perfect couple who are married and in love. But then something goes wrong. It is in this way that soap operas communicate with their audience about family life— by creating situations that violate the ideal order of the family, then, slowly, over several months working toward the restoration of the ideal.

What goes wrong in this case is that Bob becomes attracted to Julie and begins to lose interest in his wife. After a time it becomes clear to him (and to the audience) that he loves Julie, not Phyllis. There is no explanation for his changing affections. There is some talk about the changes that men go through in middle life, but that does not account for it. Bob himself does not understand why he has ceased to love Phyllis and come to love Julie. He even regrets that it has happened, but it has, and there is nothing he or anyone else can do about the situation. Here we are shown the mysterious nature of love. Love happens all by itself—it comes and goes without reason. People do not have control over it—it happens to them. Thus, even an ideal marriage in which the partners have the best intentions is not permanent or stable, for one of them may fall out of love with the other.

As Bob falls in love with Julie, he falls out of love with Phyllis. In soap operas there is no possibility of being in love with two people at the same time. It may be unclear for a while which appearance of affection is real, which one is love, but it will eventually become clear. The story tells us more about the nature of love: real love can be felt only for one person at a time.

Phyllis reacts violently to the loss of Bob's love and the dissolution of their marriage: she becomes irrational. She believes that Julie is evil and has taken Bob from her. She even begins to think about killing Julie. We are shown that it is insane to believe love can be controlled by acts of will, or that Julie could take Bob's love from Phyllis, or that Phyllis could get it back by killing Julie. Rational, sane human beings know it is no one's fault, and there is nothing anyone can do about it.

Bob, who is now in love with Julie, proposes marriage to her. It is quite natural, in fact inevitable, to want to marry a person one is in love with. (After all, love and marriage go together like a horse and carriage.) Julie decides to marry Bob even though she doesn't love him, because he offers her security. The chances of such a marriage being successful are slim, because, we are told, as marriage is the natural outcome of love, a marriage cannot be successful unless built on love. Julie's marriage to Bob will work only if, mysteriously, she falls in love with him. The audience is prepared for problems between Julie and Bob.

The story of Bob and Julie and Phyllis is about love and marriage. It demonstrates that love is a mysterious force beyond our control, an emotion that can be felt only for one person at a time, the natural basis for marriage. Marriage, unlike love, is within our control. We can choose to marry and to divorce, but we cannot choose to love.

Another triangle from "Search for Tomorrow" (CBS):

> Eunice and Doug, a lawyer, are happily married and have a baby girl to whom they are devoted. Eunice decides she would like to fill her spare time, and takes a job as a writer on a local magazine. Her boss, John, is also a lawyer, in fact, Doug's chief rival. Doug disapproves of Eunice's working because it takes her away from their family. After a time he becomes convinced that Eunice is having an affair with John, a belief that has no foundation in fact. He refuses to believe that Eunice is innocent and that she loves only him. Doug asks for a divorce, but Eunice still hopes for a reconciliation. In her misery, Eunice is drawn to John, who offers her advice and consolation. In fact, John is in love with Eunice. The final blow comes when, because of the malicious meddling of outsiders, Doug is crippled in an accident which paralyzes him from the waist down. The love Eunice shows for him is now interpreted by Doug as pity. He refuses to have anything to do with her and the divorce is finalized. John, who is still very much in love with Eunice, urges her to marry him. She is tempted to accept because any future with Doug now seems hopeless. Eunice marries John but does she really love him or is she still in love with Doug?

Again we begin with a situation that appears to be ideal: a loving couple devoted to their baby girl. (It should be noted that there is another long story of how Doug and Eunice achieved their ideal but short-lived bliss.) Doug comes to believe that Eunice is having an affair with John. Doug's suspicions are unfounded. Here we learn that the ideal relationship between a man and a woman includes sex as well as love and marriage. Because they are married, Eunice's sexual involvement should be with Doug alone, because to have it otherwise is a violation of the marriage. It is adultery, but worse than that, it is a symptom that love is felt for another. Sexual involvement is the natural expression of love, just as marriage is the culmination of love. Sex is a sign of love.

From this triangle we also learn something about the nature of love. Doug's belief that his wife was involved with another man led to the ruin of their marriage. The result was as bad as if she really had been involved with another man. Love is something to be exchanged. Just as it can be destroyed when one ceases to give love, it may also be destroyed when one ceases to accept love. The latter, however, is much more unusual, perhaps even evidence of an unbalanced mind. Normal people need love so much they are often tempted, though it is somewhat unethical, to accept love from one to whom they cannot give it (as Eunice is tempted to do with John). As usual, it is easier, if not better, to receive than to give. But Doug is unable to accept Eunice's love, and so he asks for a divorce. He is now saying that, more than being unwilling to accept love from Eunice, he is also unwilling to give love to her, in spite of the fact that there is evidence that he feels love for her. Eunice, who has a normal need for love, is drawn to John, who offers her comfort, friendship, and love. Love, then, is something to be exchanged, to be mutually given and received between a man and a woman.

Doug's subsequent paralysis tells us something more about the relationship between sex and love since he becomes paralyzed from the waist down. Until then he has been only an emotional cripple, unable to give love to his wife even though he loves her. Now, unable to be sexually involved with her, he believes that because he is "less than a man" she can feel only pity and sympathy for him, not love. He has confused the sign (sex) with that which it is a sign of (love). Just as he believed that Eunice was sexually involved with John and therefore no longer loved him, now he believes that since he cannot have sex with Eunice, she can no longer love him. Doug is an emotional and physical cripple. Eunice, who is quite healthy, is drawn closer to John by her need for love.

From the story of Doug and Eunice and John, we learn about the nature of love as something to be exchanged, given and received. A refusal to give or receive destroys the relationship. Because it is easier to receive than to give, what usually goes wrong is that one ceases to give love. Doug is unusual, perhaps abnormal, in being unable to accept love. We also learn about sex. Sex is a sign of love; it is the natural expression of the love between a man and a woman. But it is only a sign and should not be taken for the real thing, as Doug mistakenly does. The connection is a powerful one, but not necessary. Sexual involvement should be restricted to the married couple, who should be in love with each other.

Triangles demonstrate the ingredients, and the connections between the ingredients in the ideal relationship between a man and a woman: the co-occurrence of love, marriage, and sex. Love is the basic ingredient on which the ideal relationship is built. Marriage (which temporally should come second) is the desired cultural culmination of love; sex is its natural expression. Love can only really be felt for one person at a time. Therefore, sex (love's sign), and, of course, marriage (its culmination) should be engaged in only with one person at a time. Sex and marriage are matters of choice, but one cannot choose to love or not to love.

A triangle is a violation of the ideal. The three ingredients do not coincide, but are placed in conflict by being bestowed on different individuals. Thus, Bob is married to Phyllis, but in love with Julie. Eunice is married to Doug, but Doug thinks she is having an affair with John. When the ideal order is lost, the power of love to entail both sex and marriage causes events to move toward the recreation of the ideal order in a new relationship. But the basic dilemma is built in. While the ideal is the everlasting coincidence of love, marriage, and sex, it is in the nature of love to come and go mysteriously; and love is powerful (it conquers all). This is why the triangle is eternal.

PROBLEMS OF PARENTAGE

The second most frequent problem plaguing soap opera characters concerns their relationships with their children. Consider the story of Steven, Alice, Rachel, and Jamie on "Another World" (NBC):

Steven and Alice are married. They are blissfully happy for a while. They would like to have a family but Alice is unable to have children. Steven decides to be more of a father to his natural son, Jamie with whom, until this time, he has had little contact. He arranges to contribute to

Jamie's support and to spend time with him. Rachel, Jamie's mother, is delighted, seeing this as an opportunity to get closer to Steven through their child. Alice is jealous of Steven's relationship with his natural son. Rachel arranges for Alice to discover her alone with Steven in suspicious circumstances. Alice, sure that Steven is involved with Rachel, becomes distraught and disappears with no explanation. Rachel succeeds in her plot. After a time Steven decides to marry her, mainly so that he can be a real father to his son. Eventually Alice returns. Steven and Alice realize they still love each other. With great resistance from Rachel, Steven manages to get a divorce. Steven and Alice remarry. Disputes over the custody of Jamie begin. Jamie is torn between his love for his mother and his love for his father.

Steven and Alice are happily married. But there is a serious flaw in their happiness. Alice cannot have children. Alice's feeling of inadequacy and her consequent insecurity in her relationship with Steven indicate something about the nature of marriage. Marriage is more than the culmination of the love between a man and a woman (as the triangles have shown). It is the basis on which families are built. Put more strongly, its purpose is to create families. A married couple alone is incomplete.

Indeed, Alice has more to worry about than her inability to produce a family, for Steven has the ingredients for a real family that does not include her. He has a natural son, Jamie. And there is Rachel, Jamie's mother, who would be more than happy to have him.

We are shown by the juxtaposition of these two imperfect situations how things should be. Steven and Alice are in love and married, but cannot have children. Rachel's love for Steven is not reciprocated, and they are not married, but they have a child. The ideal, then, is a man and woman in love and married with a child who is the product of their sexual union. This is a family.

Both Alice and Rachel see in Steven's closeness to Jamie a potential for closeness to Rachel, Jamie's mother. Alice fears it; Rachel feeds it. They believe that the shared creation of a child whom they both love will bring the parents together and make them love each other. The triangles revealed that the ways of love are mysterious and beyond our control. However, the bonds between the parents based on their mutual love for a child, who is tied by blood to each of them, seem to be strong enough to be mistaken for love (Alice), or transformable into love (Rachel), or substitutable for love (Steven). Rachel attempts to capitalize on these beliefs, and she is successful for a time. Alice is convinced that Steven is having an affair with Rachel, and Steven eventually decides to try to make a real family with Rachel and their son by marrying her. But it cannot work, for although Rachel and Steven are married and have a child, Steven does not really love Rachel and the arrangement is doomed to failure. Failure is realized when Alice returns and she and Steven reaffirm their love. Rachel has lost Steven to Alice. We have been shown that the basic ingredient of the family is love between a man and a woman. Without that a family cannot successfully be built.

The problem now is what to do about Jamie. Who will get custody? That the problem arises at all tells us several things about the ideal family. This problem emerges only when Jamie's parents split up, indicating that their relationship to Jamie should be as a unit and not as individuals: They should share in his upbringing. The relationship should be between parents and child, not between mother and child, on the one hand, and father and child, on the other. Jamie's reaction to his parents' separation makes this explicit. For a time he will not speak with his father, because he thinks his father is mistreating his mother. At one point he runs away. Later there is a reconciliation with his father. Jamie's distress is acute. Parents are supposed to be together, a unit. But Jamie's parents are separated and he must relate to them individually but he does not know how.

That custody for Jamie is disputed by his parents indicates something else about the relationship between parent and child. Both Steven and Rachel wish to have legal custody of Jamie because they both love him and want the right to raise him. They base their dispute on the fact that they are equally Jamie's parents. They are both his natural parents, having contributed equally to his conception. Their divorce precludes raising him together as ideally they should; they must compete for him. The ties of blood and love are held separately. The right to raise their son, recognized in legal custody, is different from the ties of blood and love. This is something that parents should hold as a unit. It is clearly undesirable, although possible, for them to have separate social/legal rights and duties with regard to their son.

We learn more about the family from the story of Steve, Carolee, and Eric from "The Doctors" (NBC):

> Steve and Carolee are happily married, and have a daughter of their own, and Steve's son, Eric, from a previous marriage. Eric and his mother were in a plane crash. He was rescued, but she was declared missing and presumed dead. Eric is about 8 years old now and has grown up thinking Carolee is his real mother. Carolee and Steve have decided that she should adopt Eric and become his legal mother. Just as they are about to let Eric know that they have done so, Eric tells them how glad he is that he has a real mommy and daddy and wasn't adopted like one of his friends. With some trepidation, somewhat later, Steve and Carolee tell Eric that Carolee is his adoptive mother, not his natural mother. He seems to take it well, but then one day when Carolee scolds him, he complains that she loves Stephanie, his half sister, more than she loves him. Soon after he runs away.

Eric, whose natural mother is presumed dead, is living with his father and his father's wife, Carolee. Carolee loves him and treats him as her own, but she is not his legal or natural mother. Through the power of the courts she acquires the legal right to raise him, but, of course, she cannot become his natural mother. This is a fact of biology that cannot be changed. Through the juxtaposition of these different kinds of parent-child relations, three aspects of the relationship between parent and child emerge: being a parent (a biological fact), acting like a parent ("raising" a child, a right and duty usually sanctioned by law), and feeling like a parent (love).

Eric had thought that both of his parents, Steve and Carolee, were his natural (biological) as well as his loving and nurturing father and mother. He lets it be known that parents who legally raise and love a child but are not biologically related (i.e., adoptive parents) are not real parents. Through Eric's reaction a relationship among the three ingredients of parenthood is established. The natural connection is presented as basic; the ties of love and nurturing are secondary.

Further, Eric, now knowing that Carolee is not his natural mother, concludes that Carolee loves his half sister (her natural child) more than she loves him. From this we learn something more about the relationship among the three ingredients of parenthood. Parental love is derivative and its sources are known (unlike romantic love, the source of which is mysterious). There are two sources: the biological connection between natural parent and child, and the care given by the parent. Eric's reaction indicates that the first source of love is more powerful than the second, Finally, Eric's attempt to run away is testimony to the importance of the biological connection between parent and child and the profound disturbance caused when it is discovered that the relationship is not what it should be, because, although there are social and loving ties between both parents and their child, the natural bond is defective because it exists with only one parent.

There is an interesting contrast here between the parent-child and man-woman relationships. In the relationship between man and woman, the ideal of a couple united by love, marriage, and sex may be destroyed and recreated over and over. The ideal relationship between parent and child, however, rests on a blood tie which, of course, cannot be recreated. If the blood tie is not present, the relationship between parent and child must rest on love derived from the social tie. Eric believes that this is second best. What he must (and presumably will) learn is that a relationship built on love derived from nurturing is just as good as one built on a blood tie. That is, love as the basis of the parent-child relationship is a substitute for the real thing (blood), but it is a very good substitute.

These two stories tell us about the way relationships between parents and children should be. There are three ingredients that should be present: a blood tie, a social tie, and a bond of love. The blood tie is basic. The love of a parent for his or her child is not as mysterious as romantic love. Its sources are two: the blood tie, and the nurturant relationship between parent and child. The context in which the parent-child relationship should occur is the family. The purpose of marriage is to create families, the integrity of which is ultimately based on the love between husband and wife. Here a connection between triangles and parent-child problems is established. The latter are derived from triangles where sex, marriage, and love are not exclusively held between husband and wife. As in the triangles, these out-or-order relationships between parents and children, and the efforts of the characters to restore order, show us how things should be in the American family.

THE AMERICAN FAMILY

According to the soap operas, then, the American family is built on two sets of relationships: one between husband and wife, and the second between parents and child. Both of these relationships ought to be dyadic. This is obviously so in the case of husband and wife, but also true in the case of parents and child: mother and father should function as a unit in relation to their child. Problems result when relationships that ought to be dyadic become triadic. That is, when the husband or wife becomes involved with another (a triangle), or when the parents do not relate to their child as a unit, but separately as mother and father.

Each dyadic relationship should contain three basic ingredients. A man and a woman should be united by love, marriage, and sex. Parents and child should be united by blood, love, and nurturing. Love is an element in both relationships, but the love between parent and child is different from the love between husband and wife. The former is parental or familial love derived from the blood tie between parent and child, and the nurturing of a child by its parent. It has a beginning but no end. To stop loving your child would be unnatural in the worst sense of the word. The love between husband and wife is romantic love, the source of which is mysterious so that it may begin and may end suddenly. It just happens to people (one falls, not jumps). The two kinds of love are sharply differentiated and people who share familial love are prohibited from sharing romantic love by the incest taboo.

Just as there are two kinds of love, so there are two kinds of biological relationship. The biological connection between parent and child is based on birth and blood, and once it is established it is permanent. The biological connection between husband and wife is sexual union, which is transitory. One may choose (except in the case of rape) whether or not to be sexually involved with another person.

Similarly, there are two kinds of social bond, one between parent and child, and one between husband and wife. Marriage and custody are the legal recognition of social relationships between husband and wife, and parent and child, respectively. Both of these can be initiated or dissolved by participants in the relationship with the approval of society, represented by the courts.

The relationship among the elements of the husband-wife dyad may be contrasted with those of the parent-child dyad. Both are based on natural phenomena, in one case emotional (romantic love), in the other biological (blood). Both have natural expressions, one in sex as an expression or sign of romantic love, the other in parental love as the expression of the blood tie. Just as romantic love may be temporary, so may sexual involvement. Just as a blood tie is permanent, so is its expression in parental love. Only what is natural (but not all of what is natural) can be enduring, and so the social relationships may be given or taken away by society (marriage, divorce, awarding custody).[3]

THE BEGINNING IS THE END

So far we have looked at the family as a static phenomenon. But it has an ongoing aspect too, which is also dealt with in the soap operas. New families are created by the personnel of old families. The old must, in part at least, be destroyed or transformed by the new. There are proper ways to accomplish this: Some things ought to be given up, some must be maintained.

The most interesting soap opera plots are concerned with this problem. They are the most interesting because they are the furthest removed from the empirical realities of social life, and most clearly demonstrate that soap operas operate not with the actualities of family life, but with the principles on which it is based. Most often these plots occur as complications of the ones discussed so far. There are at least three varieties of plot that deal with the ongoing aspect of family life: brother-sister incest (a rare but fascinating problem), the triangle involving blood relatives (e.g., mother and daughter involved with the same man, or brothers involved with the same woman), and the mother-in-law. I will comment only on the last of these.

Three versions of the mother-in-law problem are offered. Version one, from "The Doctors" (NBC):

> Steve Aldrich is a young successful doctor from an upper-class Boston family. He and his wife Carolee are happily married. Steve's mother, Mona, has been traveling in Europe for several years, leading a carefree, sophisticated life. Suddenly she wires Steve to expect her for a visit. Steve and his mother were very close during his childhood, but as peers. She never liked the role of mother very much. Steve has always called her by her first name. He is delighted that she will visit. Some months pass and it becomes evident first to the audience and then to Carolee that Mona is doing everything she can to break up their marriage. First she tries throwing Steve together with a childhood sweetheart also from a fine Boston family. Then she tries to lure Steve back to an upper-class Boston practice so that he will see for himself that Carolee is not the sort of girl for him. She hopes he will give up Carolee, and stay in Boston with her. Her plot does not succeed. Steve stays with Carolee and Mona goes to Boston alone.

Version two from "Love of Life" (CBS):

> Dan is a young successful doctor from a well-to-do family

in Boston. After a stormy courtship he marries Kate, a nice girl from a working class background. But Kate has problems: she was raped by a former lover and is pregnant. Dan's mother, Mrs. Phillips, arrives on the scene, and tries to find a way to break up the marriage. She believes that the baby Kate will have is not Dan's and tries to convince him to get a divorce. When she learns the baby is Dan's she becomes involved in seamy schemes with Kate's ex-lover to keep the information from Kate and Dan. But Dan, even though he believes Kate's baby is not his, goes to Kate and declares his love for her and the child and asks her to let him come back.

Version three from "Search for Tomorrow" (CBS):

Len is a young successful doctor. Len's mother, a business woman, after having lived in Paris for many years, returns home. Len calls her by her first name, Andrea. She is a lonely possessive woman. Len is married to Patti. Because Patti cannot have children, she and Len arrange to adopt a child. Unknown to Patti, Len and Andrea arrange to adopt a baby boy, who is Len's natural son. Andrea, wrongly, thinks that Patti is an incompetent mother and is endangering her grandchild, who is not even Patti's real child. She becomes involved in unsavory plots with a psychotic woman, who is jealous of Patti, to destroy Len and Patti's marriage. She wants Len to divorce Patti and get custody of her grandson, his natural son. She plans to move in with Len and help him raise the child. The outcome of many additional complications is that Andrea's scheme is unsuccessful. Len realizes that Patti is a good mother after all. Patti and Len and the baby move away, leaving a sadder, but wiser Andrea behind.

All of these stories concern the relationships between a mother, her son, and her daughter-in-law. The son, a young doctor, is married to a nice girl. The young doctor's mother arrives on the scene, alone. Because she's "not good enough for him," the mother does not approve of her son's wife and does everything in her power to destroy the marriage.

In these stories two women are placed in competition with

each other for a man—the son and husband. The mother wishes to keep him in her family; the wife wishes to take him to form a new family. The son plays a passive role, remaining unaware of what is going on between his wife and his mother. The wife is a nice, relatively powerless victim; the mother is a powerful meddler, with questionable motives. The audience's sympathies lie with the wife and, in the end, the mother is defeated and the young doctor and his bride are happy (for a month or two at least).

The interesting figure in these plots is the older woman. She enters the scene alone. If she has a husband or other children they remain in the shadows. Mona and Andrea have no husbands, and Mrs. Phillips' husband appears only briefly, attempting to discourage her from interfering with their son's marriage. Len is Andrea's only surviving child; Mrs. Phillips has no other children; and Mona's other child does not appear in the story. These mothers have no one but their sons. Each is so resentful of her son's attachment to his wife that she will try almost anything in order to get him to leave his wife.

Mona and Andrea are worldly women, sophisticated, well traveled, youthful, and fashionable: not the motherly type at all. They regard their sons more as peers than as children. Now that they are older and alone, they wish to have their sons to themselves as friends and companions. Mrs. Phillips, on the other hand, thinks she has the right to dictate her son's choice of a wife. She wants to retain control over her grown son.

We learn something interesting about love from these episodes. The bonds between mother and son include blood, parental love, and nurturing. Dan's mother, Mrs. Phillips, wishes to keep all these ties intact. It is clear that she is in the wrong, and that she must give up custody and control over Dan so that he can form a new family. Mona and Andrea also wish to keep their sons but their approach and proposed solution is different: they are willing to give up mothering. They never liked it much anyway, preferring to lead worldly, sophisticated lives. They wish to transform the bond of parental love into something dangerously close to romantic love, thereby remaining or becoming their sons' chief companion. Familial love and romantic love are supposed to be distinct and mutually exclusive. But Mona and Andrea confuse the two, indicating that in some basic way familial love and romantic love are very much alike.

Dan's mother is unwilling to have things change; Andrea and Mona want change but to a state that is not culturally acceptable. None wishes to give up her son, but they each must. The mother who has given birth to the son cannot in later life have him for a consort or keep him as a child. He must become an adult and he must go elsewhere for a mate. So the soap operas contain a kind of social theory of the function of the incest taboo (not unlike Tylor's, Lévi-Strauss's, and White's). The mother must give up her son to another woman.

Thus, unlike the bonds of love, marriage, and sex, which (ideally at least) once established, unite a man and a woman until "death do us part," the bonds that unite parent and child do not remain unchanged. The ties of blood and love remain, but parents must give up nurturing when their children are grown. It is only by letting them go that new families can be formed.

CONCLUSION

The soap operas contain a coherent expression of the principles on which the American family is based. Their immense popularity indicates that the picture they present is at least meaningful, and probably very significant, to a large number of Americans. This analysis has demonstrated how the principles on which family life is based are revealed in dramatic dilemmas that violate the ideal order. Elements that belong together in the same relationship are opposed in different relationships. A man is married to one woman but in love with another; a child's natural mother and its legal and loving mother are different women. Resolution is sought in the restoration of the ideal, where this is possible, by uniting the several elements in a single relationship—the man marries the woman he loves; the child learns to accept his legal and loving mother as if she were his natural mother. The analysis of the most common of these dilemmas, the romantic triangles and problems of parentage, reveal the concepts and relations among them that are central to American ideas about the family: romantic and parental love, sex and marriage, blood and nurturing. The analysis of soap operas, then, provides another approach to the study of American kinship, which uses a previously untapped source of data on American ideas about the family.

Notes

I would like to thank my colleagues Emily M. Ahern and Harold W. Scheffler for their comments on earlier drafts of this paper.

1. In 1974.

2. It is also likely that the middle-class uniformity of soap opera characters and settings is the result of an almost exclusive concern in soap operas with the women's domain. The men's domain, the achievement of socioeconomic success only rarely occurs as an ingredient in soap opera plots. Rather, its successful achievement occurs as a given, a backdrop against which the drama of the female domain is played.

3. Marriage is easy to get and not too difficult to get rid of; custody is hard to get (unless you come by it naturally), and no one wants (or should want) to give it away.

References

Edmonson, Madeleine and D. Rounds, 1974, *The Soaps*. New York: Stein and Day.

Goodlad, J. S. B., 1971, *The Sociology of Popular Drama*. London: Heinemann Educational Books Ltd.

Laub, Bryna R., ed., 1974, *Daytime Serial Newsletter*. (Post Office Box 6, Mountain View, California 94042).

Warner, W. Lloyd, 1948, "The Radio Day Time Serial: A Symbolic Analysis." *Genetic Psychology Monographs* 37:3-71.

HOW NANCY GETS HER MAN

An Investigation of Success Models in American Adolescent Pulp Literature

SUSAN P. MONTAGUE

This paper investigates success models in American culture. The data are drawn from adolescent pulp literature, with specific attention paid to Horatio Alger and Nancy Drew stories. Baldly stated, the aim of the paper is to explain why in a society once so attracted to Alger's success model, as evidenced by his sales, Nancy Drew, who violates it, sustains an equally great appeal. That this question initially seems trivial or at best somewhat irrelevant to the serious student of American culture is a sad commentary on our views of popular media. It is only recently that anthropologists are attempting to treat mass media seriously as a data source. In large part this stems from ethnocentrism, from the fact that pulp media are defined by us native Americans as frivolous, nor serious stuff, intended for leisure relaxation. Actually it is precisely the fact that mass media *is* aimed at leisure time, and *is* voluntarily bought by its audience that ought to lead us to the realization that it contains information that its buyers find particularly timely and topical. I thus hope that this paper not only explicates a particular historical shift in success ideology in American culture, but in addition that it provides a convincing demonstration of the utility of mass media material as a data base for significant cultural analysis.

The best-known body of didactic success literature is a series of stories written in the second half of the nineteenth century by Horatio Alger, Jr. They were, indeed, so successful, that

Horatio Alger has become an American synonym for success. The books are "how to" manuals, guides to assist young men to properly program their course through adult life. The plots are uniform: A poor youth sets out to find fame and fortune, the rewards given by society to the successful actor. By following aspirants as they seek success, the reader is educated in their methods. He learns the success formula. Alger's formula is simple: Its basic tenets are hard work, self-denial, and altruism. Let us look at each of these in turn.

Alger heroes are enjoined to seek rewards through work. Work means holding a paying job in the world of commerce, or business. The heroes are exhorted to devote their lives to work. Devotion is demonstrated by not only holding a job, but also by devoting off hours to improving work skills. It is not uncommon for an Alger hero to attend night school while working during the day. Ragged Dick goes so far as to take in an impoverished but educated boy and pay his lodging in return for tutoring (Alger, 1972). Alger heroes are always happy to spend time with successful older men, learning of and from their business experiences.

In addition, dedication to work also means a certain type of performance on the job. Alger heroes are diligent at their work. They appear on time, and work overtime if necessary. When they find themselves unoccupied they eagerly seek out new tasks to perform. They make sure that each task is done thoroughly and correctly, admitting their failures and attempting to compensate through increased effort.

Dedication to work involves *self-denial,* the second element in the formula. Work is portrayed as both physically and mentally taxing. It strains the individual's resources and tires him. In short, far from gratifying, work does the opposite: it drains. It is the *result* of the worker's effort that gratifies him, not the effort itself. This means that there is always the temptation of more directly pleasurable activities, which might lead the worker away from his tasks. The model therefore discriminates between legitimate and illegitimate gratification. Legitimate gratification comes after the work is completed, and consists of the actor's satisfaction from a job well done, along with society's recognition of that same fact. Society's recognition consists of fame (good repute) and money. Alger defines fame as the most valuable reward. However, these stories are called "from rags to riches" stories because the plots actually center on the search for wealth. Good reputation may in theory be the most important, but without the accompanying wealth the hero would feel deprived, because it is money that tells him and others that his efforts are truly appreciated. Fame and fortune thus ideally go together, fortune validating fame. However, Alger is aware that money may be had illegitimately, and that actors who legitimately make money may later become evil people, and it is for these reasons that he emphasizes good repute while his heroes actually look for dollars.

Illegitimate gratification means using one's resources in ways that render them unavailable for work. Alger defines the most tempting forms of illegitimate gratification as smoking, drinking, and gambling. Smoking is wasteful of money and injurious to health, but of the three is the least pernicious. Whereas in *Mark, the Match Boy* the secondary hero is persuaded to "leave off smoking–a habit which he had formed in the streets of New York" (1962: 382), in *Digging for Gold* the secondary hero smokes and nothing is made of the fact (1968). Drinking is worse. The heroes do not drink, and excessive drinking is used as one of the signs of the antihero.

Gambling is the worst temptation. It wastes time, money, and can lead to theft to cover financial losses. But these are not the main reasons that gambling is so pernicious. Rather it is that the gambler is opposed to the work ethic: he wants to get something for nothing. Smoking and drinking may injure the actor's work capacity, but indulgence in these activities does not necessarily mean that the actor opposes work. With gambling, however, there can be no question. The man who recognizes the proper relationship between work and money cannot gamble, and conversely, the gambler cannot be a truly dedicated worker. Ragged Dick gambles, but only because he believes that he will never amount to more than a poor bootblack. When he decides that he can better himself and seek success, he overtly repudiates gambling, although he apparently still smokes (1962:

75, 110). In *Digging for Gold* the hero, who has a job in a restaurant, is accused of gambling and is at pains to try and clear himself because if thought guilty he will be fired (1968: 88-105).

Thus far, the element of altruism has not entered into the model. Getting rich and famous hardly seems altruistic. However, altruism is in fact the key component. The success is the actor who devotes his life to helping others. Wealth and fame are the expressions of a grateful society, grateful for his efforts on its behalf. It is crucial that Alger defines work as *labor that benefits society*. The hero deserves success because he dedicates his life to assisting others. He is rewarded both for his accomplishments in this line and for the fact that he is willing to routinely forego self-gratification in order to devote himself to his work. One of the most often heard criticisms of Alger books is that the heroes do not really get rich by working hard, but through dramatically helping wealthy actors in nonbusiness crises. Rescuing the banker's drowning daughter, preventing a train crash, or reuniting a man with his long lost son—these are the kinds of actions that earn lavish reward. But this criticism misses the point. Alger maintains that the actor who thinks of others first will always get ahead because he possesses moral character, and is thus deserving. Opportunity will knock at his door.

Achieving success does not permit any relaxation of altruism. The boy who struggles upward in one book is the wealthy patron of another struggling boy in the next. When offered $1000 reward, the already successful Richard Hunter takes it, saying: "Then I will keep it as a charity fund, and whenever I have an opportunity of helping along a boy who is struggling upward as I once had to struggle, I will do it." His benefactor replies: "A noble resolution, Mr. Hunter! You have found out the best use of money" (1962: 381).

The popularity and pervasiveness of the Horatio Alger model is undeniable. Not only did it sell well in the pulp business, but it is striking that *the* American sport, football, is virtually an enactment of this model, to the extent that Vince Lombardi spent his off seasons lecturing businessmen on how to improve worker attitudes and thereby increase profits.

Thus far my data present no problems. Horatio Alger's success formula is simple in its tenets, and has an internal logical consistency. However, difficulties arise when we look at some other adolescent pulp literature. The difficulties concern the role of women. Alger's model is not aimed at women. Rather, women function as the hero's ultimate reward. This is submerged in the stories in the sense that the heroes are always actively seeking reputation and money; but the reason they do this is so that they may support a family either by taking on support of a widowed mother or marrying the sweetheart of their dreams. Women do not actively figure in the stories because they do not compete in the business world: They do not work. Theirs is the complementary realm of the home, and for them, to work is a hardship. It means either that they are too unattractive to attract a husband, or that through misfortune they have been stranded without one. As Huber puts it:

> A cynic once remarked that "a man is a success if he can make more money than his wife can spend." The rejoinder might be: "Yes, and a woman is a success if she can find such a man." A wife not only took the name of her husband, but also her rate of mobility from him. However, one did not speak of a housewife as a "success." A housewife didn't get promoted. There was no way of measuring her achievement. (1971: 5)

We would expect, considering the Alger stories, that there would be a complementary literature aimed at telling girls how to go about finding and attracting a successful man, and that such literature would be centered on domestic roles. In fact there was and is that type of didactic female oriented adolescent pulp literature, but the best-selling series in the United States for the last 45 years has been the Nancy Drew series, and it does not conform to these expectations.

Nancy Drew is but one of many creations of Edward Stratemeyer. Stratemeyer began his career writing Horatio Alger stories after Alger's death, and came into his own with the Tom Swift series. He wound up as *the* teen pulp writer for Grosset and Dunlap, turning out over 800 books under sixty-five pseudonyms (Prager, 1971: 102). As Laura Lee Hope he wrote *The Bobbsey Twins,* as Franklyn W. Dixon, *The Hardy Boys,* and as Carolyn Keene, *Nancy Drew.* Stratemeyer began writing Nancy Drew stories in 1930. To date, over 30 million Drew books have been sold, while Alger sold only around 17 million (Prager, 1971: 73; Alger, 1962: 7). As adolescents hand them around Nancy Drew books have probably been read by some 60 million American girls and women in the last 45 years. Why?

An examination of the content of the stories indicates that adolescent girls *too* are interested in success, for that is the basic topic. The books document the adventures and achievements of an extremely talented and capable heroine. What are some of Nancy's accomplishments? Well, to start with, she is an expert on Shakespeare, ancient Greece, Chaucer, obscure pottery marks and manufacture, and Mayan cryptography. And as Prager explains:

> For all her intellectual attainments, Nancy is no bluestocking. She rides and swims in Olympic style . . . on one occasion leaping into a bayou with all her clothes on and doing a rapid 500 yards to the shore. She can fix a balky outboard motor with a bobby pin. With no effort, she climbs a rose trellis to the second floor. Pursuing an escaped crook she puts the police on his trail by drawing a perfect likeness of him for them. When the River Heights Women's Club charity show faces disaster because of the defection of its leading lady, Nancy steps in at a moment's notice and wins general kudos with a creditable ballet, although she is recuperating from a sprained ankle. At 100 yards, she plugs a lynx three times with a Colt .44 revolver. Her delphiniums win first prize at a flower show. She floors "Zany" Shaw, a fullgrown law breaker, with a right to the jaw. She is always a barrel of fun at a party, and she ". . . received a lot of applause for her impersonation of Helena Hawley, a motion-picture star who played parts in old-time westerns." What hero or heroine of modern fiction can top that (1971: 78)?

And indeed, even the most successful Alger hero falls short. But these capabilities are merely the window dressing, the backdrop for Nancy's true success arena, criminal detection. Nancy is an accomplished teenage detective, who routinely solves mysteries that baffle the official experts.

Stratemeyer, like Alger, is overtly didactic. He claims that by observing Nancy anyone can learn to succeed as she does in the area of crime detection. The implicit message is that since Nancy's methods do not vary from activity to activity, one can generalize from the explicit model of how she catches criminals to how to succeed in any undertaking.

How does Nancy solve crimes? First, like Alger heroes, she has prepared herself:

> No doubt all of us have scores of times rubbed elbows with some refugee from justice, or have figured in some unimportant incident which actually was one link in a long chain of mystery and adventure. Few of us, though, have trained our powers of observation and deduction as Nancy had, although by studying her methods it should not be at all impossible for any intelligent reader to learn them. (1933: 13)

Second, Nancy is completely dedicated to her task. Stratemeyer states:

> There was something about a mystery which aroused Nancy's interest and she was never content until it was solved. (1930: 6)

> "Where there's a will, there's a way," she quoted whimsically. "That old proverb is doubly true in the Crowly case. If there actually is a second will, I'm going to find it!" (1930: 23)

Nancy pursues the solution despite all costs or discomforts. She spends enough time on pleasurable activities to be acceptably sociable, but she is forever leaving a party early to return to the chase.

Nancy is also altruistic. She works to help people, not for reward. She is always modest about her accomplishments, taking true pleasure from the knowledge that she has been useful to others.

In short, Nancy Drew is essentially an Alger success model hero; she functions in the role and according to the standards that he outlined for men. Instead of standing on the sidelines cheering, she is in the heart of the battle. Instead of staying home, she goes out after criminals. How can this be? Why is it that a society that found the Alger model so compelling also supports Nancy Drew? One obvious possibility is that there was a cultural change and that by 1930 women's roles had been redefined so that women might legitimately function in either or both slots of the Alger model. To investigate this hypothesis let us look at how Stratemeyer presents Nancy, the person, and the other most prominent women in the series.

In the first volume, *The Secret of the Old Clock* (1930), the reader is told that Nancy's mother died when Nancy was 9 years old. At that time Nancy took over the adult woman's traditional domestic role of running the household. This included supervising the servants and planning the menus. To her father's surprise she performed this role with an adult's competency. Recognizing that her unusual talents indicated a high intelligence, he encouraged her to develop her mental skills. And since he had no son, but rather an exceptional daughter, he raised her to follow in his professional footsteps:

> From her father she had acquired the habit of thinking things through to their logical conclusion. Frequently Carson Drew had assured her that she went at a thing "like a detective." (1930: 6)

> Carson Drew, a widower, showered a great deal of affection upon his daughter; it was his secret boast that he had taught her to think for herself and to think logically. Since he knew that Nancy could be trusted with confidential information, he frequently discussed his interesting cases with her. (1930: 6)

> Of course, Nancy had an advantage in being so conversant with the professional secrets of Carson Drew, the celebrated criminal lawyer. (1933: 13)

It is thus the combination of (1) exceptional intelligence and (2) an unusually close paternal relationship or masculine identification that results in Nancy's professional interest and capability. However, this is not consonant with the theme of Stratemeyer's didacticism, for he argues that any *ordinary* girl might succeed like Nancy, and it is clear that she is far from ordinary. By the third or fourth volume he downplays this explanation, and instead establishes Nancy's credentials through favorably contrasting her with two other girls, her chums Bess and George.

Bess Marvin and George Fayne are presented as polar types on a scale of femininity. Bess is overly feminine. Physically she is plump with long, curly hair. She has a predilection for food, frilly dresses, and physical comfort. She does not like dirt, danger, and adventure. George, as her name implies, is a tomboy. She has short hair, is boyish of figure, and tends toward foolhardy daring. She constantly gets into physical difficulty through her rashness; her worst tendency is to fall into mudholes. Nancy stands between the two and strikes the ideal feminine mean. She is physically perfect; not too plump, athletic but not boyish. Like George she likes adventure, but she is not foolhardy. Like Bess she likes feminine frills and comforts, but not to the extent of letting them interfere with her activities. This contrast solves Stratemeyer's problem. Outstanding intelligence is dropped as a qualification, as is excessive masculine identification. Rather, Stratemeyer indicates that it is Bess' and George's extreme types of feminine identity that interfere with their competent performance as detectives. He thus ties *work competency* to what society recognizes as *correct femininity.* However, this is sleight of hand. Correct femininity is actually being defined in terms of what the traditional Alger male looks for in a home-centered, admiring consort. Bess and George are undesirably feminine in that they come close to being unappealing to traditional men: Bess threatens to undermine their masculinity with her overfemininity; George threatens to undermine their masculinity with her own. Nancy is the perfect consort, pretty and practical, the very girl Alger defines as the ideal wife and mother, the domestic complement to the successful male.

Stratemeyer is taking advantage of the fact that the traditional definition of the ideal woman involves two components: physical attributes, expressed in face, figure, and dress; and action orientation, expressed in home management. The two are symbolically tied together. Physical attributes are used as indicators of what sort of wife and mother a woman is apt to be. Stratemeyer's sleight of hand lies in substituting a nondomestic job, criminal detection, for home. By applying the physically expressed attributes that conventionally indicate the desirable wife to performance as a detective, he makes it seem natural and acceptable that the ideal woman and the successful detective should be one and the same.[1]

The fact that Stratemeyer made Nancy a girl who is raised like a boy and had to go to such devious lengths to make her seem both the ideal girl and competent worker indicates that by 1930 it was still not legitimate for women to function in the male slot of Alger's model. And there are other instances in the Nancy Drew stories that support this conclusion. For all her activities outside the home, she retains the traditional feminine home role. She directs the servants, tends the garden, cooks on occasion, and acts as her father's hostess. While her work is outside the home, she does not go outside to seek work. Instead it comes to her at home in the person of her father and his clients. And while she works like a professional, she maintains an amateur status by refusing to work for money. Her father supports her, and it is implied that later on Ned, her boyfriend, will do the same.

Nancy's relationship with Ned is also significant. He appears early in the series in the role of an Alger hero. He attends a university, is doing well in his classwork, and is the star quarterback on the football team. He belongs to a prestigious fraternity and is extremely popular with the brothers. When Nancy visits him on campus it is in the traditional Alger girlfriend-consort role: Her beauty and other feminine charms make her a high-status prize for Ned, and her presence on his arm as his admirer after he has scored the winning touchdown is visible proof of his success. But Ned is not the only winner in this situation. If Nancy is the visible reward for Ned's achievement, in turn, the fact that he wants her validates her own extreme feminine desirability.

While on campus Ned achieves, Nancy admires. Off campus the situation is reversed since it is Nancy who is out solving the mysteries. To salvage Ned's masculinity, he is given an excuse for his inferior performance as a detective. He cannot solve the crimes because he cannot be physically present. He is either off at school or working as a camp counselor. This means that he actually sees Nancy only on rare occasions for very brief periods of time. The fact that Stratemeyer uses Ned to verify Nancy's femininity, and yet does not present her in a realistic romantic relationship again indicates that Nancy's success role is anomalous.

There is additional direct evidence for this conclusion in Stratemeyer's other male-oriented work. The Hardy Boys series provides a good example, particularly since it was written at the same time as Nancy Drew. Like Nancy, the Hardy brothers are teenage detectives. And just as she has a boyfriend, they both have girlfriends. But these girls are not like Nancy. Rather, they are wholly old-fashioned, domestically oriented girls. While the boys go out and solve mysteries, they stay home and bake. Their basic function in life is to provide food for picnics and parties. They never have adventures themselves, but cheer Frank's and Joe's accomplishments. While again Stratemeyer does not really develop the interpersonal male-female relationship, the reason here is not that of anomalous sex roles. Instead, it is because the series is aimed at 9- to 12-year-old boys, who are assumed to reject any mushy love stuff.[2]

Thus there exists a real cultural contradiction. It really is the case that American culture has simultaneously contained a success model defining different, complementary male and female roles, along with a popular literature in violation of that model. How did this situation arise?

The desire of women to enter the labor market following upon the industrial revolution has been thoroughly documented, but as a cultural development it has not been adequately analyzed. Let us jump ahead and look at the modern feminist argument, again as presented to adolescents. In *Girls Are Equal Too,* Dale Carson argues that society should allow and encourage every member to grow and develop as fully as possible

(1973). This she equates with becoming an individual with a strong self-identity. How does one grow and develop? By preparing oneself for and then working at a career job. Marriage and housework, she argues, do not provide adequate identity:

> The two saddest results of the double-sex standard are that: one, girls are too often kept from useful work and from fulfilling themselves as people as well as wives and mothers. (1973: 18)

> And believe me, being Mrs. Somebody is not the same as being somebody yourself. There's not much sense of personal identity in it and not much pride. (1973: 20)

> . . . everybody, not just boys, should be allowed the pride and sense of identity that comes with knowing how to earn a living at work one chooses to do, at being treated as an adult human being. (1973: 21)

> . . . there is one thing nobody can take care of for someone else. And that is, the sense of one's own worth. And what is it worth, in the long run, to have the cleanest kitchen floor in the neighborhood? (1973: 67)

Thus the feminist model sees nondomestic, career work as the basis of all self-identity, not just something appropriate to males. Although in the 1930s Nancy Drew stories the argument is not yet couched in terms of self-identity, it is clear that the connection between nondomestic, career work and *the* valuable social persona has been made. And the connection is strong enough to appear in adolescent literature despite the fact that it violates the traditional sex role ethos seen to lie at the very core of the organization of American society. Where did this new idea come from that it had the power to challenge the fundamental postulates of the traditional social organization?

I would suggest that this idea is a product of the nineteenth-early-twentieth-century shift away from the religious model of human society to the scientific-physicalist model,[3] and that that shift involved a partial redefinition of the actor's relationship to his work.   Nineteenth-century pulp literature, including Alger, uses a religiously based model of human society, wherein man's existence is plagued by his character flaw, the propensity to sin. Sin equals greed, the desire to act for one's self at the expense of one's fellow human beings. The ideal actor is the person who combats this meance by orienting himself toward the good of others.   He possesses moral character insofar as he exercises self-control to overcome or avoid his own sinful tendencies. Alger heroes demonstrate their moral character through their dedication to work.   The more menial their tasks, the more self-discipline they manifest by performing them.

However, by the mid-nineteenth century another model of human society was well developed in academic circles, and was attracting considerable public attention: the scientific-physicalist model.   Malthus, Spenser, and Darwin were among those who argued that the true laws governing all existence are the physical laws of nature. Far from being known or knowable through an oracle, God, these laws remain to be discovered through careful examination of the physical world. The physicalists did not destroy the model of man's flawed character. They added to it. Man's existence is plagued not only by greed, but also by ignorance, and both of these must be combatted if human society is to run properly. The successful actor under either model is the person who devotes his life to contributing to the fight to keep society on the right track.

With the shift from God to nature, the quality of what constitutes significant contribution also shifts, from performing one's duty, however menial, in the face of temptation, to confronting the challenge of the unknown, and by the creative application of one's mind, rendering it known. The ideal worker moves from the dedicated altruistic drudge to the creative thinker. Whereas Alger heroes are rewarded for being good clerks, miners, and busboys, Stratemeyer's heroes are explorers, scientists, inventors, and detectives. They are rewarded for their intellectual feats, for their ability to see solutions missed by other actors.

The shift from work as an expression of moral character to work as an expression of creativity affects women in two ways. First, a new option is open to men that is denied to women in their home-centered role. Whereas women express only their altruism in their labor, men in addition use their work to express their mental interests and abilities. The housewife is stuck virtuously scrubbing floors while her husband, equally virtuous, has the thrill of inventing penicillin, exploring darkest Africa, of being the first to fly over the South Pole. Being cheated of the fun and adventure of discovery is a prominent feminist theme. It is coupled with the fear of being thought a bore for not having had exciting adventures. Second, and more important, while the scientific-physicalist model does not deny the need for moral character, it removes it from the realm of the problematical so far as men are concerned. This is because as work becomes the vehicle or self-expression, the lure of temptation decreases. Work is no longer drudgery, but is exciting and interesting. The actor no longer needs to be rewarded for disciplining himself to work, because he enjoys working. Stratemeyer's heroes cannot be distracted from their work because it is the most pleasurable pastime they can imagine. It is no longer only the results of working that are rewarding, but doing the work itself. As maintaining proper work orientation ceases to constitute a problem, the possession of moral character ceases to be the distinctive feature of the outstanding actor. The problematical quality shifts to intellectual ability, and it is this that is rewarded by society. Women laboring at home are left struggling to achieve social value in terms of a quality which, for men, has been devalued and superseded by another. So long as both sexes were rated on the performance of their respective roles by the same criterion, moral character, the division of labor did not necessarily mean that the sexes differed in social worth. Being Mrs. Somebody *was* the same as being Somebody one's self, be cause Mrs. Somebody was worthy of her outstanding husband only insofar as she too had demonstrated her excellent moral character. Turn-of-the-century pulp such as *Poppea of the Post Office* (Wright, 1909) and *Girl of the Limberlost* (Porter, 1909) does not treat women as lacking social value or identity. Instead it deals with the development of the woman's moral character through correct performance of domestic roles, and it looks for the moral woman to match the moral man. But as the work model changed, woman became socially inferior to men, denied by the division of labor the chance to utilize and demonstrate their intellectual capabilities, and struggling instead to attain the devalued attribute of moral character. And we find Nancy Drew trying to straddle the old model of what it means to be a woman and the new model of what it means to be a valuable social actor.

Nancy is transitional between the two models, and it is striking that a transitional figure has lasted so long. However, 45 years after her inception she still outsells all other pulp literature for girls. This is largely because the cultural conflict between the traditional moral ethos and the changed work ethic defies any easy resolution, and continues to pose a real problem for Americans of both sexes. The devaluation of the female role leaves women with two unappealing choices: to sacrifice self-identity, or by moving into the male work arena, to deny their femininity. Men are confronted with the question of how to define masculinity in the face of female intrusions. But it is interesting that Nancy outsells more modern pulp, which presumably would more accurately reflect the state of the question in current society.

Although I have not conducted an exhaustive survey of the adolescent pulp of the 1950s and 1960s, what little I have read does indeed propose a different solution to the problem. Donna Parker may be taken as a typical case. The formula is superficially the same as Nancy Drew: the heroine is a teenage girl detective confronted with a mystery. But there the resemblance ends. In *Mystery at Arawak* (Martin, 1957), Donna has been given a job as a camp counselor. She is concerned about her ability to perform the job adequately, a concern that Nancy never manifests. She is also concerned about her feminine desirability. One of the other counselors is extremely pretty and in heavy demand for dating. Donna envies this girl. Another counselor is extremely smart, but shunned by the boys. Donna sympathizes with her. In the conclusion Donna realizes that the pretty girl feels handicapped by her looks, just as the bright girl feels handicapped by her brains. Donna concludes that she herself is lucky to be adequate looking, but not beautiful, and adequately smart, but not brilliant, and thus socially acceptable.

The solution here involves manipulation of the same symbols used by Stratemeyer. The pretty girl is in a bind because her feminine looks, which make her attractive to men, also signal the traditional feminine domestic orientation. This constitutes a problem now openly recognized by literature: the equation of domesticity and lack of intellectual creativity. Being defined as femininely desirable also means being defined as stupid or at best vacuous. The bright girl suffers the bind in reverse. Just as the feminine girl cannot be smart, the smart girl cannot be feminine. She is left desexed, and effectively ostracized from male-female social relationships.

This literature defines the problem much more clearly than did the earlier, in that it states the issues rather than glossing over them. But unfortunately, direct statement of the issue does not facilitate a satisfactory solution. The tactic that Martin invokes is simple compromise. If it is impossible to be both perfectly feminine and truly creative, perhaps it is possible to be somewhat feminine and somewhat creative. Donna retains enough feminine attributes to attract at least some men, and also enjoys the modicum of creativity that will not actually threaten their masculinity and hence repel them. But the solution is inadequate because Donna winds up in the same bind that constitutes the essence of the problem in the first place: She is second rate. She does not even get to solve the mystery! Martin leaves it to the smart girl to do that. Donna may bridge the gap between being a real woman and being creative, but she cannot close it. Nancy, for all Stratemeyer's sleight of hand, remains the more appealing character precisely because she enjoys the best of both worlds, the preferable solution however much he had to juggle his symbols to attain it.

SUMMARY

This paper documents a partial shift in success models in American culture due to changing definitions of meaningful work. As the definition of meaningful work went from performance of routine tasks to discovery and mastery of the unknown, a chain reaction was set off. Desirable actor qualities shifted, leading to a reassessment of the sexual division of labor. Because the sexual division of labor lay at the core of American social organization, this created a severe conflict, which still plagues us today. Girls' adolescent pulp literature deals with this conflict because its subject matter is women's roles in society. However, it is confronted with a heavy task. To take on the problem squarely is either to deny American social organization by rejecting the definitions on which it is constructed, or to repudiate the moral base around which American society operates by denying the scientific-physicalist model of the universe, which asserts that the valuable social actor equals the creative worker dedicated to conquering the unknown. The pulp literature has been unwilling to do either of these, and instead has attempted various compromise solutions, all of them inadequate because the two postulates really are irreconcilable. As the very recent girls' feminist literature indicates, there is a current move toward a genuine solution through repudiation of the traditional social organization. However, the continued popularity of Nancy Drew literature, which masks the contradiction and essentially wishes it away, is an indication of the magnitude of difficulties that confront so radical an undertaking, and the corresponding reluctance with which Americans approach it.

Notes

I am grateful to Julia Hecht, David Kemnitzer, John Kirkpatrick, Roy Wagner, and Madeline Schwenk for their comments on earlier drafts of this paper.

1. A further indicator of the sleight of hand is that the girls' feminine identities are, in the final accounting, the result of their parentages. Bess and George are first cousins. Their mothers are sisters. Nancy has no mother. Bess has learned to be over-feminine from her mother, while George is in rebellion against hers. Nancy, the example of perfect femininity, is untouched by motherly influence, and somehow mysteriously achieved her perfection without any adult female role model on whom to pattern herself.

2. Prager offers a more complete summary of the Hardy Boys series in *Rascals at Large.*

3. I am indebted to John Kirkpatrick for the term "physicalist."

References

Alger, Horatio Jr., 1962, *Ragged Dick and Mark, the Match Boy.* New York: Collier.

—1968, *Digging for Gold: A Story of California.* New York: Collier.

Carson, Dale, 1973, *Girls are Equal Too: The Women's Movement for Teenagers.* New York: Atheneum.

Huber, Richard M., 1971, *The American Idea of Success.* New York: McGraw-Hill.

Keene, Carolyn (Edward Stratemeyer), 1930, *The Secret of the Old Clock.* New York: Grosset & Dunlap.

—1933, *The Sign of the Twisted Candles.* New York: Grosset & Dunlap.

Martin, Marcia, 1957, *Mystery at Arawak.* New York: Whitman.

Porter, Gene Stratton, 1909, *Girl of the Limberlost.* New York: Grosset & Dunlap.

Prager, Arthur, 1971, *Rascals at Large, Or The Clue in the Old Nostalgia.* Garden City, N. Y.: Doubleday & Co., Inc.

Wright, Mabel Osgood, 1909, *Poppea of the Post Office.* New York: Grosset & Dunlap.

CHAOS TRIUMPHANT

Archetypes and Symbols in The Exorcist

JOHN W. BURTON
and
DAVID HICKS

Just as analyzing the folk tales, legends, and myths of pre-literate people provides insights into their patterns of thought, so a study of the themes of movies, novels, and TV plays helps us understand the collective psyche of literate folk. Best sellers and hit movies merit anthropological attention. Best seller *and* hit movie, *The Exorcist* ranks high among the most profitable works of the imagination offered to the American public in the last few years. Its complex of motifs lays bare certain ideas and principles fundamental to our collective thought. Many of these ideas we share with peoples of preliterate cultures.

To think at all, we must first classify. The simplest way of classifying follows the operation of the digital computer—binary contrast. Something is either pigeonholed in category x or put in category y, its polar contrast. Societies can construct systems of thought so controlled by the principles of *opposition* and *complementarity* that almost all their major categories are arranged as complementary oppositions or binary contrasts. No place exists in such a schema for a straddling category that is only partly x or partly y. It would be out of place—an anomaly. Granted recognition, such a classificatory monster would break down the sharply defined line separating x and y, and substitute for the clear-cut binary system an amorphous confoundation. Confusion would displace disciplined thought; chaos would possess order. Consciously or unconsciously, humans everywhere appreciate their need for order and fear its converse. Psychologically, chaos is manifested in insanity—a state in which the afflicted person's mental cosmos is overwhelmed by the forces of disorder, and all is confused. This is why we feel uneasy in the presence of things that can't be placed in the conventional pigeonholes established by our society; or in the face of behavior inconsistent with declared norms; or listening to irrational discourse. Because the contrast between order and chaos is vital for human thought and society, the tension required to bring together, yet also repel, polar categories is frequently exploited for dramatic effect in narratives—written and visual—as a device for arousing emotion in the minds of those entertained by them. This arousal partly—though not entirely—accounts for the popularity enjoyed by *The Exorcist*. Certain complementary oppositions crop up so regularly in narratives and rituals the world over that they—like the principles of complementarity and opposition from which they derive—seem to be universals in human experience. Needham would call them natural symbols; Jung, archetypes. Capable of evoking intense emotion in the right dramatic context, they are the symbols through which *The Exorcist's* theme—the attempt to restore order from chaos—reveals itself.

Jamming a *white* crucifix down into her *bloody* vagina, the possessed adolescent, Regan, luridly enacts the motif of order overcome by chaos, which dominates the story. Although complementarity and opposition don't pervade American thought as comprehensively as they do those of some other communities, and lack their systematic power to order categories, they do arrange some of them into contrasts significant for us. A few of these surface continually throughout *The Exorcist: order/ chaos, good/evil, human/beast, male/female, sane/insane, creation/destruction* and, taking second place in *The Exorcist* only to the distinction *order/chaos—secular/sacred*. The sociologist, Durkheim, says of the distinction between secular (or profane) and sacred: "In all the history of human thought there exists no other example of two categories of things so profoundly differentiated or so radically opposed to one another." (Emile

Durkheim, 1965, p. 52). This has been substantiated by many fieldworkers in various parts of the world.

As the first scenes of the drama unfold, secular and sacred are discrete categories. But soon Regan shows signs that their separation is ending. By the time she abuses herself with the crucifix they have fused. Regan is the prime symbol of chaos. A human, she belongs to the secular world, but as a demon she pertains to the sacred world. Since her actions are hostile to human interests she is a monster of evil. Her ambivalent cosmological nature is symbolically impacted by her being the focus of other confounded polar contrasts. Although an 11-year-old *child,* Regan speaks in a *mature* voice and possesses tremendous (perhaps even superhuman) strength. A *female,* her voice is *manly. Human,* she utters *animal* noises. *Innocent,* she voices *obscenities.* Whether or not it is true that human beings prohibit incest because it confounds social relationships that they prefer keeping unambiguous, incest symbolizes the notion of confoundation—as does lesbianism. Thus by pressing the face of Chris, her mother, into her vulva, Regan creates a double ambiguity with her own body. The blood covering her shattered hymen and spreading to Chris's face adds a third.

Another natural symbol, blood, often conveys the idea of opposites fusing or the notion of a conceptual bridge linking them. To establish contact with their spirits, persons typically offer blood sacrifices. Sometimes the blood must be that of a virgin. Blood's ambiguity makes it an apt covering for Regan's vulva, especially since the product of a life-enhancing act (copulation) will, for her, be not life, but death. Blood's most striking sensory property is its color, and we find that in many symbolic systems red and blood convey the same meaning.

Not all ambiguities devolve upon the masturbation scene, though. Regan urinates in a most inappropriate location (the floor of her mother's living room); and describing some of the fiend's traits Merrin (the exorcist) says to Karras (his priestly assistant): "The demon is a *liar.* He will lie to *confuse* us; but he will also mix lies with the truth to attack us" (p. 229, italics added).

One way societies have of suggesting that the order of the

world has been subverted is by ritually inverting the previously orderly categories. Several instances of this technique appear in the book/movie *The Exorcist*. Regan makes birds that are upside down; she speaks English reversed; her head reverses itself; and the head on a corpse is reversed.

The most instructive example of ambiguity and confusion occurs in a Washington church. There, some pervert (Regan?) has defaced the *white* statue of the Virgin Mary by adding protuberant breasts (more befitting a harlot [or *scarlet* woman] than a saint) and an engorged, *red* penis. Hermaphrodites, certainly, represent ambiguity. In a recent essay (Hicks, 1975) it is demonstrated how the Tetum of Timor make ritual use of such figures. Here, its value is expressive rather than instrumental. The impressive dimensions of this bisexual's carnal apparatus imply prodigious sexuality that lacks discrimination—the last thing to be displayed in God's house, where chastity and order should reign. The juxtaposition of the colors red and white compose another symbol of chaos. Representing males (semen is white) and females (mother's milk), secular and sacred, good and evil, white (like red) is ambivalent—as Melville's discourse on white symbolism makes beautifully clear in *Moby Dick*. Unlike red, which is the color of *impurity*, white is *pure*. A (virgin) bride's dress, angels, the Holy Eucharist, the Lamb of God, and other things Christianity associates with purity are white. In *The Exorcist*, while both colors represent ambiguity, red is a symbol manipulated by the demon for evil ends, whereas white is exploited by the exorcist (and God—the power behind the rite of expulsion) for good. But both are symbolic bridges. The fiend (a sacred being) can possess Regan (a secular creature) only by crossing the cosmic gulf dividing their respective categories. The exorcist can expel the demon only by grappling with it. Merrin must establish a bridge between him and the sacred world, whose representative is domiciled in Regan's body. The demon's bridges include blood and the color red. The exorcist's include holy water and the color white. Blood, red, holy water, and a white crucifix—all at one time or another lodge on or in Regan, further emphasizing her ambivalence. Daubed with the white-red combination, the defiled statue of the Virgin (and we must not forget that Regan is a virgin herself until the demon deflowers her) symbolically duplicates the girl's body.

By fusing with Regan, the fiend has turned her and itself into a monster. So, too, is the exorcist—one, however, who is good, who is literally on the side of the angels. These heavenly messengers are also monsters—spirits (sacred) who resemble humans (secular) with wings of birds (beasts). Their evil counterparts are typified by Pazuzu, a Grünewald nightmare, whose dominion is sickness and disease (i.e., personal chaos)—"ragged wings, taloned feet, bulbous, jutting, stubby penis and a mouth stretching taut in a feral grin" (p. 7).

The exorcist is male, but celibate. Eunuchlike, he is a contradiction; by nature, sexual; morally, sexless. Thus in his symbolically neuter character as a priest, Merrin is the polar contrast of his enemy. Christ (half-man, half-God) had the same sexual nature as the exorcist, and they are equated here. Like Christ, Merrin before his ordeal encounters the demon in the desert. The fiend sneers at the exorcist: "Go back to the mountaintop and speak to your only equal!" (p. 307). Unlike the too-human Karras, but again after the manner of Christ, Merrin lacks emotional, family ties. He is devoid of social entanglements in the secular world. In chiding him, the demon says: "where is your humility, Merrin? In the desert? in the ruins? in the tombs where you fled to escape your fellowman? to escape from your inferiors, from the halt and the lame of mind? Do you speak to *men?"* (p. 307). All priests should ideally possess these qualities, but (as Karras shows) the ideal and practical reality do not always merge. Karras worries guiltily over his mother; worries about reacting to importunate drunks; and becomes involved with Regan because he feels sorry for Chris. But in Merrin they *do* merge. This is why he, and not Karras, is the exorcist. Too involved in secular life to effect a bridge between the secular and sacred, Karras' ties with the world of sacred beings—both evil (the demon) and good (God)—are so tenuous he must struggle with himself to retain faith in either. Indeed, his weakening faith provides the drama with a secondary theme. One of the several unresolved puzzles is whether or not Karras dies with his faith restored. The exorcist, on the other hand, never doubts God, the demon, or the powers invested in his own priestly office.

So, two confident, polar ambiguities (demon-Regan and Christ-the exorcist) clash over the body and personality of Regan: "You care nothing at *all* for the pig. You care *nothing!* You have *made her a contest between us!*" (p. 307). So says the demon. Confrontation is necessary to restore order to the world of Regan and those close to her, and the attempt to reassert order over the chaos into which it has lapsed is the theme of *The Exorcist*. The restoration of order can be brought about only by the expulsion of the demon by the exorcist—an act that is symbolically the same as relocating the line between the confused oppositions, secular/sacred, male/female, good/evil, human/beast, creation/destruction, and—most critical of all—order/ chaos. Merrin's faith never flags, but his body (secular) can't match the demands made by his spirit (sacred). In this drama, as well as in the symbolic classification of preliterate peoples, health equals order, illness equals temporary chaos, and death equals permanent and ultimate chaos. The exorcist's death signals the total triumph of chaos over order.

It's a resounding climax, of course, and from the point of view of classificatory logic, conclusive. The drama could (perhaps should) have ended at that point. But however logically sound the conclusion, had the author ended his story there his readers (and, to a greater degree, his cinema audiences) would have left it with a feeling of considerable disquiet. The demon would remain inside Regan. Merrin was not just an ordinary priest, but an experienced exorcist of tremendous intellect and compelling personality, so with him out of the way Regan would have died, and the demon would have been encouraged to continue its depredations among us. Put another way, chaos would have supplanted order *permanently*. As it is, a number of psychologists criticize the movie on the grounds that it is dangerous to the sanity of those who see it. In our myths—as in those or preliterate cultures—order must subjugate disorder. It must have the last word. Otherwise, we're in trouble.

So, by a literary device, a concession is made to our thirst for order, and readers close the book and movie goers leave the theater satisfied that order still rules their world. By an ironic twist of fate, the faith-weakened Karras is responsible for Regan's restoration to health (i.e., for the return to order). But the concession is mixed. True, it seems the demon quit her body because of Karras' taunting challenge, but its evacuation is voluntary, and—the ultimate chaos—the priest dies, like Merrin. The attempt to reestablish order has failed, because there has been no exorcism: Even at the end chaos triumphs.

References

Blatty, William P., 1971, *The Exorcist*. N. Y.: Harper & Row.

Durkheim, Emile, 1965, *The Elementary Forms of the Religious Life*. N. Y.: The Free Press.

Hicks, David, 1975, "A Slow and Orderly Dying." *Human Behavior* 4, no. 3:17-22.

THE BAGEL

Symbol and Ritual at the Breakfast Table

STANLEY REGELSON

What could be more American than apple pie? And what could be more Irish than corned beef and cabbage, more Italian than pizza, or more Jewish than bagels and lox? Yet, these foods have become "typical" ethnic dishes only in America; in their native lands, they lack equivalent notoriety.

Food, like any other element of material culture, has a variety of implications. However, American anthropologists, reflecting this culture's puritanical attitude toward food and eating, have concentrated on nutritional and ecological considerations while regarding an interest in flavor and symbolism as frivolous. In contrast, this essay follows the examples of Lévi-Strauss (1963) and Leach (1964) and adopts a symbolic analysis. Specifically I intend to comment on the remarkable growth of the custom among American Jews of eating lox and cream cheese on a bagel on Sunday morning. The symbolic value of this secular ritual demands attention since it can not be explained in relation to economics, nutrition, or ecology. The practice may in fact be a weekly ritual enactment of an ancient belief by means of which many contemporary American Jews maintain their sense of religious affiliation and identity.

JEWISH FOOD CATEGORIES

Before addressing the bagel ritual itself, it is appropriate to offer some background information on traditional Jewish food categories. This specific topic has been of interest to many scholars because the categories have survived for many centuries over a wide area without substantial change. Also, they are part of an explicit and patterned fabric of permitted and taboo behaviors; and they are regarded as central to their religion by the Jews themselves. The Jewish food laws can be divided into four elements: (1) All animal and vegetable components of food must be derived from approved species; (2) warm-blooded animals must be ritually slaughtered; (3) blood of slaughtered animals must be removed by ritual soaking; and (4) dairy products and meat products may not be mixed. The first two rules are the concern of male ritual experts outside the home, and the last two are household matters, which come under the supervision of women.

Traditional Jewish labels posit the existence of two major food categories: *kosher* ("clean" or "fit") and *treyf* ("impure"). The latter derived from the Hebrew word meaning "torn," probably referring to game or carrion. Kosher foods are further divided into *pareve, milkhik,* and *fleyshik.*

Pareve foods include all *kosher* foods of plant or chemical origin; and of animal origin, honey, eggs, *kosher* insects, and *kosher* fish. These cold-blooded animals are not subject to the ban on blood, and rules for slaughter require only that the animal be spared unnecessary pain. *Pareve* foods cannot pollute other foods, and are ritually neutral. If a *milkhik* or *fleyshik* ingredient is added to a *pareve* food, it ceases to be *pareve.*

Milkhik (dairy) foods include all dairy products produced from the milk of *kosher* animals: milk, butter, cream, cheese, whey, as well as their derivatives. Any food that contains a trace of these items is defined as *milkhik.*

Fleyshik (meat) foods are those produced from the meat of *kosher* mammals and birds, which must be slaughtered by a ritual expert and drained of blood. In the home, the housewife then ritually salts and bathes all exposed surfaces of the meat to removing remaining traces of blood. Only then does it cease to be *treyf,* and is fit to be cooked and eaten.

However, it is taboo to mix *kosher milkhik* food with *kosher fleyshik* food. If the two are brought together, the result is *treyf.* Not only is the result unfit for consumption, but the vessel itself is defiled.

> In order to create a "fence around the law" the rabbis or-
> dained that the separation of meat and dairy must be as
> complete as possible. Thus, separate utensils, dishes, and
> cutlery must be used for dairy foods and meat. . . . These
> must be stored separately, and when washed, separate bowls
> (or preferably sinks) and separate dishcloths (preferably
> of different colors to avoid confusion), must be used. If
> meat and milk foods are cooked at the same time on a
> cooking range or even on an open fire in a closed oven,
> care should be taken that the dishes do not splash each
> other and that the pans are covered. (Rabinowicz, 1971:
> 40)

As a result, the life of an orthodox Jewish housewife resembles that of a nuclear chemist in a radiation laboratory. Foods
are polluted, not only if the categories are actually mixed, but
if they are consumed or prepared too close in time or space:

> According to the Talmud (Hul. 105a), one may not eat
> milk after meat in the same meal. However, strict ob-
> servance demands an interval of as long as six hours be-
> tween eating meat and dairy dishes. . . . It is permitted to
> eat meat immediately after milk dishes, provided that the
> mouth is first rinsed and some bread eaten. (Rabinowicz,
> 1971: 40)

The prohibition against mixing dairy and meat is assumed
to stem from the biblical triple injunction against boiling a kid
in its mother's milk (Ex. 23:10, 34:26, Deut. 14:21). However,
the reason for the generalization of this specific prohibition to
include all meat and dairy foods has not been demonstrated.
In approaching this problem some scholars have even argued
that the prohibition was one of the original Ten Commandments (Frazer, 1919). The broader prohibition against mixing
meat and dairy in general is no easier to explain. For example:
"Abraham ibn Ezra maintained that the reason for the prohibi-

tion of [meat with milk] was 'concealed' even from the eyes of the wise" (Rabinowicz, 1971: 46).

Some Talmudists have associated the rule with the humanitarian requirement that a parent bird be chased from her nest before the young are taken (Deut. 22:6-7). Maimonides felt that "Meat boiled in milk is undoubtedly gross food, and makes a person feel overfull" (Rabinowicz, 1971: 43). More recently, Martha Wolfenstein has linked the rule to "the impulse of the infant to bite and eat the milk-giving breast" (1955: 436); and Mary Douglas has written that the prohibition "honors the procreative process" (1971: 78). The literary critic Isaac Rosenfield (1949) has stated that a reference to sexual behavior is contained in the taboo. He draws attention to the fact that the word *treyf* applies to forbidden sexual alliance as well as forbidden food. This suggestion is pursued here and its association with the seemingly far-removed topic of bagels, lox, and cream cheese will be clarified shortly.

The rule against exogamy that labels as *treyf* marriages between Jews and gentiles is well known. Less well known are the menstrual regulations, set forth in the Bible (Lev. 15:19-14) and practiced until modern times. These require that a married woman and her husband abstain from all physical contact during her menstrual period and for at least a full week thereafter. At that time, she is expected to go to the ritual bath (*mikve*), where she is immersed in water that symbolically removes the pollution associated with menstruation. During these twelve days, when the word *treyf* is also applied to the woman, she and her husband are not only barred from sexual relations, but ideally should not touch or indeed even hand things to each other. Sexual congress between a man and a menstrous woman (*niddah*) is a mortal sin, for which death by divine retribution may be expected (Lev. 20:18). Virgins, unmarried women, and widows are not required to use the *mikve,* and are therefore always *treyf* (Ganzfried, 1928 IV:20). A bride must go to the *mikve* before the marriage is consummated; and the flood of defloration (whether it actually appears or not) is also considered defiling and requires a visit to the *mikve.* Furthermore, the role of the marriage ceremony in establishing the fitness of sexual relations is made plain. Thus Jews are instructed that: A bride without the wedding blessings is forbidden to her husband like a *niddah* (Kallah 1:1).

As indicated, animals chosen from among the *kosher* species are slaughtered ceremonially by ritual experts. First, I propose that this ritual is perceived as symbolically equivalent to the ritual of marriage with women of Jewish origin. It was also mentioned that after the meat has arrived in the household, it is ritually washed by women, which transforms it into edible food. Second, I suggest that this activity is symbolically equivalent to the *mikve* ritual. The ritual bath is perhaps the only Jewish ceremony taking place outside the home that is supervised by women.

Hence, there is an identification of the female sex with *fleyshik,* which implies a similar relationship of the male to the *milkhik* category. In other words, there is a symbolic correspondence of milk with semen and masculinity in contrast to meat with menstrual blood and femininity.

Consider the following folktale in this light:

> The milkman (or the man selling milk in the dairy) claims that his milk is perfectly kosher . . . because water which he pours into the pail is taken from the "kosher" Mikvah or Ritual Bath. (Schwarzbaum 1968: 368)

The humor is derived from a simultaneous breaking of both food and sex taboos across symbolic levels.

It is now possible to appreciate why the coming together of *milkhik* and *fleyshik* results in a substance unfit for human consumption. Two products of the same household representing different categories are not permitted to come into contact. This arrangement strongly resembles a type of rule we are all familiar with, the incest taboo. For a society with powerful symbolic precautions against marriage with outsiders, it is not surprising to find equally strong symbolic precautions against marriage with certain group members.

The original biblical prohibition against boiling a kid in its mother's milk, which seemed only dubiously related to the broader question of *milkhik/fleyshik* categories, can now be interpreted as a symbolic prohibition against the mixing of closely related members of opposite sex. "You shall not boil a kid in its mother's milk" (Deut. 14:21) emerges as the equivalent of "You shall not bring shame on your father by intercourse with your mother" (Lev. 18:6). The reason for the aforementioned triple biblical repetition of this injunction, and for the ultimate expansion of this narrow prohibition into a veritable maze of dietary rules, is now less puzzling. The set of dietary rules cited earlier is now recognizable as isomorphic (i.e., structurally equivalent) to a set of marriage rules: (1) marriage with an "outsider" is forbidden; (2) sexual relations are permitted only after a consecrated marriage; (3) sexual relations are permitted only during the period following the ritual bath; (4) marriage within the prohibited degrees of kinship is prohibited.

The relationship between food and other cultural categories should now be somewhat more recognizable, so that it is possible to approach the specific symbolic problem of lox and cream cheese from a similar perspective.

THE BAGEL RITUAL

The bagel (beygl), derived from the German *Baugel* (little bracelet) is a doughnut-shaped roll made from high-gluten flour. Simmered in boiling water for two minutes before baking, it has a unique chewy texture. Lox is smoked salmon, prepared so that it is bright red and has the texture of raw fish. There are two kinds: ordinary lox and Nova Scotia. The former is considerably saltier than the latter, but the difference between the two is not meaningful to the custom. Lox is an anglicized spelling of the German and Yiddish words for salmon (*Lachs, laks*). Cream cheese is the same high butterfat soft cheese generally available in the United States.

The bagel itself is only one of a number of traditional Jewish smallbreads. Among the others are kaiser rolls, salt stengels, and bialystokers, which have faded into obscurity as the bagel has grown more popular. Because of their odd recipe, bagels are produced by specialized bakers in bagel factories, but never at home. Bagel factories, traditionally located in cellars, are numerous wherever there is a concentrated Jewish population. Jews living far from such centers now make provision for the shipment of frozen bagels, since the chemical additive that keeps bread fresh cannot be added to bagels without destroying the characteristic texture.

Lox is only one of a wide variety of smoked and pickled fish preparations that the Jews brought with them from northeastern Europe. Herring, the fish formerly most often linked with Jewish culture, is the subject of innumerable Jewish jokes, usually on the theme of fish as "brain food." Unlike herring, a food of the poor, lox has always been a costly luxury.

Cream cheese, a western European product, is not part of the material culture that the east European Jews brought with them to America. However, farmer cheese and pot cheese were traditional to this immigrant group. The substitution of cream cheese for pot cheese in traditional Jewish recipes has resulted in another felicitous development, cream cheese cake.

In questioning older Jews, both immigrant and American born, about the traditional Sunday morning combination of lox with cream cheese on bagels, they often become uneasy. They answer, "Bagels and cream cheese, yes. Lox and bagels, of course. Bagels on Sunday morning, why not?" However, what they are uneasy about is the realization that the wide distribution of the custom that we are discussing is primarily a post-World War II American phenomenon. In fact, there is nothing traditional or European about this specific food combination or its ritualized consumption. The explosion of its popularity among American Jews is a contemporary cultural development.

The suggestion that flavor accounts for the popularity of the combination is not very helpful. Although this is the reason most often expressed by informants, the rationale is undermined by the fact that quite different flavors may be produced depending on the type of lox used. Consequently, the explanation must lie elsewhere.

In recent years, the term "bagels-and-lox Judaism" has become a favorite theme of rabbinical sermons in the United States. It is used to refer pejoratively to those Jews who avoid the synagogue and neglect traditional religious practices, yet adhere strongly to "frivolous" secular customs. Concretely, this translates into the fact that there are many Jews who will never voluntarily enter a synagogue, but manage to perform the bagel ritual every week. Despite the self-consciously secular nature of this ritual, it is possible to show a direct relation to traditional Jewish religious symbolism involving the principle of *havdalah* ("distinction"), which is a basic element of Jewish cosmology.

The prime reference of the word *havdalah* is the distinction between the Sabbath and the week, the name of the weekly ceremony performed at the close of the Sabbath, intended to "draw a clear line" between the sacred and profane portions of the week. The *havdalah* prayer reads in part:

> "Blessed are Thou . . . who makest a distinction between holy and profane, between light and darkness, between Israel and other nations, between the seventh day and the six working days. Blessed art Thou, O Lord, who makest a distinction between holy and profane." (*Services* . . . 1928: 433)

Other "distinctions" include the previously mentioned dichotomies between *kosher* and *treyf,* heaven and earth, eternity and time, male and female. Eternity in this instance refers to the "end of time" or "end of days," the period following the coming of the Messiah and the raising of the dead. The set also includes the distinction between the upper and lower parts of the human body: "If no garment or girdle separates the upper part of his body from the lower [a man] is not allowed to utter anything holy" (Ganzfried, 1928 1:12).

In this regard the navel (*pupik*) is traditionally seen as the midpoint of the body, connecting the upper portion with the lower. As such, it is an important landmark of Jewish folk anatomy, so that the word *pupik* occurs frequently in jokes and metaphors. For instance, a recent television special on Yiddish culture repeatedly jump-cut in shots of a navel, with the label "PUPIK" as an easy laugh-getter.

The following joke illustrates the navel's folk anatomical function:

> A man was born with a gold screw in his navel. Considering it a disfigurement, he traveled all over the world inquiring how to remove it, to no avail. Finally a rabbi told him, "You should accept the fate you were born to. But if you cannot, go home and go to sleep. You will dream that there is a golden screwdriver under your pillow. Use it to unscrew your navel. When you wake up, the screw will be gone." Everything happened as the rabbi had said. On waking, the man walked to the window, took a deep breath . . . and his behind fell off.

The navel connects the sacred and profane parts of a human being in two dimensions—one natural and one supernatural. First, it marks the juncture of the upper part of the body with its mental (godlike) functions and lower part with its physical animal functions. Second, the navel marks the link between the invisible soul and the visible body. At the moment of birth, each human being is marked with a navel, which spiritually binds body and soul into a single unit. The Jewish mother often worries lest her newborn infant cry too energetically. "He might rupture his *pupik*," that is, the link between spirit and flesh might be sundered.

The world is conceived as having a structure similar to the human body, with the holy city Jerusalem perceived as the navel. Thus, to the ancient Jews and later to medieval mapmakers, Jerusalem was located at the physical center of the world. Furthermore, it is believed that the earth and heaven are actually connected at the site of the temple in Jerusalem, making it the place most suitable for prayer.

> Associated with [the] description of the temple and Jerusalem is the idea that the place is also the center of the world and the *tabbur ha-avez* ["the navel of the earth"] . . . .

> As the navel is set in the middle of a person, so is Erez Israel located in the center of the world, Jerusalem in the

132

center of Erez Israel, the Temple in the center of Jerusalem, the *heikhal* ["altar"] in the center of the Temple, the ark in the center of the *heikhal*, and in front of the *heikhal* is the *even shetivyah* ["foundation stone"] from which the world was started. (*Encyclopedia Judaica Jerusalem*, 1971 9:1557-1558)

Thus, it was believed that this foundation stone was the physical spot at which eternity is joined to time. Furthermore, "According to one view, Adam was created from . . . the site of the Temple" (*Encyclopedia Judaica Jerusalem*, 1971 9:1557). This conception of Adam (who, having a navel, must have been umbilically linked directly to the Creator) repeats and unifies the same references (cf. Eliade, 1959).

Therefore, as the *havdalah* ceremony mediates between the Sabbath and the new week, the navel mediates between soul and body, and the Temple mediates between heaven and earth.

Furthermore, in Jewish culture, bread of any kind signifies man's material needs and is specifically seen as the symbol of earth itself. The prayer over bread refers to it as being brought forth from the earth, and also contains a reference to the first man, since the word for earth (*adamah*) contains Adam's name. Similar to a simplified folkview of the human body, or like the map of the world mentioned above, the shape of the bagel symbolically represents a navel mediating between the earthly and the divine. It is not surprising, therefore, that the first written reference to the bagel was in "the Community Regulations of Cracow, Poland, for the year 1610, which stated that bagels would be given to any woman in childbirth (Rosten, 1968: 26).

THE END OF TIME

A basic teaching of Judaism is that at the end of time, in the days of the Messiah, the distinction between the material and the spiritual, the profane and the sacred, will cease to exist. In fact, the cessation may be seen as a precondition to the coming of the Messiah, as in the following tale:

A rabbi returns home and finds his wife in bed with a peasant. In reply to his reprimand, she says: "Rabbi, you have told me that the Messiah will come only at one of two moments—when all men are good, or when all men are bad. I know the time can never come when all men are good, so I am doing my share to bring about the second alternative."

This joke expresses the underlying logic of Shabbatism and Frankism, heretical movements of seventeenth- and eighteenth-century Judaism, which declared that the "End of Days" had come. This heresy, *antinomianism,* also avowed that the serious sins of Judaism were actually meritorious. This inversion of standard morality was based on the Talmudic assumption that with the coming of the Messiah the commandments would be abolished and fasts converted into feasts (Scholem, 1971). "Indeed, some say that all the animals that are unclean in this world will be declared clean by the Holy One in time to come" (Midrash Tehillim 164:4).

At the beginning of time, we are told, God created the distinctions that made a primal chaos "without form and void" (Gen. 1:1) into light and darkness, heaven and earth, sea and dry land. Undermining these distinctions prematurely would restore the world to chaos. But at the end of time, signaled by the coming of the Messiah, the obliteration of the opposed domains will mark the coming of a higher order. In two contemporary Jewish ceremonies performed weekly in the home, the dissolution of these dichotomies is symbolized. On Friday evening the Sabbath is welcomed by the lighting of two candles; on Saturday night the new week is ushered in with a braided candle containing two wicks. Among the contrasts that would be neutralized at the end of time is that between the living and the dead since the dead would be raised in their corporeal bodies.

Hence, in the days of the Messiah, the Law that governs the temporal world will cease to hold; its burden on Israel will be lifted. The division between profane and sacred, dead and living, body and spirit, red meat and white milk, female and male, will no longer apply. Prohibitions pertaining to these divisions will also no longer be meaningful. Consequently, Shabbatai Zevi, proclaimed by his followers in the seventeenth century as the Messiah, pronounced a benediction on "Him who permits the forbidden" (Scholem, 1971: 1223), and he "abolished" the fast of Tishah be-Av and turned it into a feast. A successor to this Messiah also preached: "a complete reversal of values, symbolized by the change of the 36 prohibitions of the Torah . . . into positive commands. This included all the prohibited sexual unions and incest" (Scholem, 1971: 1246).

LOX AND CREAM CHEESE

From the perspective of this analysis lox differs from all other preserved fish preparations in one way: It is as red as blood. The glossy redness of the fish, in combination with the opaque whiteness of the cheese, results in a striking contrast. Indeed, children frequently refuse to eat lox because of its visual resemblance to raw meat. The coming together of these two foods produces a visual pun. Although a permitted combination, lox and cream cheese give the appearance of violating the strong taboo on mixing *milkhik* and *fleyshik.*

This suggestion can be supported from another direction since in many other cultures the ritual use of white and red refers to male and female, respectively. The reference to semen and menstrual blood, often perceived as the two elements required for conception in folk biology, lies just beneath the surface of this symbolic opposition. Indeed, this idea is made almost explicit in the Talmud. "The white substance . . . is supplied by the man, from whom come the child's brain, bones, and sinews; the red substance . . . is supplied by the woman, from whom comes its skin, flesh, and blood" (Niddah 31a).

The persistence of the categories red and white are apparent in association with meats and wines in our culture. Interestingly enough salmon is the only fish eaten with or prepared in red wine. However, these associations go well beyond the kitchen and dining room. The folk tradition that links the (red) rose with females and sexual passion and the (white) lily with males and divine passion is a case in point. The television commercial for a popular wine producer that involves a leering male suggesting a "little white" for him and a "little red" for his female companion and finally a "little rosé" for both of them later suggests the ability to communicate effectively at this symbolic level.

However, to return to our primary interest, it can be appreciated how through the use of salmon, a color-marked fish with a fleshlike texture, an obvious reference to meat is being made. In this case, the combination of lox and cream cheese, through a series of intermediate metaphors, can be seen as a reference not only to the breaking of the surface taboo against mixing meat and milk, but a violation of the incest taboo itself. We have often been told, by Freud and Lévi-Strauss, among others, that the incest prohibition is a denial of the individual's needs in favor of those of the group, and thus the very foundation stone of human society. Also relevant is the fact that incest was among the practices of antinomian heretics. Thus the consumption of lox and cream cheese is ritual reenactment of an anticipated event—the elimination of the distinctions that govern social behavior of this world after the coming of the Messiah.

The last question is, why should this symbolic reversal be enacted on a Sunday morning, which is normally associated with the Christian, not the Jewish, Sabbath? This paradox can be resolved by bearing in mind that in Judaism the weekly cycle ends with the Sabbath on the seventh day, the day the Almighty rested after creating the universe. Leach (1961) calls attention to the reversals often marking calendric rituals that involve a reversal of a cycle before it resumes. In the case of the Jews, we have repeated examples of this phenomenon. For example, on the weekly Sabbath the Jews, who have a strong mercantile tradition, are prohibited from handling money (Ex. 23:12). At Yom Kippur during the first days of the New Year, the most important ceremony is one at which all vows made in the previous year are declared void. Further, traditionally during the Sabbatical year, farmers were forbidden to sow their crops (Lev. 25:1-7). Following seven sabbatical cycles, every fiftieth year was a year of Jubilee. Ideally at this time slaves were restored to freedom and land restored to its original owner (Lev. 25:10). Finally, the coming of the Messiah was to result in the great overturning of all rules.

Few American Jews strictly observe the Sabbath, and the Sabbatical year and the Jubilee are almost unknown today as religious concepts. However, Sunday morning is the time of the first light after the close of the Sabbath. It is both a symbol and repetition of the moment when time began, the moment when the Creator proclaimed, "Let there be light" (Gen. 1:3). As such, it is the point at which any new era must begin. Similarly, the trumpet (*shofar*), which announces the Jewish New Year is blown not at the initial evening service but the following morning. Admittedly, few Jews who perform the Sunday bagel ritual observe all the dietary laws. Yet those who do eat bagels, lox, and cream cheese feel that in some way they are affirming their Jewishness. I submit that by symbolically breaking the incest rule at a fixed time representing the moment of Creation, these Jews are confirming their adherence to the fundamental structure of a Messianic faith.

Therefore, this meal results in the coming together of symbolically significant substances defined by certain specifically Jewish values at a time of declining interest in traditional ritual, and the abandonment of the strongest strictures upon food, sex, and marriage. In short, it is an unconscious expression of religiosity and ethnic identity.

Most of the practitioners of this ritual will be startled at the analysis presented here, and deny its validity. Yet we should be aware that anthropologists often encounter and are not surprised by unconscious representations of this type in other cultures. However, we expect that literates such as ourselves are more rational and that ideology will be close to the surface. Yet, we have evidence here that literacy is no bar to such representations or submerged symbolic statements. Indeed, it is in our own society that we may have the opportunity to study the way in which such symbolic representations come into existence.

References

Douglas, Mary, 1971, "Deciphering a Meal." In Clifford Geertz, ed. *Myth, Symbol, and Culture,* New York: Norton.

Eliade, Mircea, 1959, *The Sacred and the Profane.* New York: Harper & Row.

Encyclopedia Judaica Jerusalem, 1971, New York: Macmillan.

Frazer, James, 1919, *Folk-Lore in the Old Testament.* London: Macmillan.

Ganzfried, Solomon, 1928, *Code of Jewish Law.* (Kitzur Shulchan Aruch) New York: The Star Hebrew Book Co.

Leach, Edmund, 1961, "Two Essays Concerning the Symbolic Representation of Time." In Edmund Leach, *Rethinking Anthropology.* New York: Humanities.

   —1964, "Animal Categories and Verbal Abuse." In Eric H. Lenneberg, ed. *New Directions in the Study of Language.* Cambridge: MIT Press.

Lévi-Strauss, Claude, 1963, *Structural Anthropology.* New York: Basic Books.

Rabinowicz, H., 1971, "Modern Views of the Dietary Laws." *Encyclopedia Judaica Jerusalem,* 6:26-46.

Rosenfeld, Issac, 1949, "Adam and Eve on Delancey Street." *Commentary* 8:385-387.

Rosten, Leo, 1968, *The Joys of Yiddish.* New York: McGraw-Hill.

Scholem, Gerson, 1971, "Shabbatai Zevi." *Encyclopedia Judaica Jerusalem,* 14:1219-1254.

Schwarzbaum, Haim, 1968, *Studies in Jewish and World Folklore.* Berlin: De Gruyter.

Services for the Day of Atonement, 1928, New York: Hebrew Publishing Co.

Wolfenstein, Martha, 1955, "Two Types of Jewish Mothers." In Margaret Mead and Martha Wolfenstein, eds. *Childhood in Contemporary Cultures.* Chicago: University of Chicago Press.

Part II

SOCIAL STRATEGIES AND INSTITUTIONAL ARRANGEMENTS

COFFEE

The Bottomless Cup

LAWRENCE TAYLOR

INTRODUCTION

As these essays illustrate, the anthropologist's prerogative is to wonder about both the bizarre and the obvious. The bizarre is typically of little interest to anyone else, while to most the obvious does not call for explanation. However, the anthropologist as outsider often finds that it is precisely those practices which the members of a particular culture consider most practical and reasonable that strike him as most odd. Perhaps the ultimate fate of the anthropologist is to become a professional outsider and thus a stranger even to his own culture. In this estranged state he is liable to be suddenly amazed by those things he had once been happy enough to take for granted.

In this condition I was struck one morning with wonder at my personal, and my culture's, preoccupation with coffee. I must have been particularly outside myself, for there are few elements of American culture in which I am more avidly involved than those associated with coffee. More than an avid consumer, I am also a believer in everything I am supposed to about what coffee does for me as a social being.

What particularly caught my attention was the waitress's smiling acquiescence to my silent demand for a second cup. I merely looked up, and through the medium of silent language, she knew and responded. However, what impressed me on that

141

occasion was not that she knew I wanted more coffee, but rather that, in the market place of the restaurant, the second and subsequent cups would be free.

Consequently, later that day, I asked my class for their opinion on the "bottomless cup." The first thing they did was close their notebooks, since they reasoned that the professor was no longer talking about real anthropology. Instead he was catering to an obsession with the obvious. Why the bottomless cup of coffee? Several expert informants in the guise of former waitresses immediately volunteered to disabuse me of any fanciful anthropological explanations. Being good natives they suggested that coffee is free after the first cup for a practical reason. Coffee is made in large amounts and it will get stale if not dispensed quickly. In a similar vein, although cheaper, the labor involved in making a cup of tea might make it ultimately more expensive than coffee, so that refills must be paid for.

Like a good anthropologist, I began the investigation of a cultural phenomenon by questioning the natives. Their responses were recorded as evidence of their "system of thought," but also discounted as inadequate since all the answers were too utilitarian. Americans in particular like to think of themselves as a practical people; thus practical explanations must be immediately suspect.

Is it not possible, I queried, that the production of restaurant coffee by the vatful, as opposed to the one-cup-at-a-time tea, was the result of coffee usages, rather than the other way around? In England, I pointed out, the situation is the reverse. There, tea is made by the pot and can be had in quantity at no extra charge, while if available, coffee is typically instant and prepared by the cup. It is unlikely that the English are unaware of the possibility of mass-producing coffee, or of the convenience of tea bags. They evidently had chosen to make tea the sort of drink that coffee is to us. But what *is* coffee to us?

SYMBOLIC IMPLICATIONS

A helpful student observed that ". . . You invite someone 'over for coffee'." Everyone recognized that the phrase had symbolic as well as literal implications. In America, if someone moves into a new neighborhood and they are not shortly thereafter asked "over for coffee," they would become anxious. Certainly this is not because they are unable to brew a pot for themselves. Consequently, coffee offering has to be examined in the same fashion as any repetitive and significant behavior in an exotic culture.

As anthropologists have long recognized, exchanges are the very lifeblood of social relationships. In a particular culture the items and terms of exchange are appropriate to the specific social relationships. The gift is never pure, but rather sets in motion a process of continual giving and receiving. The recipient understands that the offering stands for a whole series of future exchanges in which he is now obliged to involve himself. A Christmas card from the Smiths requires one in return. An invitation to dinner is more than a free meal; in addition it is an obligation to reciprocate. This does not imply that people view such invitations entirely in this light, since more than likely they are happy to enter into these exchange relationships. What thrills them, if thrilled they are by the reception of the Christmas card or dinner invitation, is not that they got something for nothing. Rather, they are delighted at the prospect of a new social relationship which is implied in the gift.

In many cultures a food offering holds a particularly important place in symbolizing the quality of a social relationship. The high caste Brahmin of India is very fussy about who cooks his food for him; not for fear of poison, but of ritual pollution. Moreover, this transmittable impurity has more to do with the preparer's social position than his personal cleanliness. The exchange of particular foods thus becomes such an important aspect of a social relationship as to stand for or symbolize it. New Guinea pig feasts, for example, are often the most important means of affirming the social solidarity of large groups of people. In Ethiopia some people define those families with whom they interact daily as the "people we drink coffee with."

So it is in suburban America, where the invitation "over for coffee" initiates a socially significant system of exchange. The reason an individual becomes disconsolate at not receiving such an overture lies in the social implications of such an invitation.

143

In effect, coffee stands for, or symbolizes, a certain type of social relationship in America which we call neighborship.

Neighborship

The dictionary informs us that the word *neighbor* comes from the Old Teutonic *neagh-gebur,* meaning 'near-hut.' Neighborship therefore was a social relationship based on the proximity of one dwelling to another. The Old Teutons probably had little choice in recognizing such a tie, since in a tiny hamlet there was little chance, or sense, to remaining socially aloof from one's fellow hut-dwellers.

Neighborship is important in every culture, but its form and meaning will vary greatly. Among middle-class Americans it is not surprising that neighbor implies a very different category of person and relation than was true for the Old Teutons. In the suburbs there is a great deal of choice in the formation and maintenancy of neighborship ties. A family is surrounded by row after row of houses from which only a relative few are selected with whom to enter into neighborship. Proximity, however, remains a vital criterion; the essence and cultural justification of the neighborly relation remains the physical nearness of one dwelling to another. Americans feel that the physical nearness of abodes also calls for a degree of social nearness. The social involvement implied in the relation, however, is limited. For example, we still distinguish between friends and neighbors, both in word and in deed. The neighborly relation is initiated with the offer of coffee, which may or may not evolve into friendship. The invitation means, "Come over and begin being my neighbor." In other words, prepare to receive and reciprocate a whole series of possible exchanges, of which coffee is only the first. Others will then follow, such as the classic requests to borrow the lawnmower or cup of sugar.

Although compared to kinship or friendship, neighborship may seem a relatively insignificant social relation in America, it is nevertheless vital to our daily lives. By establishing understood relations of neighborship, the suburban family provides itself with casual access to a whole series of goods and services. Moreover, the restrictions Americans put on the closeness of neighborship may add to its usefulness. Many ties of this type can be upheld simultaneously, whereas the maintenance of an equal number of full-fledged friendships might prove socially exhausting.

It may be objected that coffee is used in many more ways than as a ritual exchange of neighborship. While this is true, the anthropologist's concern is with the cultural meaning of a particular symbol, like coffee, and this is not necessarily found in the analysis of the item's use. Experience is not quantitative, so that the ritual function of a substance does more to define its symbolic meaning than a thousand mundane uses.

Perhaps this proposition can be clarified by looking at color categories which also have symbolic meanings in all cultures. For example, blackness is strongly associated with death in American ritual contexts. However, in the course of a year, blackness is experienced in a thousand insignificant forms. Yet blackness still means death when confronted in a ritual context, such as Halloween, when the witch's black cat means "black, like death." In a similar fashion, the use of coffee to initiate neighborship, and its recurring exchange, may do more to define its meaning to us as a cultural symbol than the thousand papercupsful consumed in less meaningful social contexts.

In pursuing the coffee exchange topic in class, another student remarked that "When I was a little girl, when my mother wanted to begin gossiping with her neighbor, she would say, 'Can't you see we're having coffee?'" An anthropologist from Africa would have to assume from that remark that there is some sort of taboo against children observing their parents and other adults consuming the sacred fluid. In reality, though, the child is being asked to leave in code. Remarkably enough, the child understands very early that the meaning is, "Leave, we're about to engage in the privileged exchanges of friendship—children are not eligible." The mother in this instance used the word "coffee" to symbolize the whole range of neighborly exchanges, and the child took her meaning correctly.

What is more, coffee is the typical American non-alcoholic adult beverage. As a rule, children do not drink it, and if they do, adults may show some discomfort and are likely to comment on the oddity. Evidently the coffee-drinking child is suspect; perhaps he is faking a taste for coffee in order to seem grown-up. The "adults only" proscription may even be buttressed by bogus chemistry. One student's mother had warned her that coffee was sexually dangerous for children. Indeed, I can remember not liking coffee as a child but developing a taste for it, along with several other adult pastimes, only a few years later.

Coffee in the neighborship context is not only an adult fluid, but its exchange is between close hut-dwellers. In some communities in suburban America to fully participate in neighborship requires a home of your own, whether it be a split-level colonial or a high ranch. The Irish bachelor of forty without a farm is still a "boy" and the suburban American without a home of his own is not fully adult in the eyes of others. "Come over to my house for a cup of coffee," also means, "I have a house, too." The relationship therefore is one based upon social and economic equality as well as physical proximity.

Evidently coffee is the offering most suited for the exchange between householders. Although other items may be passed back and forth, coffee normally initiates the neighborly relationship. As with a New Guinea pig feast, a periodic repetition of the coffee exchange is felt to be necessary to proper maintenance of the relationship.

The Household Social System

How is it that in America coffee becomes the typical exchange medium in the relation between hut-dweller and hut-dweller? Looking inside the hut helps to answer the question. The ideal model of the household social system is as follows: the husband wins the bread, and the housewife makes the coffee. Which is to say, the husband provides the raw materials and the housewife cooks them for their common consumption. The food exchanges involved are numerous, and coffee is neither the most economically or nutritionally important. However, it plays a rather singular role in the three exchange ceremonies of the average American family day—breakfast, lunch and dinner. Coffee is the opening presentation which begins the domestic day. It also has the balanced opposing function, for after dinner coffee closes the expected meal exchanges.

In the household, as in neighborship, coffee occupies the unique position of symbolizing an entire series of exchanges, and TV commercials, as they so often do in America, make the point clearly. The unfortunate woman who cannot cajole her husband into taking a second cup of coffee has profoundly failed as a homemaker. This analysis does not mean that the commercial is not trying to sell a product, but there is something sensible in the choice of coffee for this sort of message. If she could not make tea, would she be a similar failure? Although such a commercial is unreal since few divorces have followed from poor coffee-making alone, the submerged message is profound. In our culture, coffee stands for the entire range of responsibilities and exchanges involved in homemaking. The inability to make a decent cup of coffee therefore implies total failure.

CONCLUSION

Thus coffee symbolizes, among other things, the household itself. If one family seeks to establish relations with another, what more appropriate invitation than "Come over for coffee"? We distinguish, as has been said, between friends and neighbors. Friendship is a social relation between individuals. You can choose your friends, as the old saw goes, but you can't choose your relatives. Can you choose your neighbors? Yes, in the sense that it is possible to select a neighborhood. But once this is done, choices are narrowed considerably, since neighborship necessarily involves physical proximity to others. Freedom to enter into the relationship is also restricted by the fact that one family member may draw others into the web of neighborship. In the absentee-husband suburbs, the housewife may more often than not choose the neighbors, and soon after whole households rather than just individuals are involved.

The bearing these cultural associations have on the price of

147

coffee in restaurants is apparent in an examination of the restaurant context. The coffeehouse customer is greeted by a "hostess," and after eating "her food" (since professional cooks are discreetly hidden in the kitchen), she offers the customer more coffee at no extra charge. The food must be paid for, since the relation between the customer and the restaurant is that of two strangers meeting in the marketplace. Yet the restaurant is evidently also trying to be a pseudo-household by giving away coffee to guests. This explains the emphasis on service and the use of such household symbols as the hostess. There is in this an invocation through the imagery of householdness. Even though socially a stranger, the customer must be made to feel, in some sense, like a neighbor, and in America only coffee can create this illusion.

What is more, Americans are willing to believe in these images. The real test of the importance of a cultural role is in the effect of its breaking. The prices on the menu may rise their predictable two percent per month and no one flinches. After all, these are affairs of strangers. But let the coffeehouse suddenly terminate the bottomless cup and the customer is outraged. What is upsetting is not the rising cost but the abrupt conclusion of neighborship.

This restaurant-customer interaction in the peculiar case of coffee is more intelligible in light of the meaning of coffee as an American symbol. Much of that meaning emerged in an examination of the symbolic social characteristics of American neighborship. The special considerations various cultures afford to specific foods are always valuable paths to understanding their social categories. No matter how sophisticated or technologically advanced, no culture perceives food only as nourishment. In other cultures, different food symbols are important, but in America, good coffee makes good neighbors.

FAIR-WEATHER FRIEND

Label and Context in Middle Class Friendships

DAVID JACOBSON

"Although social anthropologists themselves live lives in which friendship is probably just as important as kinship, and a good deal more problematic to handle, in our professional writings we dwell at length upon kinship and have much less to say about friendship." (Paine, 1969: 505). This paper on friendship in our own society aims toward closing this gap.

Much sociological and anthropological writing about friendship focuses on its properties as an interpersonal relationship. Paine's analysis of friendship, for example, concerns the conduct between friends, and in particular the rules of relevancy that determine "what is permissible or desirable in the relationship." The utility of the concept of rules of relevancy is that it moves the analysis of friendship beyond an account of the attributes of friends and of the rights and duties of friendship to the study of the dynamics of the friend relationship and its contextual variations. This paper also examines friendship contextually, but in a different sense.

Rather than view friendship simply as an interpersonal relationship, either in terms of the attributes of friends or in terms of the behavior between them, the term "friend" is considered as a label that one person attaches to another or to himself with reference to another. My concern with contextual analysis is not with the content or conduct of the relationship, but with the labeling process itself, that is, with the situations in which a person gives and takes away the label of "friend."

The analytical perspective draws on the tradition in social anthropology that emphasizes the situational selection of social identities (cf. Evans-Pritchard, 1940; Leach, 1954; Barth, 1969). In a recent and useful explication of the model Bloch (1971) distinguishes between the moral and tactical meanings of a role-word as it relates to the difference between the "right" and "wrong" conduct associated with a role and the ways in which the role-word is used to transform social relationships and social situations.[1]

Although situational analysis has been used in various anthropological studies, it constitutes a relatively unusual approach in the literature on friendship.[2] Studies of friendship range from those concerned with simply defining the term "friend" or the characteristics of friends to those focusing more on processes such as recruitment into or the formation of friendships. On this continuum, there are five major types of analysis. In the most simple sort, a single definition of the term "friend" is assumed and the primary effort is to analyze the attributes of friends within a singular context. Little attention is paid to types of friends, to contexts of interaction, or to changes in relationships. The best examples of this type are sociometric studies, in which individuals encapsulated within a population—typically a room of school children, a high school's students, or the residents of a college dormitory—are asked to name their friends within that unit, and then the sociodemographic characteristics of these choices are analyzed with reference to their similarities and differences. Common attributes are then interpreted as the basis for, or the definition of, friendship (see, for example, Thorpe, 1955, and similar studies cited by Albert and Brigante, 1962).

A related but somewhat more developed type of study takes the role "friend," still an undefined and undifferentiated category, and contrasts it with other social identities (kin and neighbors are the most common) in order to analyze the structure and functions of friendship (see Litwak and Szelenyi, 1969). This method of comparative analysis goes beyond the sociometric studies in its attempt to make explicit the rights and duties of friendship. However the category of friend remains undifferentiated, and the dynamics of the relationship, including the movement of personnel between those roles, remains unexamined. Consequently, the findings of this type of study are often ambiguous. Although the different social identities in question are distinguished analytically, little or no attention is paid to the fact that empirically the differentiation is not easily discernible, and that the same person may occupy all of them, being kinsman, neighbor, and friend simultaneously. Behavior that is attributed to kinship may be equally attributable to friendship or to the relationship between neighbors.

A third type of study is still largely definitional, but provides a more differentiated and more realistic account of friendship. Naegele (1958), for example, describes "acquaintances," "friends," and "close friends" and notes the development of a relationship as it moves from a casual personal contact to one more intimate. The movement is described as unidirectional. No attention is given to reverses in a relationship or to its termination, whatever stage of its development; process is still not a focal concern.

A fourth approach focuses more on interactional processes and deals with the dynamics of friendship (see Suttles 1970). Suttles suggests that a friend is someone who is positively evaluated as a person qua person; therefore, true friendship requires revelation of one's true self, not the self (or selves) governed by norms conventional to social situations. This line of thought leads Suttles to argue that the "logic of friendship is a simple transformation of the rules of public propriety into their opposite" (1970: 116). Although Suttles analyzes this logic, his study is still about the (normative) characteristics of the relationship—how individuals who are friends are supposed to act towards one another—and, in this sense, resembles Paine's examination of the "rules of relevancy," which are said to regulate behavior between friends.[3] Although Suttles recognizes the problems his analysis does not deal with exceptions to these rules or with the ways in which friendships begin or end.

The fifth type of study complements the others by analyzing the dissolution of friendships in order to illuminate the processes underlying their formation and maintenance. Liebow's description of the changing friendships of "streetcorner men" (1967) is one of the best of its kind. Liebow depicts their friendships in terms of a network radiating out from an Ego. In its inner part, closest to the focal individual (Ego), are "good" and "best" friends and on its outer edges are "acquaintances" and "former friends" (1967: 162-163). The category of "former friends," in particular, is important in its implication of oscillation, suggesting not only the beginnings of relationships but their endings as well. Liebow analyzes the transition from acquaintance to friend to best friend, emphasizing the motivation for the transformation, which, he suggests, is primarily instrumental. Friends exchange goods and services, necessary for survival among those who face chronic poverty. Reciprocity is promised between friends, but the reality of limited resources restrains individuals from meeting expectations, leading to the breakdown of relationships and to a corresponding reevaluation of people as "fair-weather friends." Liebow thus relates changes in the identification of friends, of those who are included and excluded under that label, to changing socioeconomic circumstances. He analyzes this labeling process among the urban poor, but it also occurs in middle-class friendships, as is evident among unemployed professional workers.

My data come largely from a study of unemployed engineers.[4] The saliency of the label "friend" in this population derives from the fact that engineers find jobs primarily through friends. In fact, whatever other rights and duties obtain between friends, it is a paramount expectation among engineers that a friend will help another who is in search of employment. Furthermore, a person who proves to be a contact in getting a job is often described as a friend, regardless of whether or not that person acts as such in other respects. Alternatively, an individual who does not offer assistance in finding a job may be described as "no friend," or, at best, as a "fair-weather friend."

The analysis, then, focuses on the term "friend" as a label, and on the contexts in which it is applied and withdrawn. The conditions under which engineers include and exclude others as members of their social world is also of particular concern.

Route 128, ringing Boston, Massachusetts has been described as the eastern center of the electronics industry in the United States. Predominant in this area are major corporations and their satellite companies involved in federally funded aerospace and defense research. Because of government funding cutbacks, between 1969 and 1972 large numbers of engineers and scientists were laid off. My interest here is in how these unemployed professional workers used their contacts with friends in the search for another job.

Before describing the process, some features of employment in these companies must be noted. To begin with, such companies typically work on projects supported by various agencies of the federal government. When a contract for a project is awarded, and sometimes in anticipation of one, a company hires the necessary scientific and technological personnel. When it is completed, the employment of those engineers and scientists is also terminated. Few of these employees are maintained on in-house funds so that tenured or permanent positions are unusual. Therefore, engineers and scientists typically find themselves having to periodically seek work or of moving between jobs, even in times of continuing governmental support and relatively full employment. Of course, at those times, employment in one company might be practically continuous, since the company may be working on several projects, simultaneously or sequentially. Even then, though, the demand for labor is not uniform, varying with phases in a project from its inception to its completion; and engineers and scientists are often moved, or have the opportunity to move, between projects, within and between companies. With this characteristic mobility between jobs, engineers and scientists participate in "occupational contact networks" (Katz, 1958), through which information about jobs is communicated between colleagues. It is in these networks that friends are important.

The concept "friend," for the engineers is a general term and implies various expectations in the relationship between those involved. Unmodified, it may connote more particular role-words, which can be verbally differentiated: for example, "close" friend, "old" friend, or "acquaintance." The term "friend," then, unspecified, refers to a range of individuals and relationships. Specific rights and duties are distributed differently among particular kinds of friends, by which they are contrasted with one another and thereby distinguished. For example, a close friend may be permitted to pay an unannounced visit to one's home—that is, to simply and informally drop in, while such behavior would be unexpected and perhaps discouraged from others. Whatever the differences between categories, however, all friends are expected to help one another in the process of getting a job, although it is recognized that different sorts of friends will go to greater or lesser lengths in providing such assistance.

The data on actual job contacts support the normative rule that friends help one another in getting a job. Asked about past job contacts (i.e., about leads to getting a job before the period of government cutbacks and unemployment), 67 percent of the engineers studied said that they got their jobs through friends. This figure is consistent with that found by other researchers. Shapero, Howell, and Tombaugh published a study describing the Los Angeles and Boston centers of the defense research and development industry. They reported that 51 percent of the engineers and scientists they interviewed found their jobs through "personal acquaintances" (1965: 50). Although "personal acquaintance" is not explicitly defined, the authors use it interchangeably with the word "friend" (1965: 50). Similar results were uncovered by Granovetter whose study of technical, professional, and managerial workers indicated that 55 percent got their jobs through "personal contacts" (1974: 19). In this instance, it is clear that personal contacts are friends (1974: 16, 41, 165). Although there are some differences in the population composition and the way in which respondents describe job contacts, the overall pattern is clear: when the job market is good for professional workers, friends are a primary source of job contacts.

When the market is bad, however, friends do not play an equally important role in getting a job. The data I have on the ways in which unemployed engineers and scientists find work support this claim. By the beginning of 1973, most (89 percent) of those I had interviewed earlier had been rehired. Of these, 31 percent had found jobs through friends, the others getting jobs through impersonal formal channels, including ads, agencies, professional associations, and direct application. This figure is close to that found in an earlier study by Mooney (1965) of job information channels among unemployed engineers and scientists. He reported that of those reemployed, 27 percent got jobs through a "friend or relative" (1965: 152).

Here, then, is the problem. When jobs are easily available and engineers and scientists are in demand, friends are important job contacts, as is evident by the fact that from one-half to two-thirds of these professional workers get their jobs through friends. When jobs are scarce, however, the percentage of jobs found through friends drops to between one-third and one-fourth.

There are at least two alternative interpretations to account for this fluctuation. The first is that assuming the category of friends includes colleagues who have more or less the same information about jobs, then friends will not have different or additional information about job possibilities and therefore will not be in a position to help. But job contacts are still made through friends, even though the number of such contacts is reduced. Thus, another hypothesis is required to account for the differential use of friends in loose and tight markets.

The second explanation is that friends who are colleagues will be in competition with one another for scarce resources, including information about prospective employment opportunities. As a result they withhold or selectively distribute information, in which case there will be some manipulation or reclassification as to who counts as a friend. This interpretation accords with the idea that the term "friend" is polysemic and has a tactical meaning reflecting changing social situations. In this sense, the word "friend," meaning in particular "close" friend, describes those who are situationally labeled as such and from whom the label is withdrawn as circumstances dictate, thereby avoiding the obligations of the relationship. These are fair-weather friends. This interpretation is supported by the following facts.

The distinction between close friend and fair-weather friend as different meanings of the word "friend" used in its unmodified form, is apparent in some of the studies already mentioned. Granovetter, for example, notes that the word "friend," as a general term used in describing job contacts, in fact refers to two kinds of friends: "social friends" and "work contacts" (1974: 41-42). This classification corresponds to the differentiation between close friend and the sort of friend whose relationship might be situationally emphasized or deemphasized. Granovetter further reports that of those getting a job through a friend, 31.4 percent involved "social" or "close" friends and 68.7 percent involved "work contacts." What is particularly interesting about the two meanings of "friend" identified by Granovetter is that if "work-contact" friends are indeed fair-weather friends, then when the demand for engineers is depressed, one would expect that such friends would drop out of the friend category. Those who remained as job contacts would be those otherwise identifiable as "close" friends. This is consistent with the difference noted before between the larger number of friends reported as job contacts under favorable circumstances and the smaller number associated with a tight market.

A similar pattern of the meanings of "friend" emerges from Laumann's study of friendship networks. Laumann found, somewhat to his surprise, that "work-based" friendships differ from "close" friendships in that while close friendships are enduring, work-based friendships are easily formed and easily broken (1973: 93-96). Although Laumann does not analyze the conditions under which work-based friendships are broken, we might predict, in light of the fair-weather friend hypothesis, that this would happen when the job market was tight or when the work situation otherwise changed.

Furthermore, the distinction between the meanings of "friend" helps to clarify certain ambiguities in recent research in Boston by Powell and Driscoll (1973) among unemployed professionals. Powell and Driscoll interviewed unemployed middle-class professionals, mostly engineers, at an employment center in Massachusetts. I worked with the same category of people, in the same place, and approximately at the same time.

Our two samples have similar sociodemographic characteristics, yet our findings of the social consequences of unemployment for these men differ as a result of the different meanings associated with "friend." Powell and Driscoll describe a progressive deterioration of friendship among these men from the onset of unemployment. At first there is no change in relations between friends; then relationships begin to break down, although here there is some ambiguity, because some friends are said to offer help while others engage in avoidance behavior; finally, relationships with others are limited to a few very close friends. The men I interviewed described the effects of unemployment on their friendships quite differently. For example, none of the men interviewed said that there had been a negative change in his friendships; 96 percent said that there had been no change at all. Although accounts from individuals in the two samples of unemployed men appear to be inconsistent, even contradictory, I think their experiences, in fact, may be quite similar and that the differences between them derive, in part from differences in the interpretations they placed on these experiences.

The major difference is associated with the meaning attributed to the term "friend." Powell and Driscoll assume that the term has a single and fixed referent. By contrast, for the men I interviewed, the concept of friendship is polysemic. "Friend," for them, involves a relatively large class or set of people, including "old" friends, "close" friends, and those who, by further specification of situation or context, would otherwise be identified as "acquaintance" or "business associate." Thus, my informants, like those of Powell and Driscoll, report that one correlation of unemployment is a restriction in the circle of friends, a limitation of interaction to those who can be described as "close" friends. These men, however, did not describe this process as a breakdown in friendships, but rather as one that involves a more rigorous, a more selective (situationally specific) definition or redefinition of who is a friend. In other words, they say that they have, and have had, a small set of friends, with whom there has been no change in relationship since becoming unemployed. There are also others, now described as "just a friend," an acquaintance, or a business associate, with whom the relationship has changed. Thus, unemployment, representing a change of circumstances or conditions, induces a change in the labeling process, a change in those identified as friend, but not in the structure of rights and duties (i.e., in the relationships between friends). This change in labeling, the contraction of the set of people described as friends, explains, I think, the ambiguity in the account of Powell and Driscoll: that some friends are said to offer help to the unemployed, but that other friends are said to avoid them. Those who offer help are counted as close friends and no change is reported in those relationships. Those who turn away—who refuse to help and who thereby fail to recognize or meet what is understood to be a characteristic and an obligation of friendship—are no longer counted among friends.

This analysis is meant to contribute to an understanding of friendship in our society. I suggest that anthropological inquiry, including semantic and situational analyses, will supplement the knowledge generated by those working within other disciplines precisely because it does not assume the meaning of a term. Rather anthropology takes as a primary task the analysis of its meanings as these vary across different social contexts.

Notes

This paper was read in draft form in the symposium "North of the Border: Anthropological Inquiries into American Culture and Society" at the 73rd Annual Meeting of the American Anthropological Association, November 1974 (Mexico City).

1. Similar to Bloch's concept of "tactical meaning" is the idea of a "metaphoric use" of a term, "based on connotative meaning . . . to imply solidarity of a sort, and a mode of conduct between the parties concerned, which is similar in some limited respect to that appropriate to [those] who are designated by [the] terms" (Scheffler and Lounsbury, 1971: 9).

2. The literature on friendship is diverse; the most useful introductions to it are Coelho (1959) and Paine (1970).

3. The analyses of Paine and Suttles differ from the sociometric studies in their emphasis on the characteristics of social relationships rather than those of the participants in them.

4. Research in 1971-1972 was supported by a grant (MH-20222-01) from the National Institute of Mental Health, to which I express my appreciation.

References

Albert, Robert S. and T. R. Brigante, 1962, "The Psychology of Friendship Relations: Social Factors." *The Journal of Social Psychology* 56:33-47.

Barth, Fredrik, 1969, *Ethnic Groups and Boundaries.* Boston: Little, Brown.

Bloch, Maurice, 1971, "The Moral and Tactical Meaning of Kinship Terms." *Man* (N.S.) 6, no. 1:79-87.

Coelho, George V., 1959, "A Guide to Literature on Friendship: A Selectively Annotated Bibliography." *Psychological Newsletter* 10:365-394.

Evans-Pritchard, E. E., 1940, *The Nuer.* London: Oxford University Press.

Granovetter, Mark S., 1974, *Getting a Job.* Cambridge, Mass.: Harvard University Press.

Katz, Fred, 1958, "Occupational Contact Networks." *Social Forces* 37: 52-58.

References (cont'd)

Shapero, Albert, Richard P. Howell, and James R. Tombaugh, 1965, *The Structure and Dynamics of the Defense R and D Industry.* Menlo Park, Calif.: Stanford Research Institute.

Suttles, Gerald, 1970, "Friendship as a Social Institution." In George McCall et. al. *Social Relationships.* Pp. 95-135. Chicago: Aldine.

Thorpe, J. G., 1955, "A Study of Some Factors in Friendship Formation." *Sociometry* 18, no. 3: 207-214.

Laumann, Edward O., 1973, *Bonds of Pluralism: The Form and Substance of Urban Social Networks.* New York: Wiley.

Leach, E. R., 1954, *Political Systems of Highland Burma.* London: Bell.

Liebow, Elliot, 1967, *Tally's Corner.* Boston: Little, Brown.

Litwak, E. and I. Szelenyi, 1969, "Primary Group Structures and Their Functions: Kin, Neighbors, and Friends." *American Sociological Review,* 34, no. 4:465-481.

Mooney, Joseph D., 1965, "Displaced Engineers and Scientists; An Analysis of the Labor Market Adjustment of Professional Personnel." Unpublished Ph.D. dissertation. Cambridge: Massachusetts Institute of Technology.

Naegele, Kaspar D., 1958, "Friendship and Acquaintances: An Exploration of Some Social Distinctions." *Harvard Educational Review* 28, no. 3:232-252.

Paine, Robert, 1969, "In Search of Friendship: An Exploratory Analysis in 'Middle-Class' Culture." *Man* (N.S.), 4, no. 4:505-524.

—"Anthropological Approaches to Friendship." *Humanitas* 6, no. 2:

Powell, Douglas H. and Paul F. Driscoll, 1973, "Middle Class Professionals Face Unemployment." *Society,* 10, no. 2:18-26.

Scheffler, Harold W. and Floyd G. Lounsbury, 1971, *A Study in Structural Semantics.* Englewood Cliffs, N. J.: Prentice Hall.

MOONSHINING IN SOUTHERN ILLINOIS

PHIL C. WEIGAND

"Told them agents that I don't drink no more moonshine. 'Course, I forgot to tell them that I don't drink
less."

—an anonymous informant

Moonshine is illegal whiskey. It is not illegal because it is of
poor quality, though it may be, but because it is neither taxed
nor licensed. Both moonshiners (the producers) and bootleggers
(the distributors) are responsible for major government revenue
losses every year. It is estimated that federal tax losses reach
$127 million annually and that the state and local figure is ap-
proximately $42 million. It is for this reason that the producers
and distributors of illegal whiskey are the object of persecution.

Moonshining is part of American folklore. As such, it is
shrouded in legend, myth, and stereotype, but the commonly
held belief that suspicion of outsiders characterizes the moonshine industry is true. Any stranger could be the proverbial
revenue agent. Consequently, the social and economic organization of the industry is a closely guarded secret. Therefore,
a study of moonshining must be partially impressionistic, as
this one is, and all places and people must be fictionalized. Good
data are hard to come by, and the traditional anthropological
approach to a field problem is not applicable. The anthropologist cannot overtly take detailed notes, photographic oppor-

tunities are clearly limited, and mapping localities is out of the question. Indeed, my own observations about moonshining in southern Illinois were made largely while I was engaged in other activities, such as an archaeological survey, following the rotating markets, or visiting friends in the countryside. I never studied moonshining as such, and the information that I was able to gather came incidentally and often accidentally. I pass the following observations along to the reader in the spirit in which they were acquired: incomplete impressions about a highly fascinating aspect of midwestern rural culture.

Only once did I see a traditional still in operation and this was entirely by accident. The details of the incident are worth recounting.

A fellow archaeologist and I were walking in the deep forests that cover the bluffs overlooking the Mississippi River, looking for Indian burial mounds. The day was beautiful, bright and warm. The wildlife was abundant, visible and noisy—jays calling, squirrels chattering, and from time to time we would see a deer in an infrequent glade. As we reentered the forest from a clearing, there was a change in nature's mood. A silence prevailed, and all we could hear were our own footfalls among the leaves and twigs. We chanced along a trail and followed it to a very small clearing surrounded by giant trees, where we were suddenly met by three men. One of them, who was carrying a shotgun, asked who we were. Our surprise was so great that neither of us could speak. When I saw the still behind them, nervousness grew to deep apprehension, and further increased when they took us by the arms and escorted us into the tiny clearing.

At that point I was finally able to say that I was an archaeologist and that we were looking for "Indian rocks." Fortunately, the youngest of the three said that he knew me from a local talk I had given, and with that the atmosphere relaxed a bit. The danger had clearly passed, and I studied the site with growing interest. The still was small and obviously of limited capacity. Camping gear and empty tin cans cluttered the area. We asked a few questions, all simple minded in retrospect, before the oldest man left the clearing and disappeared down the path. The youngest man began to tend the still, and the man with the shotgun advised us to forget what we had seen, and not to mention the incident to others. We agreed enthusiastically and, after awhile, asked if we could leave. With his permission, we reentered the forest and walked toward the bluff. We had been at the still for about 45 minutes, but at the time it seemed like the whole afternoon. After awhile, we stopped to rest and compare impressions. We both agreed that these men were not the stereotyped hillbillies who are romanticized in the movies—no floppy hats, no crockery jugs nor corncob pipes. They were town-oriented farmers, and were obviously respected members of the community. The equipment was relatively modern and used propane gas so that there would be no telltale smoke. Since there did not appear to be a road nearby, the entire still must have been back-packed or horse-packed in. The men had been polite and shown very little hostility, considering the circumstances. They were obviously experienced at this sort of intrusion.

Years later I revisited the area with another archaeologist, showing him the burial mounds that we had located before. Approaching the still site, I began to talk loudly to my companion—announcing our presence, as it turned out, to only the trees. This second visit was totally different. There were no men, no odors, and no still. The clearing was overgrown, and even the tin cans had been removed. The complete lack of artifacts gave me a momentary doubt as to whether I was in the right place. This faded when I found the still's stone foundation. Had I not known that this was a still site—had I not actually seen it in operation—I do not believe that I could have ever interpreted the locality correctly. The still was probably moved right after our discovery of it. Obviously, moonshiners and their stills are frequently moved to avoid detection. Undoubtedly, this one would be used again, because the stone foundation, the only permanent and visible feature, remained intact.

Historically, a traditional "moonshine belt" existed throughout much of the American South and Midwest. In reality, it was discontinuous and confined for the most part to isolated and inaccessible rural areas. This traditional "belt" has always had competition from commercial moonshiners, and, indeed, it is progressively being supplanted by well-organized city-oriented businessmen. As a result, traditional moonshining is becoming a thing of the past as commercial moonshining becomes more and more extensive.

There are major differences between the traditional and contemporary practices. Traditional moonshine is often a quality product, since the makers drink it themselves. It is made with meticulous care from cooked corn mash and sprouted barley or rye. Sugar is used, but in relatively small quantities. The equipment is clean, and made from metals that do not have lead contents or lead salt deposits. The crust of the fermented mash is carefully removed, and the liquid filtered through cloth or yarns to remove other impurities. The complete process may take up to a week before the whiskey is stored, transported, and marketed in glass containers. Although it is obviously not aged, colors or dyes are not added. The final product is clear, and most often above 100 proof—hence the fitting nickname, "white lightning."

Traditional stills are usually of limited capacity, normally capable of producing a few gallons per batch. The whiskey sells for $9.00 or $10.00 a gallon, though prices vary a great deal depending on availability and access to a moonshiner or bootlegger. The principal consumers are the producers themselves, their relatives and friends. The limited number of customers usually are well known to the moonshiner, and profit is not the primary objective of the transaction. Some, but usually not a major share, is sold to bootleggers and then retailed to their acquaintances and customers. Only a small portion is ever retailed in the many country taverns and stores that dot southern Illinois' highways and rural roads.

Traditional moonshine passes several major quality tests, the most important one being that the moonshiner and bootlegger will drink it and offer it to friends and relatives. This insures that it will not cause the consumer any major damage, beyond that which any legal alcoholic beverage might. Indeed, it is frequently claimed by the natives that traditional moonshine whiskey has so few impurities that it does not cause severe hang-overs. Although that statement may not be totally accurate, good moonshine is very good, and, as the song says, "them that refuse it are few." Consumption of this type of moonshine often used to mark family or local events. Though unlicensed, the producers are often masters of the distilling art who work with care and take pride in their product. The finest among them have good reputations in and far beyond their communities, and their product is occasionally sought in vain by outsiders. They are protected from revenue agents by their relatives and friends and operate with the community's sanction or at least tolerance.

The traditional moonshiners have a long and respectable history in the United States dating back to the Colonial period. In the nineteenth century, moonshiners took up arms against the federal government, and the Whiskey Rebellion was fought. While the rebellion had other overtones, the rebels fought to protect their rights to produce, distribute, and consume whiskey of their liking and manufacture without government interference, regulation, and taxation. In this century, the persistence of moonshiners was responsible in part for the repeal of the unpopular and unenforceable Prohibition Amendment, which banned the production and consumption of all alcohol. Traditional moonshine is also immoralized in American legend and song, where it is sometimes endearingly called "mountain dew."

In southern Illinois, traditional moonshining has a history that goes back to the arrival of the first settlers. At that time, moonshining was a necessity, since commercial legal products were either scarce, due to transportation difficulties, or beyond the means of the poor farmers. Another reason that stimulated home-distilling was that the early legal commercial products were often "cut," or diluted with illegal whiskey or water. Hence, the sanctioned product was often qualitatively worse and more expensive than what was available locally. As a result, moonshining became a household activity, similar to soap making, candle making, or leather tanning. In true frontier fashion, a product that was needed was produced.

When Illinois achieved statehood, the drive to regulate and

tax whiskey began in earnest, and accelerated with the establishment of local tax-paying companies. These firms pressured the state legislature for harsher restrictions on illegal production. Once federal government agencies were regionally established, southern Illinois' moonshiners were forced to go underground. Associations such as the Licensed Beverage Industries, Inc., the National Council Against Illegal Liquor, and various prohibition and church groups maintain the pressure today. Moonshiners thus have had to conceal their identities, activities, and networks.

In southern Illinois, as well as the rest of the moonshine belt, concealment means constant relocation of stills in difficult to reach or "neutral" places, which, even if discovered, cannot incriminate the still's operators. In southern Illinois, these sites are in the deep and heavily wooded ravines, the hills, and swamps. Ironically, some are located within the federally owned extensive Shawnee National Forest grounds, while others are in the abandoned farm buildings, owned by the banks, or in the "back forty." The back forty (the acreage not currently used by the farmer) can be an incriminating locality, so these stills are the first to be abandoned when pressure mounts. Certainly, almost all the major still sites have been located, as revenuers have been very active lately. But lack of personnel means that many remain in operation. However, it is only a matter of time, because revenuers are armed with the latest technological devices, such as infrared aerial photography to pick up the telltale wisps of smoke from the stills' fires. Walkie-talkies and helicopters are also used. Consequently, the numbers of traditional stills are decreasing as the pressure continues. Traditional moonshiners cannot afford continuous detection and fines, since their profits are limited. The Licensed Beverage Industries, Inc. reports that the number of stills destroyed annually is decreasing for the first time, from over 25,000 in the mid-1950s, to approximately 7,000 in the early 1970s, indicating the success of the campaign. Certainly, not all of the stills destroyed were of the traditional variety, but the traditional moonshiner is by far the most vulnerable. The commercial moonshiner is much less accessible, because he has an organizational backing with legal resources, which are not part of the social network of the traditional moonshiner.

With this background, we are in a better position to evaluate commercial moonshining and moonshiners, who are an entirely different lot. They are moonshiners for profit—the more and the faster, the better. As mentioned, they are organization men, and it is to the organization, not to their relatives and friends, to whom they owe their loyalties. Consequently, they are interested in profit and not necessarily the quality of the whiskey. Indeed, traditional moonshiners will not drink it, nor should anyone chance it. These moonshiners do not deserve romanticization, because their product is occasionally lethal. Their stills are often large, with capacities of 1,000 gallons or more per batch, which can be prepared in 3 or 4 days. These stills are seldom as remote as those of the traditional moonshiner, though they are carefully hidden. The more elaborate ones need running water and electricity. Thus, they are often located in basements, attics, or the backs of stores, and are found as frequently in towns as in the woods. They are often equipped with modern devices that cost $25,000 or more to construct. Clearly, this is a major investment, and one beyond the resources of most individuals, especially since banks or other regular sources of capital cannot be easily tapped for such enterprises.

In part, these moonshiners are the heirs of the "bathtub gin" makers of the prohibition era. This moonshine is made largely from sugar, and in order to speed up the process of fermentation, detergents are sometimes added, rather than yeast. At times, the metal equipment parts are made or adapted from automobile radiators and other similar contrivances, which have accumulated dangerous lead salts. These substances dissolve in the production process, and pose an extreme health hazard. Other considerations for health and sanitation are also lacking. As a result, this moonshine often does not pass the most crucial and critical test—the manufacturers and distributors will not consume the product, nor allow their families and friends to touch it. The customers are faceless strangers. This moonshining usually has no positive community sanctions, which is not surprising, since the resulting liquor has been known to cause blindness, convulsions and death—not to mention hangovers.

Nationwide, the National Council Against Illegal Liquor estimates that 12 million gallons of illegal whiskey are produced each year; by far, most of it is the commercial variety. Estimates for southern Illinois are not available, but it is my impression that large quantities of this type of moonshine are distilled each year and bootlegged into the towns and cities. The product is most often shipped and stored in plastic containers or metal tins. Common outlets in southern Illinois are the many road-houses, as well as the "wino" town bars. It is often sold across the bar from refilled legal bottles, though usually at a much cheaper price. It is also available in quantity through retailing for home consumption and in unlicensed bars. At times, the product is colored to provide an acceptable aged tint, and is also used to cut legal whiskey. Customers often know what they are getting, but do not or cannot care. The market is partially oriented toward town or city alcoholics, but it is some-times sold with forged or stolen labels of legal brands to the un-suspecting buyer. At least one regional brand of whiskey com-monly sold in this part of the state is particularly suspect on this score.

There are difficulties in the distribution of this type of moonshine, however. Since the trade is very lucrative, gang-land style battles have broken out over the control of the re-distributive channels. Taverns mysteriously burn down or, not so mysteriously, are dynamited to rubble. A tiny town near Carbondale, which used to have far more than its share of road-houses and bars, is now almost totally in ruins as a result of this competition. Homes of leaders are also occasionally bombed. The bootlegging part of the industry, as well as the actual sales outlets, are characterized by violence. Certainly, not all the violence in southern Illinois involves moonshine, because other illegal but associated activities abound. Gambling and prosti-tution are also involved. However, this overall pattern of com-petition and violence necessitates more and more organizational involvement. In some places, local officials and police are thought to be part of the illegal network. Perhaps not so surprisingly, it seems that the same effort at enforcement directed against the traditional moonshiners does not appear to be proportionally represented against the commercial operators and bootleggers. While the traditional moonshiners do not consider themselves criminals, commercial moonshiners and bootleggers do consider themselves outside the law and act accordingly.

Despite the difficulties in distribution and the overall poor quality of the product, the market for commercial moonshine continues to expand. As long as taxes on legal whiskey continue to rise at every political level, then the product will continue to be marketable. As long as people feel that the taxes and prices of brand names are too high, moonshine will exist. The illegal product is not really cheap, but always priced at just the right level to undersell legal, taxed whiskey, while high enough to insure a profit. One local estimate is that for every dollar invested, a return of ten can be expected. However, production costs, transportation, payoffs, and legal fees must be subtracted from this figure.

Commercial moonshining continues to make inroads on traditional moonshining because the resources and expenses for production and distribution continue to rise. In addition, organizations are needed to protect the commercial moonshiner and to distribute the product. The traditional moonshiner does not wish to belong to such an organization. In any event, the markets for the two types of moonshine are considerably different. Traditional moonshine is almost always strictly local, while commercial moonshine is regional. Hence, the art of the traditional moonshiner is dying as it becomes too expensive, inconvenient, complicated, and far too dangerous. Moonshine, in one form or another, has been with us since distilling was introduced to America by the settlers. It is with us now and probably will be until alcohol is replaced by another socially acceptable drug, available and desirable to all social classes.

POKER
AND THE
AMERICAN DREAM

REX L. JONES

Poker is an American game. Its origins, style of play, and language are all American. The draw poker clubs of Gardena in southern California recognize this fact. An advertising brochure of one of the clubs states:

> Poker is America's favorite card game. 70 million adults play cards and some 47 million prefer poker. Poker is as American as baseball and hotdogs. Many of our most famous Presidents were poker enthusiasts.

Poker is a pure expression of the American dream. Embodied in the action of the game is the ever-present notion that anyone with skill, individual initiative, patience, foresight, and a little luck can easily make the leap from rags to riches. In a recent article entitled, "Who Dealt This Mess?" Barry Golson says that poker "is as perfect a microcosm as we have of the way a free-enterprise system is *supposed* to work, except that the rich don't necessarily get richer." He goes on to say that "in a limit game . . . a grocery clerk can humiliate an oil tycoon through sheer bravado—the object being, without exception, to bankrupt the bastard across the table" (1974: 112).

Poker is an expression of the American dream in many other ways. We recognize the person who has achieved the American dream by conspicuous consumption. A house, a car, a color TV, a pocket full of credit cards, and a politician in the closet are some of the indications of success. In poker, the "winner" is easily recognized by diamonds, stickpins, car, clothes, bankroll, and the hangers on who flank him. He exudes rugged individualism—the winner at poker is his own man.

In the realization of the American dream, the arena is the system of free enterprise, where everyone has an equal chance; in the poker game, the arena is a system of free play, where all begin on equal footing. In the American dream, society is classless, anyone can play; it is the same with poker. In the American dream, the way to the top is up to you and you alone; in poker, too, winning is solely an individual effort. In the American dream, the winner takes all; in poker, there is no such thing as sharing the spoils.

The American dream and the game of poker thus have much in common. The latter is the microcosm of the former. In Gardena, this melodrama is reenacted every day from 9 A.M. until 5 A.M. the next day. Most of the people who participate are the senior citizens of America—the retired, and the widowed, or that element of our society for whom the American dream has indeed become a living nightmare, because old age and retirement have made its realization next to impossible.

Daily, elderly men, living on their pensions and savings, and elderly women, living on inheritances and insurance premiums of their deceased husbands, frequent the poker clubs, often in shared taxis or cars, to pursue their vision of the American dream. They meet their friends, share stories of winning and losing, compare notes on racing forms, watch TV, eat, drink, and participate in the "action" with people from all walks of life. Small businessmen, bartenders, teachers, construction workers, doctors, students, hustlers, prostitutes, the unemployed, and tourists intermingle with the senior citizens, who all too often in our society are confined to the sterility of old-age homes or the loneliness of their rooms.

In Gardena, the poker clubs may be many things to many people, but to the aged they are—as expressed to me by an 83-year-old woman—a "godsend." In the clubs their lives attain new meaning. In Gardena, few discuss their aches and pains or their imminent and inevitable deaths. The talk centers around

171

poker and especially winning, which few if any are able to do consistently. No matter, there is always hope, and such hope is justified every day, when a few hit a big win. Winnings are remembered for years; losses are forgotten the next day. In the process, however, the American dream is perpetuated through poker play, and even the old can participate in the myth.

POKER PLAYING IN SOUTHERN CALIFORNIA

In California there are over 400 licensed and legalized draw-poker clubs. In Gardena, a sprawling suburb of about 50,000 people, located 10 miles south of downtown Los Angeles, poker is the major industry. The poker club payrolls amount to around $5 million annually. Thousands of southern Californians are attracted to its six poker parlors every year, most of them regular players. The Gardena clubs are the largest and best equipped of any of the California draw poker clubs.

Each club is limited, by city law, to thirty-five tables; each table seats a maximum of eight players. In addition to the card tables, each club features a restaurant, lounge, and one or more color TV rooms. The restaurants serve decent food with diversified menus, at relatively low prices. Many serve weekly specials and buffets that attract hundreds of people who never sit at the poker tables. The clubs are tastefully decorated, by California standards, well lit, and provide free parking. They are located near major freeway systems and are therefore easily accessible to motor-crazed southern Californians.

Draw poker is still the number one attraction. In Gardena's clubs, as in most poker parlors in California, the house has no interest in the stakes of the games. The house provides the tables, cards, chips, game supervision, and other services, but the deal rotates among the players. Each player pays a "collection" to the house at the end of each half-hour of play, the amount being determined by the stakes of the table. The lower the stakes, the less the collection. The house then, essentially rents its services to those who wish to play poker. The collection, however, is no minor variable in terms of winning and losing.

Because of the collection at the end of each half-hour, a low-stakes game is a death wish. It took me some 1000 hours of poker playing to figure out this mathematical formula. In a game of, let's say, $1.00/$2.00 draw, the collection is $1.25 each half-hour. The "buy in," or the stakes that you are required to place in front of you on the table is $10.00. If all eight players at the table are of equal skill, and if at the end of 4 hours of play no player has won or lost at the card play, there will be no money on the table. Each and every player will be broke. Collectively, it costs $80.00 for 4 hours of play. The rent is not cheap.

As one moves to a higher-stakes game, the collection increases, but it increases disproportionately to the stakes of the game. For example, at a $10/$20 low draw game, the collection is $3.00 per half-hour. Collectively, at the end of 4 hours of play, it costs $192.00 per table to play. But the buy-in at $10/$20 low draw is $100.00. It would take from 16 to 17 hours, everything being equal, for the players at the table to go broke.

What this means for the regular players at Gardena is quite simple. Those who regularly play the low-stakes game, *even if they win at cards consistently*, will find it next to impossible to "beat the collection." They will lose money, not to the other players, but to the house. In 1970, I played regularly for 6 months in low-stakes games at Gardena, usually 1/2 high draw or 2/4 low draw. I played on the average of 50 hours a week, or a total of 1500 hours. It cost me in collection fees an average of $3.00 per hour, or a total for 6 months of some $4,500. In tabulating the amount of money I spent at Gardena during that 6-month period, I estimate expenses of $2000. Out of that $2000 also came my food, transportation, and such other things as cigarettes and drinks. Any way I calculated it, I had won at cards. I estimate my winnings at close to $3000, yet my bank account was some $2000 short. What happened to the money? It went to the house.

I am convinced that this happens to every regular player at Gardena in low stakes games.[1] This is substantiated by hundreds of interviews with people who play poker at Gardena and are aware that the house wins in the end. How else could the clubs meet a $5 million annual payroll, pay Gardena taxes, and also make a profit?

Who Plays Poker at Gardena?

As indicated, the majority of the regular players are senior citizens. Surveys of five clubs at different intervals of the day and week during the summer of 1974 revealed some of the following statistics: Out of a total sample of 1473 people at the tables, 789 (53 percent) were over 60 years of age. Of the total sample, 1089 (74 percent) were men and 384 (26 percent) were women. Of the men, 503 (46 percent) were over 60, and of the women, 286 (74 percent) were over 60 (see Appendix A). These figures indicate that the majority of players are of retirement age. Three-fourths of all women who play are at the retirement age and probably either widowed or playing their pensions or inheritances.

The surveys were backed up by some 3000 hours of participant observation at the tables over a period of 5 years. During that time, I have informally interviewed hundreds of regular players, most of whom indicated to me they were retired or living on pensions, inheritances, or savings.[2]

Furthermore, the majority of the aged and retired play low-stakes games. I estimate roughly three-fourths or more.[3] The reasons are simple. They are generally unable to afford the potential losses of high-stakes games, which at any given period of play can run into several hundred dollars or more.

In both formal and informal interview situations and during the course of hours of play, I found that consistent winners are few, probably less than 2 percent, and are of a certain type.[4] They are invariably young (between 21 and 35 years of age), male, and single.[5] These data correspond roughly to another study of poker playing in northern California by Martinez and LaFranchi (1972, 1974), who claim that the consistent winners were single or divorced, male, and younger than most of the other players. In that study, they also indicated that less than 10 percent of the players were consistent winners. They described the remainder as "break-evens," "losers," or "action players." I feel that a similar situation exists in Gardena, with one exception. In the Martinez-LaFranchi study there is no mention or analysis of the variable of the house collection. The

174

majority of Gardena players probably fall into the area of "break-evens" or "losers" in terms of the card play, but I am convinced that well over 90 percent of all people who play poker regularly in the Gardena clubs lose money, regardless of their card play.[6] I would add only one variable to Martinez and LaFranchi's description of the consistent winner, and that is that he will probably be found in the high-stakes games, especially $10/$20 draw.

The conclusion to my study is that the senior citizens who regularly play poker at Gardena lose money in one way or another. They spend their pensions or savings in order to frequent the clubs. The amount they lose is consistent with their income. The club owners recognize this, implicitly if not explicitly. As an example, last summer I played frequently at a $5/$10 low-draw game with a woman who was 76 years old and consistently lost money. In such a game, the losses can be heavy. An average win at a period of play in that game will range from $150 to $300. An average loss will amount to the same or more depending on the player. This woman knew this, because she had played the game in Gardena, in the same club, for over 20 years. She first began playing in the 1950s after moving to California from New York with her husband. Her husband, a successful businessman, died shortly after the move, leaving her with a fairly large income. After a period of boredom and loneliness, the woman soon discovered poker at Gardena, through a friend. Because she had the money, she rapidly moved to the high-stakes games, where the action was faster and more to her liking. During her play, she talked constantly, and frequently claimed that she had paid for the entire west wing of the club through collections over the years. She said that last year she had cashed $20,000 in checks at the cashier's window. At the end of the year, the owner of the club invited her into his office for a personal conference, and begged her to play at a lower-stakes game where she would not lose so much money. She refused, and said, "What else have I got to do with my money? Go on a goddamned world cruise with a bunch of old ladies? I'd rather lose it at poker!"

To the club owner, it matters little whether such people play low- or high-stakes games. The difference in the collection is not so great. What matters is keeping his customers happy and playing, regardless of their losses or winnings.[7] He feared that the woman might go broke, or anger the other players by creating disturbances over her losses, none of which were to his advantage. Thus, the conference was held to "help her out." The important thing was to keep her playing, and playing happily.

Why Poker Playing at Gardena?

As I have maintained, the people who play poker at Gardena are mostly senior citizens, and most of them lose money on a regular basis. The "diamond-studded woman" of Gardena who coldly calculates her cards and shrewdly takes in her winnings, as described by Jack Richardson (1974) in a recent Playboy article, is a rarity, if not a myth. The player you are most likely to find across the table from you is an elderly male in wrinkled slacks and a $5.00 sport shirt, losing his pension, or an elderly female with a wig and make-up, losing her inheritance or savings.

It is my contention that the aged and retired play poker in Gardena for social and recreational reasons. They are reliving the American dream, which gives meaning to their lives. Poker functions to make them young again.

The Gardena clubs take the place of home life for the aged. They function quite simply as old-age homes, but offer a more exciting and stimulating environment than do regular institutions for the aged in our society. The clubs, unlike old-age homes, are not places to go and die but places to go and live. Here the aged, the retired, and the widowed are able to interact on a one-to-one basis with thousands of young people, who frequent the clubs simply to play cards. Here the regulars meet tourists from all over the United States and Canada. They meet and interact with people from all walks of life. The clubs offer something more to the regulars than the loneliness and passivity of old-age homes, where people spend most of their time thinking about illness, misfortune, and death. Such discussions are out of place in Gardena.

176

CONCLUSION

Studies of this kind are of extreme importance to sociologists and anthropologists interested in American culture and behavior. Considering the importance of this pastime to most Americans, we should be able to add new dimensions to studies of gambling and gamblers. In the past, this area of human behavior has been left to psychologists such as Bergler (1957), who insist on describing the gambler as "compulsive" or a "psychopath." There are sociological reasons for gambling. In many instances it is a form of recreation or play (Stone, 1972), not a compulsive neurotic search for the affections of one's father or mother. Zola (1964: 247), citing studies by psychologists (Hunter and Bruner, 1928; Morris, 1957) claims that there is no convincing evidence on any number of psychological dimensions to indicate that gamblers differ significantly from nongamblers in personality characteristics. However, his studies (1964) and a select few by other sociologists (Devereaux, 1949; Carlson, 1939) show that there are significant sociological reasons that people gamble. Frequently, gambling as described by Zola (1964: 259) is a functional social activity that creates "rationality," "order," and "meaning" in the lives of alienated, frustrated, and predetermined failures. Poker playing in Gardena serves such a positive function for the aged and retired who are outside the mainstream of American social life. As one 83-year-old woman put it at the end of an interview in which she systematically pointed out the evils and absurdities of playing poker at Gardena, "Son, if they closed Gardena tomorrow, I would die."

Appendix

Head Count of Poker Players by Sex and Age in Five Different Clubs on Five Separate Days of the Week

	Club A	Club B	Club C	Club D	Club E
Total	271	400	245	234	323
Men	195	342	202	158	192
percent	(68)	(83)	(83)	(64)	(60)
Women	76	58	43	76	131
percent	(32)	(17)	(17)	(36)	(40)
Men over 60	107	138	81	69	108
percent	(55)	(41)	(41)	(44)	(56)
Women over 60	70	49	36	50	81
percent	(92)	(84)	(64)	(65)	(62)

Total Head Count of 5 Clubs: − 1473 people
  1089 (74 percent) men
   384 (26 percent) women
   503 (46 percent) men over 60
   286 (74 percent) women over 60

The numbers in the table were obtained by walking through the play-area and counting the men and women. I then repeated the walk, noting the women over 65. (In the chart, I indicate "over 60" to allow five years' difference in "guessing age".) I then did the same for men.

Although I give only the figures for 5 clubs on 5 different days, I did this 15 times in 5 different clubs (3 times each), to act as a check on my figures. The figures varied, of course, but the percentages of male to female and ages did not vary a great deal.

As a further check on my guessing of ages, I had an independent observer (an anthropologist friend of mine) do a similar head count in one evening of play. Our figures tallied very closely. Thus, although the ages are guesswork, I feel that the above checks and years of experience in Gardena make them fairly accurate guesses.

Notes

1. Such statements are extremely difficult to substantiate accurately, since players regularly talk of their winnings but are more reluctant to discuss their losses, especially over long periods of time. But based on close contact with hundreds of regular players in low-stakes games, I never came across an individual who admitted to being a consistent winner in those games. They all had excuses for losing, but generally, reluctantly admitted that the house collection was indeed the real problem.

In Gardena, the house collection is presented in such a way as to make the players believe that it is a necessary part of playing poker. Next to the cashier is a sign that reads something like: "For tax purposes, law in the city of Gardena requires each player to pay his collection on demand." This is to instill in the players the idea that most of the collection goes to the city of Gardena, rather than to the owner of the clubs. Failure to pay, therefore, makes you a tax fraud. Few are fooled by this gambit, however, and the most frequent utterance in Gardena is that "Nobody but the house wins."

2. In addition to informal interviews and acquaintances, I conducted twenty-five formal interviews with a cross section of regulars in the summer of 1974. Of all those interviewed who were over 60 (except one), all were living on either a pension or an inheritance, usually small.

3. This figure is difficult to pin down in Gardena, since the tables change personnel so frequently. It is estimated on the basis of hours of play, both in low- and high-stakes games, and comments by players themselves.

4. Two percent is an estimate, also. But of all my experience, in both playing and interview situations, I encountered only about six or eight admitted consistent winners. Four of these were "house players" (see footnote 7). All played either $10/$20 high draw or $10/$20 low "blind."

5. All admitted winners were male. I suspected one or two females of being winners who played in high-stakes games, but they would not discuss this matter.

6. This estimate is based both on my own study and that of Martinez and LaFranchi (1972, 1974).

7. The house even employs house-players to keep the games moving. The house-player usually is paid a daily wage to fill in at short tables. To be a house-player one must risk his own money at the tables, and before employment, put up a thousand dollars in the house bank. Most consistent winners I encountered were house-players.

References

Bergler, E., 1957, *The Psychology of Gambling*. New York: Hill & Wang.

Carlson, G. C., 1939, "Number Gambling—A Study of a Culture Complex." Unpublished Ph.D. dissertation, University of Michigan.

Devereaux, E. C., Jr., 1949, "Gambling and the Social Structure: A Sociological Study of Lotteries and Horse Racing in Contemporary America." Unpublished Ph.D. dissertation, Harvard.

Golson, B., 1974, "Who Dealt This Mess?" *Playboy*, November, p. 110.

Hunter, J. and A. Bruner, 1928, "Emotional Outlets of Gamblers." *Journal of Abnormal Psychology*, 23:38-39.

Martinez, T. H. and R. LaFranchi, 1972, "Why People Play Poker." In G. P. Stone, ed. *Games, Sport and Power*. Pp. 55-73. New Brunswick, N. J.: Dutton.

—1974, "What Kind of Poker Player are You?" *Gambling Quarterly* (summer): 23, 38, 39.

Morris, R. P., 1957, "An Exploratory Study of Some Personality Characteristics of Gamblers." *Journal of Clinical Psychology* 13:191-193.

Richardson, Jack, 1974, "Coming Down in Gardena." *Playboy*, November, p. 114.

Stone, G. P., ed., 1972, *Games, Sport and Power*. New Brunswick, N. J.: Dutton.

Zola, Irving R., 1964, "Observations on Gambling in a Lower-class Setting." In Harvard S. Becker, ed. *Perspectives on Deviance: The Other Side*. Pp. 247-260. London: Collier-Macmillan.

THE STRANGENESS
OF ASTROLOGY

An Ethnography of
Credibility Processes

SUZANNE M. WEDOW

INTRODUCTION

The popularity of astrology in the counterculture of the 1960s, is a historical remnant of its widespread prevalence prior to and during the Middle Ages. Then, as now, it was regarded as a form of "perennial wisdom," used as a method of divination, a means of self-discovery and self-explanation, uniting human life to the celestial realms in an unbroken unity of influence and harmony. However, since the advent of the scientific method and the ideology of science, the public authority of astrology has declined, resulting in its "exile" to the realms of private usage and personal belief. Nonetheless, despite an apparent retreat the use of astrology prevails in some quarters. Indeed, one sociologist (Truzzi, 1972) finds the use of astrology an aspect of what he terms an "occult revival."

This paradox of both retreat and revival provides an interesting example of how the use of a system of knowledge[1] persists despite public repudiation. This is similar to Kuhn's study (1970) of the process of paradigm change in the history of the natural sciences. In a similar fashion, this essay seeks to describe how astrology achieves credibility in the arena of private usage (i.e., the world of everyday life). The achievement of this sense of credibility on specific occasions when natal charts are interpreted will be described by looking at aspects of client-astrologer interaction. Although focusing specifically on the interpretation activities of astrologers and clients, there are implications for the broader issue of understanding the conditions under which a system of knowledge continues to be believed in and used as a legitimate method of investigation.

An examination of the aspects and significance of the presence and survival of occult or other unusual cultural practices is, of course, not a new theme in social science. A variety of theoretical and methodological tenets frame these discussions, many of them seeking to discover why such belief systems prevail or develop. In reviewing a few of these approaches, a major consideration in evaluating them is the extent to which other important questions and approaches have been ignored. I illustrate their inadequacy by asking a different order of questions, capitalizing on the sense of "strangeness" experienced by researchers investigating unusual phenomena.

Sociologists, led to ask why a phenomenon develops, generally attempt an analysis of the motivational or dispositional characteristics of participants in unusual movements or activities. In the study of astrology this approach is frequently supplemented by examining the biographical and sociological characteristics of those who believe in and practice astrology or other forms of divination (Cavan, 1972; Roszak, 1969; Truzzi, 1972). Sociologists typically account for belief in deviant or "alien" belief systems (Festinger, et al., 1965; Simmons, 1964) by referring to psychological processes in conjunction with such sociological characteristics as class, political affiliation, and similar variables.

Still others investigate the characteristics of astrological knowledge itself or the latent functions provided for individuals by the use of astrology as an explanatory or divinatory system (Adorno, 1974; Truzzi, 1972). Adorno's content analysis of the *Los Angeles Times* astrology column, discussed at length the characteristics of astrological advice and descriptions in relation to his own concern with authoritarianism and individual submissiveness in the modern state. Truzzi's sociological survey of the presence of occult phenomena, regards the current revival of interest as a form of popular culture. Discussing the popularity of astrology, he focused upon the latent functions of its use for progressively "committed" astrologers and believers. Some functions served by the predominance of astrology are: tension management of anxieties experienced in the present American social system; the fulfillment of economic goals that the mass-merchandising of an astrology fad affords; the availability of a cognitive belief system that transcends science and is "safe" from the sanction of or overt conflict with the major religions; ego enhancement; the creation of an in-group cohesiveness and an out-group cohesion by means of the language of astrology. Truzzi argues that "the major latent function . . . is that the adept astrologer obtains an ideological integration of his self with the perception of the universe" (1972: 20-21).

While these approaches appear to explain belief in astrology by using sociological and psychological categorizations, a neglected aspect has been the careful analysis of actual interactional scenes in which the use of a system of knowledge occurs. Access to this order of investigation is available by exploring or making self-conscious the sense of "strangeness" experienced by social investigators engaged in ethnographic research. It is common knowledge that anthropologists and sociologists alike experience a sensation of alienness or strangeness upon entering a foreign culture or describing cultural practices widely divergent from their own. This sense of strangeness can lead social scientists to question how these phenomena develop, prior to asking why they manifest particular characteristics. Looking at the widespread practice of astrology, for example, researchers can thus find themselves asking *how* astrology maintains its authority for some when it is so clearly repudiated by the evidence of scientific or even common sense logic. Focusing on this question, I believe, quite naturally leads to an ethnography of the use of a system of knowledge on specific interactional occasions.

In the case at hand, by asking how the authority of astrology occurs, I found myself attempting a study of a general process (i.e., credibility) rather than an investigator of a specific set of individuals.

ESTABLISHING CREDIBILITY

Natal or birth chart interpretation is a complex process. The astrologer, given the client's birth information (time, place, and date), draws up a horoscope indicating the position of various planets in relationship to each other. The zodiac, the basis for the chart construction, consists of twelve signs, ruled by twelve planets, which form a circular belt of influence affecting the particular individual. The twelve houses are the seats of the planets in the heavens; they control areas of an individual's life and are influenced by the effects of particular signs. Degrees note the angular relations of the planets with respect to each other within the belt of the zodiac. Clearly, astrology is person centered and geocentric in its depiction of the planets and their motions. The astrologer, having drawn up or "erected" a chart, then begins the work of chart interpretation. Each zodiac sign, house, and degree relationship has a meaning and a set of descriptive adjectives used to describe aspects of the person's biography and character. The astrologer's task is to translate these planetary locations into a complete, meaningful, and coherent description of the client. The chart is read, or interpreted for the client in this process; questions are asked and extensive discussion occurs about the specific aspects of the astrologer's interpretation. At this point the genuine work of astrology begins, for astrologers argue that the technical mechanics of drawing up a chart is not the real challenge of their profession. The genuine work is the artful interpretation the astrologer provides for the client.

Astrologers rely on a highly codified body of knowledge and set of categories for doing their interpretations. These may be found in manuals, textbooks, and popular accounts of the art. The proper reading of these categories constructs "sensible" natal chart interpretations that are not only semantically coherent but also credible. However, the translation of birth charts on these occasions must occur in an accompanying social and informational context. That is, a variety of contexts of information are displayed as an aspect of the interaction itself. The kinds of information that emerge provide the conditions for the interpretation of natal charts, the achieved credibility of those interpretations, and their maintained credibility when clients or astrologers encounter difficulties or contradictions. An examination of a number of these chart interpretations uncovered three kinds of contexts that serve as the bases for the achieved and maintained credibility of astrology: the context of information; and the context of social interaction. The contexts described below provide various levels of information that are employed to strengthen the overall credibility of the interpretation even when it appears to be challenged.

The Context of Working Claims

Studying the interpretation activities of astrologers and clients reveals a set of working claims (i.e., projected definitions about astrology and astrologers). Astrology is often termed occult, hidden, or perennial wisdom. The validity of astrologically based statements rests upon time-honored truths passed down through generations of teachers and students. Astrology is thought to reveal fundamental truths, in the form of complex descriptions about individual persons and even nations. In the settings studied, astrologers themselves referred to astrology as both a science and an art, an intuitive wisdom and a technical skill. Astrologers not only provide basic descriptions of the client's character but also make projected statements of future states of affairs and existential being.

The presentation and support of these public claims is a working activity insofar as astrologers manifest these claims in their interpretation statements. These working claims were supported in two basic ways, one involving the presentation of information and the other having to do with the settings as occasions for displaying the reality of those claims. Astrologers made statements about their individual, professional competence: how long they had studied; where and how they studied astrology. ranging from certification from the local Better Business Bureau to memory of former lives in which the astrologer remembered himself as a member of a royal court. Astrologers also provided information about how astrology could be or was to be em-

185

ployed (e.g., to master one's shortcomings through accurate self-knowledge, to overcome the unsupported claims of a rigidly scientific outlook on life, or just to achieve self-understanding). These working claims were presented and supported through the ongoing interpretation and elaboration of the client's natal chart. An additional aspect of the presentation of these claims was the use of the special vocabulary of astrology which is taught to the client during the course of the interpretation.

The analysis of tape recorded materials indicated that these claims should be regarded as interactional and cognitive practices. That is, the claims, when introduced by clients and astrologers, are practical directives requiring both to regard or "see" the world with reference to the relevant issues of astrological knowledge. Hence, these claims, both professional and general, are practices because they construct and preserve the necessary means to honor the perennial "truthfulness" of astrology. They are working claims because they project a course of affairs and a set of anticipations to be realized, as the implicit assumption behind the reading itself.

The Informational Context of Chart Interpretation

When astrologers and their clients come together during chart interpretation sessions a large amount of information is introduced in an ongoing sequence of statements, questions, and answers. The chart itself, consisting of a symbolic and numerical depiction of planetary locations, is read to the client. This I term "presented knowledge." Clients are described, told who they are by using an astrological vocabulary (e.g., "moon in Gemini means . . ."). This knowledge may be passed on to friends or researchers or anyone curious about what the astrologer told the client about himself.

Basic to the astrologer's presentation of this easily observed and heard knowledge is a schema or set of assumptions without which a coherent, sensible reading could not occur. These schemata may be idiosyncratic to the person; yet they may also be socially derived and learned. The astrologer, by displaying this foundational knowledge in interaction, sets the

186

stage for attributing validity to astrology. The heart of the coherence of the presented knowledge given to the client is a set of foundational assumptions[2] which the astrologer relies upon and occasionally directly refers to during the course of a chart reading session.

The Context of Social Interaction

Clients and astrologers have a variety of relationships with each other, extending from a one-time-only reading of the chart to a long-term consultation type of relationship for personal, business, or professional reasons. Regardless of the duration of this relationship the actual occasion of a chart reading is a special social interaction, temporally bounded from beginning to end by the presence or absence of astrological knowledge. When clients visit an astrologer the presented knowledge about the chart is built up from the first moment of the exchange of information to its termination when the client leaves. Hence, the context of social interaction for client and astrologer consists not only of the information presented during the visit (whether it be the varieties of working claims discussed above or the various aspects of presented and foundational knowledge), but also the events of that occasion itself.

Another aspect of the conditions for astrology's credibility involves the client's act of initiating the social interaction related to the chart interpretation (i.e., clients must find astrologers). This is done by consulting newspapers, friends, other astrologers, posters, bulletin boards, and even the yellow pages. Once the astrologer is found he or she is given the basic information by the client, and is then consulted for a chart reading. In an important sense the initial investment of time and energy to seek out the astrologer already involves the client in a minor though unintended search for and achievement of credibility. The agreement to read the chart, while obviously related to financial remuneration, is also a commitment of energy and a projection of an idealization on the part of the astrologer about his or her competence to perform this task.

In summary, a critical aspect of the conditions for the

achievement of astrology's credibility occurs within the context of social interaction between astrologers and their clients. This social interaction involves the interrelated use of the three contexts I have described above. On the occasion of a chart reading, statements are presented and clients and astrologers generate questions and answers for each other. During these questions and answers problems may appear, an issue that brings up another aspect of the problem of credibility: the *maintenance* of credibility when contradictions occur.

MAINTAINING CREDIBILITY

I have argued that the most important condition for the credibility of astrology is the way in which astrological knowledge is introduced and used in a social context. While this information could be regarded as the basis for a set of practices for constructing credibility it is simultaneously the basis for a set of practices for maintaining or preserving a threatened credibility. When the conditions for credibility have been established the same information used in this way may also be used to preserve credibility through the emergence of three preservative practices.

Astrologers and Clients as Collaborators

Clients, as active participants, can be described not only as learners and novice users of astrology, but also as verifiers of astrological knowledge. As astrologers and clients direct questions to each other the client is frequently cast into the position of being an affirmer of the description. One astrologer, for instance, directly asked the client if the chart description "rang a bell." When the client generally agreed, a condition for supporting this statement was provided as a pattern or schema to be projected into the future. In general on the occasions when contradictions occurred, clients were regarded as "faulty" affirmers, or poor collaborators in their own experience or biographies vis à vis the "truthfulness" of astrology. One astrologer, I noted, declared in response to a negative answer from a client that "often we do not really see ourselves." Another astrologer turned the tables a bit in substance, but not in structure, by declaring his own novice status as a professional. In either case, the effect of the invocation of the role of the interactant as an observer or participant deftly directs attention away from a challenge to the foundational assumptions of astrology toward the ways in which interactants are poorly informed about themselves or the world of astrology.

Invoking the Foundational Knowledge of Astrology

An important condition for the preserved credibility of astrology involves the active invocation of foundational knowledge itself. For example, one assumption is that of multiple influences. While newspaper horoscopes might describe a reader's daily forecast on the basis of a sun-sign, an accurate knowledge of astrology includes the idea that a multiplicity of planetary influences affect the description of an individual. When necessary an astrologer invokes this assumption as a supportive device to restore the credibility of the particular questioned fact. An example of this occurred when one client objected to a particular aspect of the description. In response, the astrologer reinterpreted his statement to include the idea that another influence had been inadequately emphasized. Including this new piece of information, while telling the client that many planets influence a chart, is a practice for continuing the ongoing construction of astrology's credibility. Hence, the astrologer introduces this assumption of multiple influence as a given truth. At the same time, stating the assumption in solving a problem is a way of demonstrating its truth without question, even though the contradiction challenges astrology's claims. In effect, the astrologer's comments are both assertions of a fundamental "given" about astrology and simultaneously a demonstration of the "given" in operation.[3]

Invoking the Context of Social Interaction

A third condition instrumental to the preservation of credibility is the use of the context of interaction as an item of information itself. Clients and astrologers, like other social interactants, are more or less totally involved in the events at hand. There are occasions in most situations when individuals stand back and reflect on and synthesize what has gone before with the aim of understanding the event and projecting expectations for the future. This idea is the basis for regarding the context of social interaction (which includes both working claims and the components of the information context) as an acceptable or useful practice for maintaining threatened credibility. This idea expresses the notion that participants can reflect upon information embedded in one set of actions and find in it new relevance or meaning for other situations. This was observed in the following instance.

On visiting one astrologer I heard him comment on the presumed tendency of the client to have frequent headaches, temper tantrums, or fevers, all related to the influence of the planet Mars in her chart. The client denied all of these characteristics. Both astrologer and client then proceeded to discuss this problem at length, with the astrologer finally invoking the assumption of multiple influences and his own failure to emphasize a countervailing tendency. Yet the problem, though seemingly resolved, seemed still to be present. Quite a few minutes later the astrologer, noting the client's ruddy complexion, casually asked the client if she was warm. When the client answered that this redness seemed typical of her appearance the astrologer's response was overwhelming and enthusiastic: "O boy, that's it, that's it, the Mars in you. O boy." The analysis shows how the meaning of an event from a prior time in the chart reading became dislodged from a temporal, social context and was reintroduced to resolve an old issue, which was related to the early discussion of the Mars influence. Neither the astrologer nor the client, of course, can be presumed to be conscious of the use of the present to alter or affirm the past. But in fact, this is what occurred. The condition for presumed credibility described here is that both the client and the astrologer can be creative innovators in employing a context of social interaction for multiple purposes.

What is perhaps most strange about this entire set of events is that clients and astrologers seem to be unaware of them. Astrologers merely reflect upon the features of the setting as they unfold and rely upon foundational knowledge as a set of preservative practices for their work. Contradiction does not produce new insights, but rather further interpretive work. Chart reading does not suddenly stop while the astrologer reassesses the credibility of astrological knowledge itself. The work goes on. And it does so while the grounds for the credibility of astrology are constantly being established and elaborated. Once a chart reading begins, the inherent logic of the interactional occasion and of the knowledge system of astrology emerge as continuous activities which establish and maintain credibility.

CONCLUSION

This discussion of the astrological knowledge system has tried to demonstrate two things: that there are alternate ways of approaching the study of social and cultural phenomena; and that astrology in particular establishes and maintains its credibility through the forms of interaction between client and astrologer.

The experience of "strangeness" encountered in first studying astrologers or the occult can be capitalized on as a way of generating a different kind of study. In this instance, because astrology's persistence initially seemed paradoxical, I focused on how astrology is interpreted in order for it to be a sensible and valid system. I suggest this perspective as an alternative to merely asking why astrology persists. I assume there is something about the system of knowledge itself that could be self-sustaining when it is used by social actors.

The credibility of this view of the world is established and maintained through the use of different orders of knowledge by astrologers and clients. These kinds of knowledge, when they are introduced, provide a context for persuasive interpretations. When contradictions appear the same assumptions or claims then operate as maintenance devices. At the same time the client is

191

cast into the position of being a collaborator in helping to achieve and maintain validity. Thus, the same aspects of the interpretation can be used by the astrologer in a variety of ways to establish credibility.

Notes

1. The concept "system of knowledge" suggests that astrology, from the point of view of astrologers, clients, and observers may be described, *from within the natural attitude,* as a system of knowledge (i.e., zodiacal categories and descriptions), which is presented as an existential aspect of our knowledge of the world. Burkhart Holzner, in *Reality Construction in Society,* refers to "bodies of knowledge" (p. 167). He says that "knowledge in social life comes in more or less coherent entities that have boundaries around them." His ideas bear an independently conceived similarity to the ideas and approach developed here. See especially his chapter, "Trust in Bodies of Knowledge."

2. In order to preserve the continuity of the essay we did not detail the different categories and features of foundational knowledge or foundational assumptions. They are listed and described briefly here: (1) multiple influences—a multiplicity of planetary influences establish the composite picture of a person's character; (2) planets as symbolic representations of human life—planets describe distinctive characteristics of human life in symbolic terms (e.g., the sign Scorpio symbolizes human sexual energy); (3) synchronistic correlation—the use of meaningful coincidences as a form of modified causality for explaining the origin and occurrence of various events; (4) the coherence of the universe—the universe and the individuals within it, with their particular unique characteristics represent a coherent unity in a gestaltist sense; (5) open-ended elaborations—revisions in astrological knowledge are possible; (6) self-evident applications—knowledge of planetary configurations is accurate knowledge about the client's personality, which is supposedly self-evident once it is described to the client, and assent to the description is assumed to be largely nonproblematic; (7) the objective character of descriptions—astrologers may differ in the adjectives each uses to describe a particular sign, yet the meaning of the particular terms used to provide descriptions of clients are independent of the universal meaning of the categories that generate those descriptions (i.e., the objectivity of the statement is not affected by variable terms used to describe that objective truth); and (8) simultaneous use of intuitive and technical skills—the use of both skills is essential to the com-

petent practice of astrology. The chart must be drawn up correctly, and the astrologer employs intuitive skills in demonstrating the validity of the interpretation.

3. Some critics might argue that in fact what is being preserved is the reputation of the astrologer or the "face" of the client. However, while this may be true, an additional aspect of this process is the fact that these reputations and "faces" rely upon a clearly available body of wisdom or knowledge, which itself is the basis for the interaction occurring as it does. The active investigation of knowledge-in-use recommends, then, not only the study of the characteristics of the interactants, but also the basis for the interaction itself as an encounter or event resting upon common interests, knowledge, or information.

References

Adorno, Theodore, 1974, "The Stars Down to Earth." *Telos* 19 (spring): 13-91.

Casteneda, Carlos, 1971, *A Separate Reality, Further Conversations with Don Juan.* New York: Simon & Schuster.

Cavan, Sherri, 1972, *Hippies of the Haight.* St. Louis: New Critic's Press.

Festinger, Leon, Henry W. Riecken, and Stanley Schacter, 1965, *When Prophecy Fails.* New York: Harper & Row.

Holzner, Burkhart, 1972, *Reality Construction in Society.* Cambridge: Schenkman.

Kuhn, Thomas, 1970, *The Structure of Scientific Revolutions.* Chicago: University of Chicago Press.

Roszak, Theodore, 1969, *The Making of a Counter-Culture.* Garden City; N. Y.: Doubleday.

Simmons, Jerry, 1964, "On Maintaining Deviant Belief Systems." *Social Problems* 11: 250-256.

Truzzi, Marcello, 1972, "The Occult Revival as Popular Culture: Some Random Observations on the Old and the Nouveau Witch." *Sociological Quarterly* 13 (winter): 16-36.

Wedow, Suzanne, 1974, "Perennial Wisdom on Display: The Use of a System of Knowledge in Interaction." Unpublished Ph.D. dissertation, University of California, Santa Barbara.

VOLUNTEER FIREMAN

Altruism in Action

ALAN H. JACOBS

The historical and contemporary neglect of volunteer fire departments by social scientists has resulted in a serious gap in our knowledge of rural and suburban America. Thus my aim here is twofold: (1) to draw attention to the unique and positively vital role that these organizations play in the *total* social life of non-highly metropolitan communities; and (2) to suggest certain defects in current voluntary association theory that result from the failure of social scientists to examine and understand volunteer fire departments as "voluntary associations" par excellence.

VOLUNTEER FIREMEN

Two matters of definition before proceeding: first, in speaking of volunteer fire departments, I am not talking about paid, full-time public or civil service fire departments whose organization and functions are conventionally bureaucratic in nature and fairly well known; nor am I referring to those original volunteer fire departments which, for one reason or another, have added a few full-time, paid employees, and now subsidize their volunteer members with monetary gratuities. Rather, my remarks are addressed only to the purely unpaid volunteer fire departments whose members are all employed in other work, and who are organized on a voluntary basis as an association to protect life and property in their community from fire or other accidental life-threatening causes.

Second, whereas for the sake of convenience I shall speak of these organizations as volunteer fire departments, it should be kept in mind that their activities are not limited to fighting fires. Indeed, during the past 10 to 15 years, most have added important ambulance/rescue squad divisions to their long list of community activities. In some areas the ambulance/rescue squads operate independently or semiautonomously from the volunteer fire departments with which they are associated. While historically the emphasis has been mainly on fire fighting, it is important to appreciate that the emergency medical and rescue activities of many volunteer fire departments today often rival those of the purely fire fighting dimension both in the amount of time and importance attached to the former.

Thus, today it is possible to speak of at least three distinct types of volunteer fire department: (1) those wholly concerned with fire fighting and fire prevention; (2) those involved more or less equally in both fire and emergency medical assistance; and (3) those squads that give priority to development of emergency medical assistance, or those wholly volunteer emergency medical squads that have grown up independently but in close association with a local volunteer fire department. My use of the term volunteer fire department is intended, therefore, to cover all three of these types, even though the last is not, strictly speaking, a regular fire fighting unit.

Historical Background

Volunteer fire departments have a long and distinguished history in the United States. This history differs radically from the development of fire services elsewhere in the world, which were organized and operated along highly militaristic or bureaucratic lines, involving full-time, paid personnel. In North America, volunteer fire departments emerged in the seventeenth century in response to the very real social need for fire protection and fire prevention, a need which has generated its own rich body of folklore that still awaits systematic study.

195

Benjamin Franklin is credited with starting the first successful volunteer fire department, in 1735 in Philadelphia. George Washington, John Hancock, Paul Revere, Samuel Adams, and Alexander Hamilton are all said to have gained distinction in their local communities by their active participation and leadership roles in these associations. Indeed, Washington is alleged to have given the Friendship Volunteer Department of Alexandria, Virginia, its first "water pumper," as well as having participated on a regular basis in its routine fire calls.

During the early nineteenth century, throughout the eastern seaboard states, membership in one's local volunteer fire department was an important source of social prestige and respectability—a matter well known to volunteer firemen today and an important symbolic source of pride for their own involvement in local volunteer fire department activities. In order to raise money necessary for equipment, and to ensure a steady recruitment of new members, volunteer fire departments engaged in a wide range of social activities in their communities, including dances, parties, picnics, parades, fire fighting demonstrations and displays, community raffles, auctions, and dinners. Each of these activities provided an opportunity (as they still do today) for members of the entire community to join together in common fellowship. For those made homeless or destitute by fire, local volunteer fire departments became important early welfare agencies by providing food, clothing, and shelter until the family recovered from its misfortune. Moreover, volunteer fire stations were not only buildings to house equipment, but were also important meeting halls, where socialization and enculturation of local values took place. Indeed, so important were the fire hall and its volunteers, that community social prestige and respect were often judged by outsiders in terms of the reputation of the local volunteer fire department.

In the decades just prior to the Civil War, however, many volunteer fire departments fell into local disgrace, as a result of neighboring organizations actually fighting among themselves en route to a call, for the privilege of arriving first and putting out the fire. As a consequence, several metropolitan cities initiated full-time, paid fire departments during this period. And for a short time, many volunteer fire departments lost much of their previously enjoyed social respectability. However, following the Civil War, public support rose again, due partly to the fact that paid fire departments could not adequately cope with the increasing needs for fire protection and partly because of the important role that various volunteer fire departments played in helping to reconstruct depleted fire services in the South. Though the introduction of mechanized fire fighting equipment in the late nineteenth and early twentieth century contributed to a steady increase in numbers of full-time, paid municipal fire departments in highly metropolitan areas, even today it is estimated that 87 percent of the 22,000 fire departments in the United States are owned, operated, and manned entirely by volunteers, and that 91 percent of the estimated 2.2 million firemen in this country today are volunteers.

As indicated earlier, an additional and increasingly important contemporary function of many volunteer fire departments is the provision of mobile emergency medical units at the scene of accidents, as well as attending to life-threatening medical emergencies in areas with a scarcity of doctors. These highly trained and certified emergency ambulance/rescue squad personnel in many areas form specialized paramedic units, such as the one depicted in the popular television series, "Emergency." The program is misleading, however, in that the combined fire/medical/rescue squad activities portrayed are actually more typical of volunteer fire departments than of professional municipal fire departments. The latter are often several years behind in organization and competency in the delivery of emergency medical services in comparison to most volunteer fire departments.[1]

Volunteer Fire Departments and Community Studies

From an anthropological perspective, volunteer fire departments also play a vital and often unique role in the communities in which they exist, not simply in protecting life and property, but also by contributing social cohesion and stability to the community. This is not only the case in isolated rural communities, where their role is often critical and conspicuous, but also in many developed suburban areas, such as Bethesda and

Chevy Chase, Maryland. Unlike such other community institutions as social clubs, fraternal organizations, and churches, which tend to divide residents into competing and often exclusive groups, volunteer fire departments play a unique role in uniting residents from all social classes and ethnic categories into a single cooperative community group.

Rather surprisingly, this role of volunteer fire departments in American community life has gone unstudied by social scientists. Robert and Helen Lynd (1929) make no mention whatsoever of volunteer firemen in their classic study, *MiddleTown;* and although Warner and Lunt list the presence of volunteer "fireman auxiliaries" in their book *The Social Life of a Modern Community* (1941), they fail to devote even cursory attention to their obvious importance as an integrative community organization. The anthropologist E. Adamson Hoebel is said to have lectured frequently on volunteer fire departments as vital community voluntary associations, but I gather that he did not publish his remarks. James Smith (1974) in an unpublished Ph.D. thesis makes some reference to how the establishment of a volunteer fire department within a Canadian Ojibwa Indian reservation helped to eliminate factionalism and restore vitality to the tribal council. However, the only published reference to firemen that I have encountered is a descriptive account by Judy Woods (1972) of a paid, municipal fire department. Unfortunately, the observations contain very little that cannot be found by consulting any beginners' manual in fire fighting techniques.

Indeed, the only significant mention of volunteer fire departments that I have been able to find is a two-paragraph description in Vidich and Bensman's *Small Town in Mass Society* (1958) where, strangely enough, the authors fail to note that what made Sam Lee one of the four most important and influential members of the community was not simply his role as newspaper owner and editor (which the authors admit he sold during the study) nor his membership in the Baptist Church (which the authors admit posed further problems in analysis) but rather the altogether neglected fact that Sam Lee was also the chief of the local volunteer fire department.

The common urban image of volunteer firemen as "siren jockeys," "adolescent pyromaniacs," or "thrill seekers" no doubt plays an important part in accounting for the lack of attention given to this topic. However, these attitudes are both oversimplified and inaccurate stereotypes. True, some volunteer fire departments do occasionally show stag films, another frequent stereotype. But this is often a device to recruit new membership in communities where other procedures have failed, rather than a typical or even frequent activity. Indeed, in most volunteer fire departments of which I have personal experience, membership is extremely prudish, highly disciplined, and intolerant of reckless behavior. The so-called heroic types are carefully weeded out. Further, because of their conspicuous volunteer status, most members participate regularly in weekend training schools and drills, so that they often become more proficient and professional in essential skills than their professional paid counterparts.

Social Structure and Values

Though superficially similar in many respects to their non-volunteer counterparts, insofar as they have a chief, line officers, and internal organizational rules, it must be remembered that volunteer fire departments are wholly voluntary associations, based on organizational principles radically different from the conventional bureaucratic or militaristic features of municipal fire departments. For example, the volunteer chief is usually elected for a one-year term by the entire membership. He achieves this office and its limited authority in part by having demonstrated his technical knowledge, skill, and experience in fire fighting, but also because of the social respect accorded to him for his distinctly altruistic previous service as an ordinary volunteer. Chiefs and line officers of volunteer fire departments thus command only insofar as their membership allows them to issue orders, but they cannot demand absolute compliance simply by virtue of their office: They possess no conventional sanctions for noncompliance other than putting disputes to a collective vote, since *all* members are at all times volunteers. The vitality and success of a volunteer fire department depend, therefore, on nonmonetary inducements and rewards, which must work to stimulate a constant stream of new recruits. The volunteer chief must both possess and exert unique leadership qualities based on social esteem, and appeals to self-respect and altruism as well as professional competence. This is not the case in paid fire departments, in which the chief has more control.

Typically, the average volunteer fireman contributes 15 to 20 hours a week in maintaining equipment, attending organizational and training meetings, as well as actually responding to fire or ambulance calls. This is in addition to the time devoted to his regular employment. Indeed, the average volunteer's commitment to his local volunteer fire department or ambulance/rescue squad activities is often an all-consuming enterprise that has important recreational dimensions as well.

Kinship appears to play an interesting role in recruitment and the internal organization of many volunteer fire departments. Whereas the sons of well-respected volunteer firemen often join, they rarely reach the leadership roles possessed by their fathers because of the strongly egalitarian principles that prevail, which discourage direct inheritance of leadership roles. Rather it is the more distant avuncular principle that appears to be the dominant kinship thread, there being little or no objection to nephews eventually earning the right to take over their uncles' leadership roles.

Another important social characteristic of volunteer fire department membership is the way it cuts through existing divisions within a community, providing one of the few forums for individuals of otherwise separate and distinct social groups to participate and cooperate on a regular basis. Generally, there are no formal rules designed to include particular persons and exclude others, though I do have impressionistic data that there may be significant regional variations in actual composition. Indeed, in some communities, even the "village idiot" is given a useful and important role in washing down equipment after a fire. And contrary to popular belief in many areas, volunteer fire departments have taken the community lead in recruiting minorities. Though essentially a male-oriented activity with many of the characteristics of the so-called male bonding principle, it is important to mention that the typical volunteer fire department has a women's auxiliary, which plays a vital role in raising money for recurrent operating costs or to purchase new equipment. In fact, in many communities where most of the men are out of town during the day at their places of employment, the volunteer ambulance service is often run entirely by women and turned back to the men only after dark. Women also occasionally turn out to large daytime fires to help pull hose, refill protective-breathing apparatus, and assist in other important ways. Similarly, mixed crews of men and women work together in some volunteer ambulance departments until as late as 11:00 P.M., though the predominantly prudish values of volunteer fire departments generally tend not to tolerate all-night mixed crews.

Volunteer Fire Departments and Voluntary Association Theory

A striking aspect of contemporary theory concerning voluntary associations—as reflected, for example, in Smith and Freedman (1972)—is the inability of such theory to account for the organization and function of volunteer fire departments. Indeed, a major aim of this paper is not only to draw attention to this much neglected, but vital social institution in American society, but also to suggest that the present literature on voluntary associations is defective in certain important respects because it has ignored the existence, extraordinary vitality, and historical importance of volunteer fire departments.

A full exposition of all the theoretical issues is not possible here, and I allude only to some examples. However, the matter is of some concern due to the fairly recent resurgence of interest in voluntary associations as the result of the successes of such movements as Black Power, Nader's Raiders, and Common Cause. Interest in this topic has also been stimulated by the growing and widespread concern that government and social life generally are becoming too centralized in concentration and use of power.

Much of the contemporary literature on voluntary associations is derived from a third world perspective, and as such has assigned an important, if not crucial role, to these agencies in the political development of new nations. The studies have demonstrated that these associations are able to distribute and diversify power and influence by protecting the mass of people from the excessive pressure of elites. However, there is also a prevailing belief that voluntary associations are limited in their usefulness as instruments for rationally planned change because they are themselves the outgrowth of change.

Here it may be noted, in contrast, that volunteer fire departments in America, by virtue of their extreme public orientation and commitment, and their highly egalitarian and altruistic value structure, are in a relatively weak position within the local power structure. More importantly, they generally explicitly divorce themselves from the political, religious, economic, and social polities of their area, precisely in order to maintain their neutrality and respectability as a distinctly public service organization. Rarely is the chief of the volunteer fire department also the mayor, town clerk, police chief, minister, school board chairman, or local "landed gentry." These dual roles are clearly incompatible with the self-image of the volunteer fire department. In those few cases where they do occur, it often indicates either the imminent death or the decline in vitality of the community's volunteer fire department.

Further, as I have indicated, mainly through the example of the recent addition of ambulance/rescue activities, volunteer fire departments are capable in ways hitherto unstudied and unnoticed of providing the "cutting edge" of important changes in social services. In fact, many of these are related to necessary fund-drive activities, including community parties, picnics, parades, raffles, chimney cleaning, and other fire prevention services. Many of these programs either constitute or lead to important innovations in the social organization and cultural life in the community. Typical of this are the new paramedic training programs, which bring together persons of diverse socioeconomic and ethnic backgrounds who under many other circumstances would not regularly interact or cooperate in the community.

Social theory has also traditionally linked voluntary associations with special interest group functions, arguing that by affiliation the individual has sought to enhance and protect his own interests. Concomitantly, it is suggested that voluntary associations in America are composed mainly of middle-class membership, and thus these organizations clearly reflect and reinforce class distinctions. Such conclusions gain credibility only by continuing to ignore the history and contemporary function of volunteer fire departments in our society. The only special or individual "interests" that these organizations may be said to cater to are the desire for social esteem, public respect, and honor. The volunteer fire departments confer these rewards on individuals, in the community's name, for regular and conscientious altruistic service under hazardous conditions (i.e., regular protection of life and property against natural or accidental misfortune).

Indeed, so powerful an attraction is this altruistic need, that, perhaps more than many other voluntary associations in contemporary America, volunteer fire departments and ambulance/ rescue squads tend to crosscut all sectors of the community in their membership and activities. Moreover, by virtue perhaps of the many mechanical skills required for servicing and maintaining the equipment, volunteer fire departments generally possess a high proportion of the marginal middle class or blue-collar workers, who are traditionally thought to be the non-joiners of voluntary associations. In fact, I have data suggesting that these agencies perform a vital role for those highly mobile, marginal middle class persons who aspire to become fully middle class in their community by joining the volunteer fire department.

Thus, unlike other voluntary associations, the volunteer fire department appears to play a unique and thus far unappreciated role in integrating members at larger and more basic social institutions (e.g., church, school, ethnic groups), thereby providing an important social cohesion function, above and beyond its more obvious fire fighting and emergency medical service roles. How unique this role may be, and the full extent of its parameters can be demonstrated only by more detailed and comparative studies, an aim this essay may stimulate others to pursue.[2]

Notes

This essay is presented here in essentially the same form as given at the annual American Anthropological Association Meetings in Mexico City, December 1974. There are many points that I would have welcomed an opportunity to expand upon and a great deal of data that I have not presented to support the assertions that I make. However, other commitments prevented a more complete analysis. I present the essay in the hopes that others may be stimulated to take up research in this otherwise neglected area.

The observations and data on which this essay is based were collected in the course of 14 months of ad hoc participant observation of three volunteer fire departments and their ambulance/rescue squads, mainly in the eastern panhandle area of West Virginia, supplemented with shorter visits to similar departments in Maryland and Virginia. I am indebted to Dr. Arens for assistance in urging me to publish this essay even in its incomplete form.

1. This is obviously a judgmental statement for which a number of genuine and praiseworthy exceptions can be found. It is my impression, however, that a careful study of volunteer fire departments will reveal a greater demonstrable competency and performance record than popularly assumed.

2. Since completing this esssy, John Lozier, of the Department of Sociology and Anthropology at West Virginia University has completed a study and excellent manuscript on "Volunteer Fire Departments and Community Mobilization," which, it is hoped, will be published shortly.

References

Lynd, Robert S. and Helen M. Lynd, 1929, *Middletown*. New York: Harcourt Brace Jovanovich.

Smith, Constance and Anne Freedman, 1972, *Voluntary Associations: Perspectives on the Literature*. Cambridge, Mass.: Harvard University Press.

Smith, J. G. E., 1974, *Kindred, Clan and Conflict: Continuity and Change Among the Southwestern Ojibwa*. Unpublished Ph.D. dissertation, University of Chicago.

Vidich, Arthur J. and Joseph Bensman, 1958, *Small Town in Mass Society: Class, Power and Religion in a Rural Community*. Princeton, N. J.: Princeton University Press.

Warner, L. Lloyd and Paul S. Lunt, 1941, *The Social Life of a Modern Community*. New Haven, Conn.: Yale University Press (Yankee City Series).

Woods, Judy, 1972, "Fire Calls: Ethnography of Fire Fighters." In James Spradley and David W. McCurdy, eds. *The Cultural Experience: Ethnography in Complex Society*. Chicago: Science Research.

AMERICAN PATTERNS OF HEALTH-CARE-SEEKING BEHAVIOR

NOEL J. CHRISMAN

In all societies the response to the discomfort and anxiety of an illness is an attempt to discover some means of alleviating the condition. Responses vary along a continuum from denial or self-treatment, through obtaining suggestions from friends, to consulting a health practitioner. In many non-Western societies, individual behavior tends to reflect a more integrated system of health beliefs and practices than in our own. In other cultures there may be quantitative differences in knowledge, experience, and talent among those sought for care, but all the persons involved understand the basic premises and treatments. In more complex industrial societies such as the United States, on the other hand, there is less coherence of knowledge and beliefs relating to the management of health problems. There are qualitative differences in knowledge and expertise between the general population and the highly differentiated set of health professionals—doctors, nurses, and other specialists.

Related to the existence of such specialized health practitioners and to the high degree of specialization in all aspects of urban industrial life is the American value underlying responses to illness: When you are sick, consult a doctor. If this value were heavily influencing behavior, behavioral responses to illness would cluster at the health professional pole of the consultation continuum. However, one estimate suggests that only one third of those who are ill in any month actually consult a physician (White et al., 1961). Thus, although there is a cluster of behavioral responses to the predicted point, most responses are located elsewhere on the continuum. Unfortunately there are no data, to my knowledge, suggesting the distribution of illness responses along the consultation continuum that would enable us to gauge the relative importance of the physician value upon behavior. In addition, I know of no studies conducted in traditional settings that report on the distribution of responses along this more quantitative continuum that would allow for comparative analysis.

One approach that can be of value in gathering information about how people react to illness and whom they choose to consult is based on the concept of health-care-seeking behavior. Care seeking includes those steps taken by an individual as he attempts to solve a health problem. Because this is a descriptive notion, assumptions about the "proper" sources of health information and care are included only insofar as they are part of the native's world. Most important, health and illness behaviors are viewed within the context and under the constraints of the individual's normal lifestyle.

A number of biomedical and sociocultural factors influence the course of events in the care-seeking pattern and modify behaviors oriented by the value of physician consultation for illness. The primary biologically based element is the nature of an individual's symptoms. The relative importance of symptoms, however, is influenced by one's social and cultural position in society. Cultural definition of symptoms (Fabrega, 1973), their degree of perceived severity and ambiguity (Apple, 1960; Baumann, 1961; Mechanic, 1968), and the degree to which they hamper activities in daily life (Twaddle, 1974) combine to promote or inhibit consultation with a physician. A second constellation of factors is related to the degree of accessibility of, cost of, and beliefs about the medical care system (Andersen, 1968; Berkanovic and Reeder, 1973). These considerations are the beginning and endpoint boundaries of the care-seeking process, and each factor also has a continuing effect on the process itself.

The sequential steps of care seeking may be seen in terms of an individual's negotiations with his or her social environment as the identity shift from "person" to "patient" occurs. This shift of identity and the accompanying statuses and roles (Goodenough, 1965) essentially follows Parsons' (1951) suggestions in his discussion of sick role behavior (see also Suchman, 1965a); that is, the ill person may be exempted from some or all of his social obligations provided there is a reciprocal commitment to seek competent help in order to recover. Those individuals who allow the sick person to alter the existing patterns of rights and obligations may also aid in discovering or validating the source of help.

The sociocultural system within which bargaining and consulting occurs is the *lay referral system* (Freidson, 1970). This system is composed of two dimensions: "the particular culture or knowledge people have about health and health agents" (which includes the two boundary areas discussed above) and "the interrelationships of the laymen from whom advice and referral are sought" (Freidson, 1970: 290). Freidson discusses the cultural dimension in terms of the degree of congruence between the patient's cultural beliefs about health and the health system, and those of the scientific practitioner. Lower-class persons with less scientific knowledge, inadequate knowledge of the body and its functions, and possessing "antiquated notions still exploited by patent-medicine advertisements" (Freidson, 1970: 287) are less likely to use medical services than are higher-class persons with a system of health beliefs more consonant with that of scientific health practitioners. A third cultural perspective influencing the choice to consult a scientific health practitioner is occasionally found among ethnic groups who maintain all or part of a homeland folk medical system. As Clark (1970) and others have pointed out, some members of groups such as Mexican-Americans continue to diagnose maladies using traditional rural Mexican categories, and treatments for such symptoms are requested from traditional health practitioners rather than from professionals in the scientific system.

In categorizing these diverse systems of health beliefs and attitudes toward health practitioners, I have found the following distinctions to be useful. In order to contrast the specialized scientific health system with beliefs common among the remainder of the (nonprofessional) population, we may distinguish the *scientific, lay,* and *traditional* health systems. The variety of health beliefs, practices, and practitioners among the general population may be categorized according to their origins, or reference worlds (Shibutani, 1955); *Traditional* health systems are derived from traditional or folk practices of peoples (ethnic groups) included within the population. The *lay* health system is based upon lay understanding and reworking of the scientific system. These systems are similar in that both are found among members of the public (in some instances including scientific health personnel). However, the content of beliefs and practices differs depending upon the reference world. A traditional health system, for example, refers to an existing (or previously existing) system common among members of the culture from which the ethnic group is drawn. Health practitioner roles are similarly drawn from that system (e.g., the *curandera* of Mexican folk medicine).

The lay health system, on the other hand, refers to (and is ultimately based upon) the scientific health system maintained practiced, and promoted by specialized health professionals. The source of health knowledge is the set of health practitioners trained in the scientific sphere. Like the traditional system, there is variability in the lay system in the degree to which health knowledge and beliefs approximate the complex information possessed by health practitioners. But the lay system differs in that a distinct and specialized reference group exists outside the daily life experiences of the population. Suchman (1966) has characterized the poles of the lay system as "popular" and "scientific" depending on the degree of similarity with the scientific system.

The second and more structural dimension of the lay referral system refers to the internal composition of social groups and the nature of their external relationships. Freidson describes one type of lay referral structure as cohesive and extended (1970: 291), more characteristic of people in the lower classes; the other type is loose and truncated, and characteristic of the higher social classes. Referring only to the social network properties, the former is tight knit with a restricted range of outside contacts; the latter is loose knit with extensive outside contacts. Relating these network structures to lifestyle, the round of daily activities and their meanings, we may refer to a "parochial" lifestyle, in whith the lay referral system is "intensified by its cohesiveness and by its strongly localized character, kin and friends living together in a local area with little experience outside the area and with a great deal of mutually reinforcing interaction" (Freidson, 1970: 291) "Cosmopolitans," on the other hand, participate in and recruit their networks from a wide variety of interaction settings. They are much more likely to make health decisions independently, perhaps consulting other household members. Suchman succinctly characterizes the parochial style as "ethnocentric, traditional, closed, shared, affectual, as opposed to cosmopolitan, e.g., progressive, open, individualistic, instrumental . . ." (1966: 98). Obviously, ethnographic research is necessary to describe the variation between these polar types.

The differences in these lifestyles, the structural variation of social networks maintained by parochials and cosmopolitans, and the degree of adherence to the scientific end of the lay health system underlie differences in the ways individuals seek care when they are ill. In this short paper I cannot examine in detail how these differences influence the care-seeking process. Generally, however, parochials are more likely to delay in seeking a doctor's aid, relying instead upon treatments and other suggestions from their network of lay consultants. Cosmopolitans are "more prone to make decisions about medical care without the aid of lay consultants outside the household, more familiar with abstract criteria for professional qualifications, better acquainted with a number of professional practices, if only by his residential mobility, and more knowledgeable about illness itself," (Freidson, 1970: 291) and are likely to have more confidence in their own diagnoses. If a cosmopolitan were to consult more widely, his knowledgeable contacts would expand alternatives available within the scientific health system.

In an attempt to generate more detailed data concerning the elements in the care-seeking process in preparation for a future comparative study of health practices, I interviewed fourteen new patients in a family practice clinic located in the University (of Washington) Hospital. Thus far, half of these people have been interviewed at greater length to gather data on their urban lifestyles. Only one of these patients could be characterized as parochial, and she fits few of the criteria because of her social isolation in a public housing project. None of these new patients was suffering from an acute illness, suggesting that each had a great amount of latitude in deciding how to gain care for his or her problem. Thus, this group of patients fell generally within the cosmopolitan category, had nonacute health problems, and had just chosen a new source of medical care.

The majority of these patients, eleven of the fourteen, had discussed their symptoms with others prior to consulting the doctor. The three who engaged in little or no lay consultation were all single women (one other member of the sample was a single woman). The one woman of these three who was interviewed intensively described a life with only infrequent contact with her friendship network. The remainder of the patients had discussed their symptoms with their spouses (see Twadle, 1969). The single woman who had discussed her symptoms with others had recently divorced her husband and maintained frequent contact with her friendship network. A majority of the consulters (seven of the eleven) also discussed their symptoms with family members other than the spouse. Which family contacts were included depended upon proximity and frequency of visiting. Those who did not discuss their symptoms with other family members simply had not had the opportunity to do so. Four people in this sample also discussed their symptoms with friends.

Judging primarily from the intensive interview data, discussions of symptoms with family members or friends occur in the context of normal visiting patterns. One stimulus to such a discussion is the visibility of symptoms. For example, Mrs. Davidson and Miss Johnson had lingering or frequent coughs. Friends could not help but notice and comment upon the symptom. Another stimulus to discussions of illness is commonality of experience with the disease. Citywide outbreaks of flu and the like occasion passing comments among co-sufferers.

According to the Richardsons, one of the intensively inter-

211

viewed couples, children's diseases and what the doctors prescribed arose relatively frequently in their discussions with friends. Mrs. Richardson said that some of these conversations expanded to include adult complaints, particularly with one woman. Mrs. Richardson believed that these discussions were essentially unproductive for providing solutions, but continued such conversations so she would not offend the person. Although the Richardsons did not turn to friends for advice about how to respond to symptoms, information deriving from conversations was remembered. For example, Mrs. Richardson had learned much about the effects of a mastectomy through her friend's mother's experience with the operation. Miss Johnson also gained information from friends' experiences. Parents, too, were significant sources of information. Mrs. Richardson identified her belief that a temperature of 102° or more was serious as being derived from her parents. Miss Johnson and the Peraltas possessed a great deal of information about their parents' diseases.

Previous experience with physicians or other health professionals also raised the level of knowledge possessed by individuals (Suchman, 1965b). In addition, patients expected to learn from encounters with doctors. Symptoms were to be identified with diseases or other bodily conditions and plans for ridding the body of these problems was to be carried out. A middle-aged man who had visited the clinic with a series of generalized complaints said he "just wanted to go to a clinic where they could put me through a grinder and say it's all meat." Another man expressed strong appreciation that his doctor has given him a great deal of information about breast cancer in men. Reflecting on experiences when she received little or no information, his wife said "when someone comes on sort of cold and professional and standing there like he has a whole pocketful of secrets, I just say crap."

The most recent suggestion to visit the doctor, and the choice of the family clinic can be assigned to two categories, both of which contain the element of trust. The basis of this trust differs, however, and serves to distinguish the categories. Half of the fourteen patients followed the recommendation of a family member or close friend in order to choose the family clinic as a source of care. Five of these seven were convinced of the need to consult a doctor at that time by the same source. The other stimulus category is best labeled "institutional." This includes those who were drawn to the clinic through referral from another unit in University Hospital or because of the good reputation enjoyed by the hospital complex. Six of the remaining seven fit this category. The seventh person was referred by her psychiatrist; thus it was a professional referral. But she took the advice because of the great degree of *personal* trust she felt for the man. This patient therefore illustrates a mixture of the two types.

Using these scanty data, some suggestions can be made about care-seeking patterns among cosmopolitans within the lay health system. All the people in this study adhered to the value of consulting a physician when they had a health problem. However, only one person sought care immediately following the appearance of symptoms. Among the remainder, delays of up to two years were reported. Such delays are not uncommon, and none of these health problems was acute, requiring immediate care. In addition, most informants believed that doctors were busy people not to be bothered by minor problems.

Informant behaviors during the period in which they were making the decision to consult a doctor can be examined using Freidson's lay referral system framework. Health beliefs among this group fell toward the scientific end of the continuum of beliefs in the lay health system. To a large degree, adherence to this set of health beliefs is derived from people's childhood experiences. Family use of a physician, in contrast to an alternate health practitioner or reliance on self-medication with patent medicines, creates a positive attitude in the young family member. Maintenance of this orientation throughout adulthood depends upon at least two sets of experiences, both of which are related to the acquisition of information.

Among these cosmopolitans (and the same is probably true for parochials), health issues arose as topics of conversation on the job or during informal visiting. These discussions served as important sources of information about the characteristics of illnesses. Only one of the informants followed a friend's suggestion for treating a health problem; thus treatments, even those prescribed by a doctor, are learned along with symptoms and other aspects of disease. But treatments, and all the other information, are held as the individual's own knowledge either for self-diagnosis and treatment or for evaluating physician behavior. It is important to note that the health information circulating in these cosmopolitan networks is closely linked to physician behavior. People report on symptoms as they were diagnosed by a doctor, for example. This style of communicating indirectly reinforces the central position of the physician.

The second kind of information-gathering experience is the doctor-patient interaction. Informants expressed appreciation for those doctors who carefully explained the medical situation in terms they could understand. When information was not forthcoming, informants did not always ask for details, but would nonetheless felt that there was no reason for the doctor to hide his "pocketful of secrets."

For cosmopolitans, then, much of their behavior in the lay health system is directly related to the scientific health practitioner. Information about illness is both directly and indirectly drawn from this source. In contrast to what has been reported for some parochials, I found very little evidence of group-stimulated lay treatment patterns. These informants treated themselves (and their spouses) or visited the doctor. They evidently feel that they control as much knowledge as their friends and would rather take individual responsibility for treatment. Once an illness is defined as beyond a person's competence, the only source of care is a doctor—and not an alternate health practitioner.

Information is also important in the process of choosing a doctor. The general health discussions noted above can include an evaluative aspect, as when the speaker's physician is characterized as warm or cold, competent or incompetent. Of greater importance in choosing a new physician is *trust*. As I mentioned above, people in this study turned to either institutional or personal sources for a suggestion about a new doctor. The major institutional source—the University Hospital complex—was trusted for its reputation as a technically competent source of medical care. Trust among personal contacts was only marginally related to that person's medical competence. Instead, this trust was one aspect of the close affective links among friends or kin. Informants seemed to evaluate trusted contacts on the basis of the extent to which the contacts had experienced the scientific health system. But this was not the central concern. It was more important that the informant and his or her trusted contact shared common perspectives on other matters, which in turn added credence to the suggestion of a doctor.

SUMMARY

Participants in this small study can be generally characterized as having cosmopolitan life styles and loose-knit social networks, and sets of health beliefs clustering at the scientific end of the lay health system. All of the informants subscribed to the value that a physician should be consulted in cases of illness. However, most of these people procrastinated before consulting the doctor. Events during this period of delay when symptoms are present are probably not much different from events when a person is not explicitly seeking care. As Freidson's lay referral system model suggests, cosmopolitans with their loose-knit and wide-ranging networks, have access to a great deal of information about health. In addition, the individuals in this study desired information from the doctor, resenting the practitioner when information was not delivered. Health knowledge among people such as those in this study is drawn directly or indirectly from physicians, allowing these practitioners to be important reference persons in the lay health system.

Like information, trust is a significant dimension for understanding the care-seeking process. In this study the element of trust emerged in conjunction with the final steps in care seeking. That is, individuals with their stored knowledge and experience could make decisions about how to deal with symptoms. In addition, physicians were seen as legitimate persons to consult. However, the final step, choosing the doctor (or making an appointment), requires more than just information; the source of information is also evaluated.

Comparative research is necessary among people with differing lifestyles and network structures in order to determine variations in amount and content of information, relevant health practitioners, the role of trust in care seeking, and an element not discussed here, the types of support found among differently constituted social networks.

Notes

Some of the research upon which this paper is based was carried out in collaboration with Richard Baker, M.D. We are grateful to the directors and staff of the Family Medical Center at the University of Washington for their aid in completing this project. I also received support and assistance from the Office for Research Facilitation in the School of Nursing, Marjorie Batey, Ph.D., Director. (project #NU 00369)

References

Andersen, Ronald, 1968, *A Behavioral Model of Families' Use of Health Services.* Chicago: Center for Health Administration Studies. Research Series, No. 25.

Apple, Dorrian, 1960, "How Laymen Define Illness." *Journal of Health and Human Behavior* 1:219-225.

Baumann, Barbara O., 1961, "Diversities in Conceptions of Health and Physical Fitness." *Journal of Health and Human Behavior* 2:39-46.

Berkanovic, Emil and Leo G. Reeder, 1973, "Ethnic, Economic, and Social Psychological Factors in the Source of Medical Care." *Social Problems* 21, no. 2:246-259.

216

References (cont'd)

Clark, Margaret, 1970, *Health in the Mexican-American Culture.* Berkeley and Los Angeles: University of California Press.

Fabrega, Horacio, 1973, "Toward a Model of Illness Behavior." *Medical Care* 11, no. 6:470-484.

Freidson, Eliot, 1970, *Profession of Medicine: A Study of the Sociology of Applied Knowledge.* New York: Dodd, Mead.

Goodenough, Ward, 1965, "Rethinking 'Status and Role': Toward a General Model of the Cultural Organization of Social Relationships." In Michael Banton, Ed. *The Relevance of Models for Social Anthropology* A.S.A. Monograph No. 1 London: Tavistock.

Mechanic, David, 1968, *Medical Sociology: A Selective View.* New York: Free Press.

Parsons, Talcott, 1951, *The Social System.* Glencoe, Ill.: Free Press.

Shibutani, Tamotsu, 1955, "Reference Groups as Perspectives." *American Journal of Sociology* 60:562-569.

Suchman, Edward, 1965a, "Stages of Illness and Medical Care." *Journal of Health and Human Behavior* 6:114-128.

—1965b, "Social Patterns of Illness and Medical Care." *Journal of Health and Human Behavior* 6:2-16.

—1966, "Health Orientation and Medical Care." *American Journal of Public Health* 56, no. 1:97-105.

Twaddle, Andrew C., 1969, "Health Decisions and Sick Role Variations: An Exploration." *Journal of Health and Social Behavior* 10, no. 2: 105-115.

—1974, "The Concept of Health Status." *Social Science and Medicine* 8:29-38.

White, Kerr L., T. Franklin Williams, and Bernard G. Greenberg, 1961, "The Ecology of Medical Care." *The New England Journal of Medicine* 265, no. 18:885-892.

Postscript

The introduction suggests that there is some general lesson to be learned about the human condition by studying ourselves. Our task in this postscript is to consider if our venture was indeed worth the effort or whether we have merely enticed the reader into a confrontation with another culture with which he already has some familiarity. Although reporting of social and symbolic systems lies at the core of the anthropological inquiry, this activity is not in itself sufficient to justify the existence of a discipline which claims to be the *study* of man. By definition we also are a proper subject of inquiry, but there must be more to the endeavor than simply looking at ourselves. If it is to be a success, the process must also uncover those characteristics which we share with others separated from us in time and space.

Anthropology came into existence with this explicit assumption—that beneath the obvious and superficial differences there was an essential unity shared by all the representatives of our species. In the attempt to validate this assumption, students of this new art were dispatched to the farthest corners of the globe. Paradoxically, they returned with reports of other people which unwittingly generated a view of the universe which emphasized the differences rather than the similarities among those who shared the planet. Although this may have been a perversion of the practitioners' original intent, the results were in line

219

with what was expected by those who encouraged the project. To the established governments, commercial interests, and religious orthodoxies, an emphasis on what separated "them" from "us" was taken as a literal representation of the gap between civilization and savagery. In effect, anthropology emerged as the study of what came to be known as "primitive" man rather than mankind. The process has culminated in contemporary "scientific" studies of ritual in the New Guinea highlands based upon theoretical assumptions and approaches totally inapplicable to the study of religion in our own society. This would imply that either they or we are not truly human beings.

Thus, one of our main tasks in this volume has been to take advantage of those ideas and techniques initially employed elsewhere and apply them to our own culture. From this perspective, our essays represent no new fad, but instead an attempt to rescue from oblivion anthropology's original and laudable ambition: to study universal man. Reflecting on the analysis of our amusements, art forms, diet, and views of the natural and supernatural world may make us somewhat self-conscious. But at the same time such reflection should convince us that we share a common humanity with those we have read about with a degree of bemused fascination. The preceding discussions validate anew that, for better or worse, there is nothing about "them" that we cannot recognize in ourselves. It becomes clear, and in retrospect sometimes painfully obvious, that rather than great disparities between cultures, there is nothing more than a differential elaboration of similar themes. The implications and conclusions of these essays indicate that a deliberate effort is required to continue to disassociate ourselves from others. We can no longer blithely assume that they have myth while we have history, that they have superstition while we have religion, and that they have magic while we have science. We are not implying that superstition, magic, myth, and ritual do not exist in other cultures, for clearly this is the case. However, what we hope to have demonstrated is that it is not very difficult to locate the same phenomena in our midst. Once this is recognized, we are in a better position to appreciate other people's reactions to those symbolic systems and customs. The belief in witchcraft in another culture does not mean that the people involved live in constant fear of the supernatural, anymore than Americans are morally paralyzed because we accept the existence of the devil. Both supernatural creatures have their culturally limited roles to play. Thus, both the witch and devil restrict their appearances to the appropriate situations, which usually require an explanation for the unexplainable. At the same time, the function of myths, morality tales, and other oral literature among nonliterate peoples can be more properly assessed when we consider the subliminal messages of our fantasies, whether couched in the future world of star trek, the present of soap operas, or the over-romanticized versions of our historical past. These essays validate what we have learned from our experiences with other cultures. Now we can more fully appreciate how we are shaped into what our culture considers to be moral creatures by the contents of seemingly meaningless amusements.

We believe that, to some extent at least, we have achieved our original objective of expanding our appreciation of the varieties of the human experience by seeing ourselves more clearly. In the process, the essays have also helped us to identify those approaches and problems which truly belong to anthropology, which we believe to be the study of all men.

DATE DUE

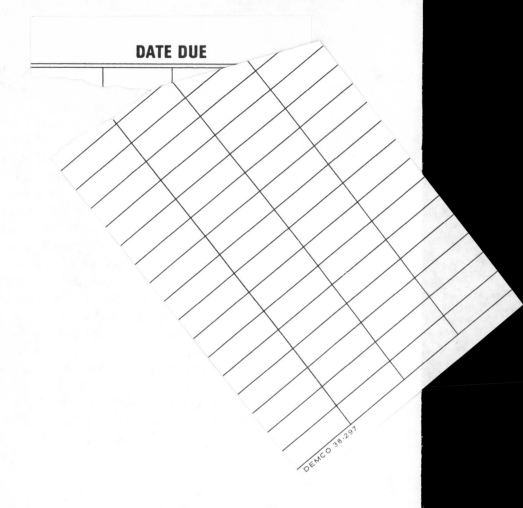

DEMCO 38-297